IN10TIONALITY
IT IS FINISHED

The End is not Near the end is Here.

JANINE DO CABO

Title: IN10TIONALITY: The end is not near, the end is here.

ISBN: 978-0-7961-3763-0

Author has paraphrased some passages of Scripture at the author's discretion for emphasis.

Published by: JDC EXEC (Pty) Ltd | JDCEXEC.com

To order additional copies of this book contact:
Janine Do Cabo,
Website: www.janinedocabo.co.za
Email: janine@jdcexec.com
Facebook: janinedocabo

Cover designed by Janine Do Cabo
Book Layout and Typesetting by Mariëtte Martin
www.mariettemartin.co.za
Edited by Magda de Korte

"There's a crown of righteousness waiting
in heaven for me, and I know that
my Lord will reward me on His day of
righteous judgment. And this crown is not
only waiting for me, but for all who love
and long for his unveiling."

2 Timothy 4 : 8 (TPT)

Dedication

I dedicate this book to

This book is dedicated to my grandmother, Anet de Koker:

Your stories, your wisdom, and your unwavering faith have been my guidance in many ways in life, in raising my children, faith and marriage. Time spent with you, are some of my most cherished memories. Your example of how to serve God and your intimate relationship with the Holy Spirit, driven by a profound spiritual experience, instilled in me the importance of purpose and commitment to my eternal call.

Every Bible verse you shared, every prayer you prayed, and our simple morning routines have left an indelible mark on my life. Through you, I've come to understand devotion, love, and the power of faith.

This book is a tribute to the lessons you've taught me and the love you've shown us as a family. Never forgetting the gentle smiles given to me by you in abundance. Even though you're no longer here, your influence remains.

Knowing what I know about heaven now, you are reading this

and I can even see your face. Thank you for being part of the great cloud of witnesses cheering me on. Until I see you again — very soon!

"As for us, we have all of these great witnesses who encircle us like clouds. So we must let go of every wound that has pierced us and the sin we so easily fall into. Then we will be able to run life's marathon race with passion and determination, for the path has been already marked out before us. We look away from the natural realm and we focus our attention and expectation onto Jesus who birthed faith within us and who leads us forward into faith's perfection. His example is this: Because his heart was focused on the joy of knowing that you would be his, he endured the agony of the cross and conquered its humiliation, and now sits exalted at the right hand of the throne of God!" Hebrews 12:1-2 (TPT)

With gratitude and love,
Janine do Cabo

Acknowledgements
Thank you to:

My gratitude is deeply rooted in the heart of my family and my husband. Their unparalleled courage in sharing the intricate tales of our encounters with cancer, death, the ethereal touch of Heaven and divine grace, has provided this book its soul and essence.

A heartfelt note of gratitude goes out to my children. Your youthful enthusiasm, your candid insights, and your childlike faith have breathed life into this book in ways I had never imagined. The tapestry of this narrative is richer for your involvement.

To my spiritual parents, your unwavering support and belief in the divine call upon my life have been my guiding compass. Your mentorship has been instrumental in leading me toward my destiny, nurturing my purpose every step of the way.

And to my faithful readers and the vibrant **IN10TIONALISTS** community: I am humbled by your support. May the wisdom and insights you gather from these pages blossom into a bountiful future. Remember, the lessons you've gleaned are not mere words but seeds of **IN10TION**, ready to be sown into the fertile grounds of your tomorrows.

Love and gratitude.
Janine Do Cabo

Foreword

by Pastor Lillian van der Westhuizen

I have known Janine since 2011. From the moment I met her, I knew that this beautiful woman had greatness inside of her - a woman with great tenacity, power and influence. Everything she does is IN10TIONAL, and she wants to only do what is right in the sight of her Savior. As a spiritual daughter in our church (NBCFC), she has shown consistency, walking by faith in a supernatural way, with a great servant's heart.

Through the years, I have seen how God has shaped her for His glory, through her life story. She lives with such a spirit of IN10TIONALITY, that she always sees possibilities in every situation.

Her writing style is very uplifting and impactful, drawing you closer to the Father's heart. My favorite part of the book is where she writes about prayer, something I hold dear to my heart. I believe prayer is your most important relationship you will ever have in this life. Janine gives valuable principles on prayer which will propel you into a very personal relationship with Jesus Christ.

This book "It Is Finished", will take you on a journey to increase your faith walk with God. It will not only change you but everyone around you.

Enjoy reading one of the greatest investments towards attaining your destiny.

Dr. Lillian van der Westhuizen
Co-Founder and Senior Pastor of NBCFC

Foreword II

by Dr. Vivian Rodgers

As I began to peruse the pages of this thought provoking book, IN10TIONALITY It Is Finished, I noticed a uniqueness in the style of writing that captivates the heart of the reader through the authors transparency as she shares with us her own real life moments in time. Dr Janine Do Cabo gives us the realities of her own personal life experiences, that clearly places on exhibit a person who has gleaned some of the most valuable lessons of life through every season that she has encountered.

We all encounter different seasons throughout our lifetime. Some can be painful while others may be filled with joy. The genius in Dr Janines work presented to us in this book, reveals that she is a woman of great wisdom who has mastered the skill of taking out of every memorable season, the wisdom that is most needed to empower others who have faced the same. There is a great possibility that you may be currently going through similar circumstances or could have gone through this already. Either way, this one thing I know is that you will be so glad that you did not ignore that urge to pick this up!

The chapter synopsis puts her on a mark above many as she craftily gives the reader a tantalizing taste of what to expect. Like an hors d'oeuvre before the main course, Dr Janine keeps you hungry for more! To miss this part of the book will be rather sad for any reader. due to the fact that it clearly reveals that she has put a lot of effort into captivating the heart of the reader. Chapter after chapter is filled with highly inspirational thoughts that oozes from her heart, revealing her passion to make a great impact before you close in on the final moments at the end.

The chapters that cover the end time message is unique in placing on display her dreams and visions, together with precise interpretations. Few have been able to see through their own personal dreams and visions concerning this subject. Every moment in these pages will ignite such hope and joy that will create within you a desire to listen to the times when God is speaking to you through dreams and visions.

I have enjoyed every moment of my time with this author over the recent years of getting to know her personally. Her determination to make an impact in the lives of others has constantly come to the surface in every conversation. Her passion to raise people up towards achieving their own goals is an unselfish trait that she has always kept burning deep within her heart.

Dr Janine is a woman of remarkable Godly character & unwavering faith, who ignites a hunger for us all to pursue our destiny no matter what may stand in our way. She is the perfect example of the kind of relationships that many ought to pursue if you want to reach your dreams in the shortest space of time. Without the right relationships, everything in life will become extended seasons of constant frustrations.

May these pages bring you the reader to the point of becoming IN10TIONAL in every season, so that your life could become the book that others will one day read!

Dear Dr Janine.. I do hope that these few words will do enough justice to your remarkable work…

Dr. Vivian Rodgers (PhD)
Founder & President:
Excellence International & Mentorship
In Business Excellence
President & Dean:
Destiny College International
Executive Life Coach
Author

Contents

CHAPTER SYNOPSIS

IN10TIONALITY - Unlocking Your Potential, Reigning in Life, and Embracing the Supernatural

Welcome to the captivating world of IN10TIONALITY, where living a rewarding and intentional life is within your grasp. In my previous book, IN10TIONALITY, I delved into the Ten life hacks that can help individuals not just navigate life but truly reign over it. Now, in this sequel, we embark on a profound journey that takes us deeper into the realm of the soul, exploring what moves, heals, and expands its capacity.

Chapter 1: The Soul – The Gateway to Divine Connection

In the opening chapter, we embark on a soul-stirring exploration of how to cultivate a profound relationship with God and develop a life-transforming prayer practice. Through relatable analogies, such as withdrawing from an ATM compared to withdrawing from Heaven in faith.

We uncover the power of prayer and learn how to effectively ask for our needs on Earth. Supported by scriptural wisdom and practical implementation, you are prepared to witness your prayers manifest in remarkable ways. As Isaiah prophesied, *"So shall My word be that goes forth from My mouth; It shall not return to Me void, but it shall accomplish what I please, and it shall prosper in the thing for which I sent it."* (Isaiah 55:11 NKJV).

Discover what ignites its passion, learn how to heal its wounds, and unlock its untapped potential. By cultivating an intentional understanding of the soul's workings, we empower ourselves to navigate life's challenges and nurture our spiritual growth.

The mind is a powerful tool that shapes our reality. In this chapter, we explore the transformative practice of IN10TIONAL thinking. By intentionally aligning our thoughts with our goals, dreams, and desires, we unleash the true potential of our minds. Through practical techniques and insightful exercises, we cultivate a mindset that propels us toward success, abundance, and fulfillment.

Chapter 2: Heavenly Encounters - Unlocking the Supernatural

Prepare to embark on a breath-taking journey into the realm of the supernatural. From personal encounters with divine beings to glimpses of heaven and revelations about the nature of hell, we explore the limitless wonders that await those who live a life of intimacy with God. Break free from limited perspectives and embrace the supernatural realm that transcends time, space, and matter. Experience the miraculous signs of God's boundless love and power.

Chapter 3: Angels - Guardians of Divine Intervention

In this chapter, we delve into the fascinating realm of angels and their purpose in our lives. Gain a profound understanding of the different types of angels and their role in God's divine plan. Explore remarkable stories of angelic encounters that will ignite your faith and inspire you to embrace the protection, guidance, and assistance of these celestial beings.

Chapter 4: Confronting Dark World - Demons and Spiritual Warfare

As we journey into the depths of the supernatural, we must confront the reality of spiritual warfare. Uncover the various types and ranks of demons and gain insights into their strategies. Equip yourself with the armor of God and learn how to overcome their influence. Through IN10TIONAL thinking and a deepening spiritual connection, we stand firm in the face of darkness and emerge victorious.

Chapter 5: Embracing God's World - Restoring Wholeness and Divine Health

Witness the extraordinary power of supernatural healing as we explore stories of miraculous recoveries and restoration. From overcoming cancerous reports to receiving divine intervention in times of immense hardship, the chapter on supernatural healing reveals the incredible potential for divine intervention in our lives. Through the power of IN10TIONAL thinking, we tap into the limitless healing power of God and open ourselves to the miraculous transformations that await us.

Chapter 6: The Summit to Success - Thriving with IN10TIONALITY

Success is not a mere coincidence but a deliberate pursuit. In this chapter, we uncover the secrets to achieving success that goes beyond worldly measures. By embracing obedience, cultivating a Christlike identity, and practicing daily discipline, we unlock the door to true significance and summit. Discover how IN10TIONAL thinking propels us towards a life of purpose, impact, and lasting success.

Chapter 7: Devine Insights into the Prophetic Future - Unveiling the End Times

In this thought-provoking chapter, we delve into the intriguing subject of the end times and the signs that indicate we are living in a pivotal era. From exploring the rapture of the church to unravelling the mysteries surrounding the mark of the beast and artificial intelligence, we gain profound insights into the prophetic future. Through IN10TIONAL thinking, we navigate through the storms of life with wisdom and discernment.

Chapter 8: Exploring your IN10TIONAL Revolution

As we near the conclusion of this transformative journey, we reflect on the significance of our personal identity and purpose. By shedding societal expectations and aligning with our true desires, we unlock the full potential of our IN10TIONAL. Discover the joy of pursuing new hobbies, developing meaningful relationships, and creating a future filled with purpose and fulfillment.

INTRODUCTION
UNLOCKING THE EXTRAORDINARY

A Real Life-Story of IN10TIONAL Change and Triumph

"But whose delight is in the law of the Lord, and who meditates on his law day and night. That person is like a tree planted by streams of water, which yields its fruit in season and whose leaf does not wither - whatever they do prosper." Psalms 1:2-3 (NIV).

Growing up, my childhood was full of adventure and various sports activities like tennis, athletics, netball, and hockey. However, I purposely avoided long-distance running, as it seemed daunting and required a level of effort that overwhelmed my young mind.

I had a tendency to do just enough to get by, studying to pass exams and attending practices without giving my best. This mindset carried me through most of my school and university life until I encountered a string of challenges: depression, divorce, loss of income, and becoming a mother.

It was during this time that I realized life demanded more than mediocrity. I had to change, but I had no idea where to start. I had neglected my untapped potential and the purpose for which I was called. A spiritual mentor's statement, "make peace with your process," awakened me to the fact that shortcuts and minimal effort wouldn't lead to fulfillment.

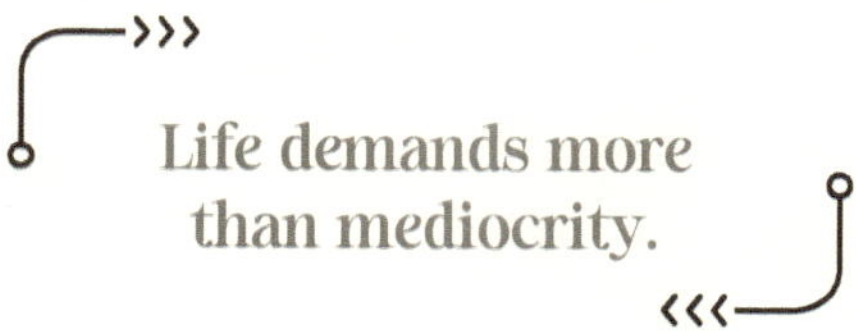

I embarked on a journey of self-discovery and personal growth, learning to appreciate the process and embrace the long haul. Understanding the importance of paying attention to details and respecting the journey, I recognized that progress often eludes those who don't comprehend the significance of the process.

Rebuilding my self-confidence, I focused on my God-given gifts and talents. I had to start afresh, unlearn negative beliefs, and reprogram my mindset. It was crucial for me to develop intentional habits aligned with my aspirations and create a balance between spiritual, mental, and physical well-being.

I also sought to understand my identity, disregarding societal pressures and aligning my choices with my true desires. Exploring new hobbies and engaging in activities that required dedication and commitment allowed me to rediscover the joy of personal growth.

In the business world, I shifted my focus from short-term gains to long-term strategies with eternal purpose. Understanding my identity in Christ empowered me with humility and a sense of purpose. I realized there is limitless potential in God's goodness and love, and together, united in our identity, we can make a significant impact for the Kingdom.

Through my journey, I embraced the concept of living intentionally, thriving daily, and embracing progress over time. Now, it's your turn to embark on your own intentional journey. What are you waiting for? What steps will you take to start your process?

On February 3, 2013, I received a prophecy that initially brought doubt and a return to old habits. However, I recognized that one of the gifts revealed to me was the ability to write books, despite English not being my first language. To fulfill this prophecy, I understood the need to be entirely intentional and focused.

In that same year, I enrolled as a John Maxwell leadership coach, unaware of how transformative this experience would be and how it aligned with my unfolding journey. This decision led to a series of supernatural events, some of which are both astonishing and hard to believe as I reflect on them now.

With each turn of the page, IN10TIONALITY invites you to embark on a life-transforming journey of self-discovery, divine connection, and supernatural encounters. By embracing the power of IN10TIONAL thinking, you unlock the limitless potential within you and align yourself with God's purpose for your life. It is time to rise above mediocrity, break free from limitations, and live a life that reflects the fullness of who you are meant to be.

Open your heart, mind, and soul to the wonders of IN10TIONALITY, and watch as your life unfolds in extraordinary ways. It is time to step into your destiny and embrace the abundant life that awaits you. The world is waiting for you to embrace your IN10TIONAL journey.

1.1 Unlocking the Supernatural: Empowering Believers to Walk in Power

I have grown up spiritually in a supernatural church. And what seems so difficult for others to grasp comes naturally to me. Not because I am special, just because I came to a place in my life where I knew there had to be more in God and so I asked God, "Lord, show me more."

It was in the early morning hours, when my daughter woke me up for another feed. It gets very quiet when you are forced to sit still by yourself and just feed. I got confronted with all the thoughts I used to run and hide from. The quietness bounced off the walls and I could not handle it. As I stared down into my daughter's beautiful little face and admired how perfect God made her, I prayed an earnest, heartfelt prayer.

"Daddy, there has to be more. There just has to be more?" With tears rolling down my face, I continued to pray. "More to life, more to You, more to the supernatural. I cannot think that you and Your greatness stop here, at this moment. Show me more, Lord. Show me Your greatness. I am ready and I am willing to learn."

I finished the feed and went back to sleep. I woke up with a heavy heart the next morning. I was almost disappointed that nothing had happened with my very emotional moment with God.

But God. Is all I can say. His promises are always Yes and Amen. Behind the scenes, He was setting me up. He was making a way for me to find my new spiritual home. I was in a new city, and I tried to connect with various churches and find a spiritual home, I just could not find the right one.

Not long after that, I got a call from a lady, who now is a good friend of mine. She needed Bible Bags branded for their church conference. It was around Wednesday, and she needed it by Friday. That was a silly deadline if I think about it now, but I got it done. I laugh now when I tell the story because that was the first miracle.

A few months later, I got another call from the church, asking if I can come through and quote them on some branding at church. I went through and spoke to Renier. We stood outside the church and spoke about the requirements. Every now and then his phone rang, and he spoke to the pastor of the church. I knew that because he told me that his pastor is on a trip in Israel and he has a couple of things he needs to do for him quickly.

We finished our meeting after the call. As I left, I asked him: "By the way, what do you do here?" I laugh about it now, but as humble as Renier is, he answered me with so much understanding of my silly question. He explained with so much passion what the church stands for and what they believe. I did not hear the words as clear as I felt his zeal for the house of God. I knew I needed to come here. "I asked him, what time is your services?" and followed it up with him. "I will see you Sunday."

This was 2011. My family and I are home. We have grown up in the house of God. We are still growing, and we are loving every moment. Passion for your house, Lord has consumed me. We are planted. *"But whose delight is in the law of the Lord, and who meditates on his law day and night. That person is like a tree planted by streams of water, which yields its fruit in season and whose leaf does not wither - whatever they do prosper."* Psalm 1:2-3(NIV).

I want to take a moment to honor my spiritual parents Apostle Nicky and Lillian van der Westhuizen. Thank you for always praying for us. Thank you for always pushing us to accomplish more in God. To stay hungry for God's presence. To push deeper into God. Thank you for loving our family so much. Thank you for sound advice, wisdom, and Word over our life. We look forward with great anticipation to what the future holds.

Apostle Nicky always says, "Tears don't move God. Faith moves God." My tears did not move God that early morning. My faith in God moved Him.

What I know about the supernatural I have learned from my spiritual parents. They have taught me that we are here to activate the next generation with the supernatural power of God. The supernatural is a concept that many deem demonic, only because of a lack of understanding. "The supernatural goes beyond time, space, and matter. Miracles is the sign language of God that He loves you," says Apostle Nicky. Apostle Nicky is the leader of The Movement of the Supernatural. He believes that faith is the access point to the supernatural.

People easily hinder or quench the work of the Holy Spirit in their lives by the enemies of the supernatural, namely:

- The spirit of reason.
- The spirit of conformity.
- The organization of man (methods and programs).
- The spirit of religion. (Van der Westhuizen, 2016)

The supernatural can be activated in all our lives by faith through the demonstration of the power of God. The supernatural is displayed by signs, miracles, and wonders. As children of God, we have a mandate from heaven to spread the gospel, heal the sick, and cast out demons as in Matthew 10.

"And as you go, preach this message: 'Heaven's kingdom realm is accessible, close enough to touch.' You must continually bring healing to lepers and to those who are sick, and make it your habit to break off the demonic presence from people, and raise the dead back to life. Freely you have received the power of the kingdom, so freely release it to others." Matthew 10:7-8 (TPT)

Heavens Kingdom realm is accessible, close enough to touch. Is this not the best news you have ever heard? We have been given the power and authority by God to heal, deliver, and raise people from the dead. We have been freely activated with power from above and we can freely share this gift with others.

We will take a walk in the lives, stories, and testimonies of people who have experienced the supernatural power of God.

Topics such as dreams, visions, the supernatural, heaven and hell are explored. I answer troublesome questions such as;

- Will I meet my loved ones in Heaven?
- What happens to babies in Heaven?
- Will we have animals in Heaven?
- Will we have our own homes in Heaven?
- What rewards awaits us in Heaven?
- Will I be married in Heaven?
- What is the difference between a dream and a vision?
- Is there really a place called hell?
- What does hell look like? What does Heaven look like?
- Can a born again child of God be demon possessed?
- What is the supernatural?
- What role do angels have on Earth?
- Will demons torment us in hell?

- Why is the word rapture not mentioned in the Bible?
- When will Jesus be returning?
- How can I prepare my family?
- How can I help my loved ones to be ready the for the coming of Jesus.
- Is AI and cryptocurrencies part of the mark of the beast?
- What is the next pandemic that is coming?
- Will the church be around for the mark of the beast?

My prayer for you is that you will understand and use the knowledge easily to enrich the lives of people around you as well as your own. May your heart be opened, your spirit strengthened and the truth of God minister to you throughout the pages.

My spiritual Father, Apostle Nicky, taught me, and I confess this over my life often: "I carry the favor of God. I am distinct by my knowledge, favor, and wisdom." People will recognize that I am different, that I am full of wisdom and knowledge and humility. When I walk into a room, the atmosphere of Heaven enters with me. I have favor with God, and I have favor with man."

When I leave a conversation, an eternal imprint of the goodness and favor of God stays behind in their lives. I leave the residue of Heaven behind. Because of this, your life will change for the better, not because of me, but because you will meet Jesus in the coming pages.

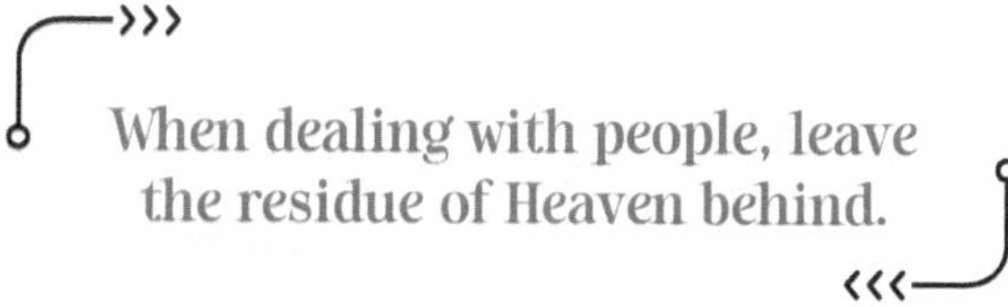

Apply wisdom and discernment in all areas of your life. May you download wisdom from heaven as you read the pages and may your life be filled with knowledge.

"Never mistake knowledge for wisdom. The one helps you make a living the other helps you make a life."
- Sandra Kerry

Wisdom in Hebrew means, skilled in living. It requires time, years, and discipline to make it happen. Billy Graham believes that, "knowledge is horizontal, and wisdom is vertical, it comes down from above."

"To know what to do with what you know is the essence of wisdom. Wisdom is knowing what to do and skill is knowing how to do it - virtue is doing it. Knowledge is proud because it knows so much, wisdom is humble because it knows so little. Today there is a lot of means but little meaning, lots of knowing but little know why, and lots of sight but little of insight," these wise words were said by my friend John C. Maxwell.

"Any fool can know - the point is to understand."
- Albert Einstein

One of my mentors, Dr. Vivian Rodgers, said: "Wisdom is the application of knowledge." My prayer is that you will apply the wisdom in the coming pages to your own life. I also pray that this wisdom will enable you to grow in intimacy with God, Godly integrity, stature, and influence.

Note from the author: I purposefully employ various versions of the Bible as a valuable tool to enhance people's understanding and effectively convey my message. Each scripture I include is carefully chosen and used within the context of the subject being discussed. I firmly believe that all translations of the Bible hold inherent truth and have evolved over centuries to aid our comprehension. It is important to note that utilizing different translations does not diminish the meaning or power of God's word. On the contrary, the Word of God remains potent and impactful, always achieving its intended purpose, regardless of the specific translation employed.

1.2 Unlocking Destiny: Live a Life of Purpose on Purpose

The simplest translation of the word purpose is to live a life of purpose (meaning) on purpose.

According to Google (Google, n.d.), **IN10TIONALITY** means: The fact of being deliberate or on purpose. The quality of mental states (e.g., thoughts, beliefs, desires, hopes) consists in their being directed toward some object or state of affairs. It derives from the word intentional of Latin origin and has been used since the mid-16th century, which means doing something on purpose or deliberately.

Accordingly, we can see that nothing about **IN10TIONALITY** is done by chance. It is done deliberately. It is very much intended and even calculated. It is well planned and done on purpose while being conscious of it. This was the birthplace of **IN-10-TIO-NALITY** and 10 Ways to Live a Rewarding and **IN10TIONAL** Life.

By intentionally improving the quality of decisions, choices, and habits we make and develop daily, we can improve our life quality and status.

> By intentionally improving the quality of decisions, choices, and habits, we improve our life quality and overall status.

Even the number 10 in **IN10TIONALITY** is written intentionally. Ten is the number of the divine order or the number of the Creator's Divine law. Making this number the perfect number. This is a way of adopting it into our own lives. The words "God said" are repeated ten times throughout in Genesis. We also say when something is perfect, it is "a perfect ten". When we do well, it is "10/10". We even measure certain things on a scale of 1 to 10. We have ten fingers to easily remember the ten things on which we will be focusing.

In primary school, one Sunday morning, the children were called to the front of the church. The minister at that time explained the ten commandments in such a way that I can still remember it because of the images he used. I am not proposing that these are the ten commandments, but I trust that you will create a picture of each of the ten intentional points in your mind to last you a lifetime.

In the Bible, the number ten is mentioned 242 times. The number ten also symbolizes a tenth. In this regard, many believers believe and give a tenth of their income. This also makes ten a number of the divine economy, placing believers in a position of power and provision. I refer you to Malachi 3:10, a very well-known scripture about the tithe.

"Bring all the tithes (the whole tenth of your income) into the storehouse, that there may be food in My house, and prove Me now by it, says the Lord of hosts, if I will not open the windows of Heaven for you and pour you out a blessing, that there shall not be room enough to receive it. And I will rebuke the devourer [insects and plagues] for your sakes, and he shall not destroy the fruits of your ground, neither shall your vine drop its fruit before the time in the field, says the Lord of hosts. And all nations shall call you happy and blessed, for you shall be a land of delight, says the Lord of hosts" Malachi 3:10-12 (AMPC).

This is one of the only scriptures where God invites us to put Him to the test. He has also promised protection, health, provision, blessings, and happiness. I believe that opening the windows of Heaven means more than financial prosperity. The purpose of a window is two-fold. It is there for one to look through and to let light in. When looking through a window, I believe we will see windows of opportunity open before us.

As light flows in through the windows in the form of the presence of

God, and Godly wisdom, revelation will flow out. As a result, we will be able to interpret opportunities correctly and be successful in our ventures.

We are undoubtedly dealing with a potent combination of natural and supernatural events. In my mind, this says 10 to 1. We are in for something out of this world. Join me as you discover this phenomenon further.

IN10TIONALITY is the message every successful motivational speaker delivers at every single event. But, unfortunately, most **UN-IN10TIONAL** listeners fail to realise that the underlying message is the same each time.

It is marketed cleverly with different bows and wrappings to draw you in. However, they are selling you the mindset that you can have whatever you want - the house, the career, the car, or life, by simply being **IN10TIONAL** about your everyday life. That means living life purposefully and not allowing life to happen to you.

Contrary to popular belief, unhappiness is not the result of what one does and does not possess. Instead is the consequence of failing to control people, circumstances, and events. The desire to dictate how any of those mentioned earlier would change because you want them to is a reactive way of life because no one has or would ever have control over them. The result, therefore, would entail submitting to a sub-standard life devoid of happiness.

Being **IN10TIONAL** means using the God-given right we have to choose differently, and in so doing, you can create wealth and sculpt a better life.

> Being IN10TIONAL means using the God-given right we have to choose differently, and in so doing, you can create wealth and sculpt a better life.

May your journey of **IN10TIONALITY** be one of performance, promotion, and pride in what you do. I always strive to do things with passion, power, and purpose.

One thing is for sure, you cannot outgrow your own personal growth.

Your journey of personal growth may involve:

- Mastering a skill and stretching beyond yourself.
- Perhaps developing the social skills, you may not currently have.
- Choosing different responses to what is beyond your control.

It could be having an additional income stream, changing careers, or better still, becoming your own boss. The choices are yours, and these are choices you will need to make repeatedly until they become habits.

Keeping in mind that **IN10TIONALITY** is far greater than motivation.

Where motivation provides the match that lights the fire, **IN10TIONALITY** is the fuel that keeps the fire burning well after the emotions have dissipated. It is not great men that change the world, but weak men in the hands of God.

1.3 IN10TIONAL Thinking

Use the **IN10TIONAL Thinking** sections to practice being **IN10TIONAL** with your soul.

Look for what I call "aha" moments. These are those moments of revelation or enlightenment you come across during the reading of this book. Write them down, journal them, draw your conclusions, and use them to make practical applications.

What are the 10 areas you can be **IN10TIONAL** in:

- Be **IN10TIONAL** about your **SOUL**
- Be **IN10TIONAL** about your **RELATIONSHIPS**
- Be **IN10TIONAL** about your **COMMUNITY**
- Be **IN10TIONAL** about your **HAPPINESS**
- Be **IN10TIONAL** about your **MONEY**
- Be **IN10TIONAL** about what makes you **GREATER**
- Be **IN10TIONAL** about what makes your **STRONGER**
- Be **IN10TIONAL** about what makes your mind **HEALTHIER**
- Be **IN10TIONAL** about your future and **PLAN AHEAD**
- Be **IN10TIONAL** about your **TEAM**

For any of the other **IN10TIONAL** points, you can purchase the book on **IN10TIONALITY** from Amazon, Takealot, and other leading places where books are sold.

From here on out we will focus solely on the soul and how to be **IN10TIONAL** with your soul so that you can prosper as your soul prospers.

In the chapters, sections end with **IN10TIONAL** Thinking and a prayer to activate the supernatural upon your life. This is to put what you have just learned into action.

IN10TIONALITY is **IN10TIONAL** and requires your action. Your first task is to get a notebook. Leave it open as you work through this book.

I **IN10TIONALLY** added thought-provoking questions throughout the chapters for you to answer.

I want you to be a part of this journey. As you read, write down the questions and meditate on the questions and your answers. Pray the prayers out loud.

Then, review them, and with time, they will change as part of your ongoing process.

Once you have completed your journey, you will know yourself and where you are heading in your spiritual direction.

The direction in life awaits. Identity awaits. Health awaits. Happiness awaits. Flourishing relationships await. Your future awaits and your new identity in Christ awaits.

My aim once you have completed this reading and did the practical applications, is not to say "Wow, what an incredible book this was," but rather, "Wow, look how much better I became after reading and applying the principles in this book. My life has turned out so much better than I thought, and I got so much more out of life than I expected.

Chapter I

IN10TIONALITY - A FASCINATION WITH THE DEEPER THINGS IN LIFE

"But the one who endures to the end will be saved. And the Good News about the Kingdom will be preached throughout the whole world, so that all nations will hear it; and then the end will come." Matthew 24:13-14 (NLT).

I have always had a fascination with heaven, angels, and supernatural occurrences. I just never knew that what seemed normal for me was not normal for people around me. It is called the supernatural. It was indeed super and totally natural for me. For most people the supernatural is labeled as evil and scary and they stay far away from it.

People relate the supernatural with sorcery, witchcraft and demon possession. The devil is an imitator and cannot produce anything original, so he is simply imitating evil in a way that is Holy and created by God. Society has painted us a very warped picture of what the supernatural is and what the supernatural power of God is.

As a child I remember being around six years of age and playing with angels was a normal occurrence for me. We lived in Bottlebrush Street and our backyard was my kingdom. I played outside as much as I could and I was never alone. I pretended to camp and played in our sand pit, hung on the grapevines and climbed on the jungle gym my dad and grandfather had built for me. Sitting in the sand pit, I was always having conversations with the angels I played with and those that surrounded me.

It has always been a desire for me to experience and make the supernatural part of my daily life without being weird. My desire is to operate at the standards and expectations of eternity not the standards and expectations of this world.

> Operate at the standards and expectations of eternity not the standards and expectations of this world.

I started writing this book during the launch of my previous book, **IN10TIONALITY**, living a rewarding and **IN10TIONAL** life. In complete dependence on God, every step of this journey opened up a world of angelic and glorious events.

I often dream at night and know when morning comes that these dreams are significant. I prayerfully consider the meaning of these dreams and ask the Holy Spirit for interpretation. I want only to know His thoughts toward me.

"I will praise the Lord, who counsels me; even at night my heart instructs me." Psalm 16:7 (NIV).

One such dream I had was when I was playing a netball game. In the middle of the match as I jumped for the ball my clothes started to tear. With each jump it tore more. The color of my clothes where black and I found that to be odd for this game. In the dream I realized this is not good, yet I kept playing and knew that no one else could see that my clothes were tearing.

The significance of this dream was that it symbolizes the season of life I was in and the game of life I was playing. I was winning. In the dream I was outmanoeuvring every other player and they had no chance to get the ball, despite my clothing situation.

This was what it meant for me at that time, I was going to, or I am in a place where I will outmaneuver my opponents in the game of life. I was winning.

The clothing represented my spiritual state of readiness. I was clothed with Christ. The color black on clothing normally means mourning, in the past that could have been true. The truth now is I am being stripped of the mourning and I am being clothed with Christ.

> Be stripped of mourning and be clothed with Christ.

Praise God, He is preparing me for the next season in my life.
How does God speak to you? What do you say or ask God to answer you? In dreams, visions, or maybe a still small voice? Some people wake up in the middle of the night or early hours of the morning and spend time with God in prayer, meditation, worship and in the

Word. How can you relate? What and when is your sweet spot full of supernatural conversations?

How I relate is talking … talking to God all day long … in my thoughts and even out loud at times. I dream and I have visions. He answers me all the time. He is such an amazing God and knows my sweet spot is definitely not mornings. It takes me a really long time to actually be awake. Yet, I can absolutely sense His presence and feel Him right there with me.

For a long time there was a specific place where I prayed in the mornings. I would sit on a specific couch to read, pray and worship. For many months that was just my spot. Then my routine changed and so did my spot. I moved to my room just because it felt more private. One morning I walked into the living room where I used to pray. The presence of God hit me in a unique and powerful way I have never experienced before. There was Jesus, on my couch, waiting for me. I remember so clearly how he said: "Good morning my girl, I have been waiting for you."

The words ran through my body like electricity. The presence was tangible, and the moment was one where Heaven meets earth. The words, "my girl" meant so much to me. My gran used to call me this. There was just so much love in those words.

I sat right next to Jesus and soaked up the moment. I would worship and pray, and for long moments just became quiet within myself. What felt like mere minutes was actually hours passing. When I finally got up and carried on with my day it was more than five hours later.

This experience showed me that Jesus loves it when we set out a time and place to spend time with Him. He loves it so much, He even looks forward to it and makes sure He is there. In person. Not in a dream. I read a book called, "Seeing the voice of God by Laura Harris Smith

(Smith, 2014), where she explains that if we sleep 6-8 hours a night by the age of 50, we have slept for almost 20 years of our life. Why would God not speak to us for 20 years of our lives? That thought was insane and hard to grasp. How could I not speak or communicate with God for such a long time? Even in my sleep as my body rests, my soul is still awake and receiving.

God spoke to prominent men in the Bible through dreams and visions. To Daniel God showed a vision and gave him the interpretation of a dream an answer, a solution. What do you need an answer for, or a solution to? Ask God. Have you ever wrestled with a problem and then one day you just wake up with the answer? Now you know where it is coming from, or rather from "Who" it is coming from.

"Then the secret was revealed to Daniel in a vision of the night, and Daniel blessed the God of heaven. Daniel answered, Blessed be the name of God forever and ever! For wisdom and might are His! He changes the times and the seasons; He removes kings and sets up kings. He gives wisdom to the wise and knowledge to those who have understanding!" Daniël 4:35

"He reveals the deep and secret things; He knows what is in the darkness, and the light dwells with Him!" (Job 15:8; Ps. 25:14; Matt. 6:6)

"I thank You and praise You, O God of my fathers, Who has given me wisdom and might and has made known to me now what we desired of You, for You have made known to us the solution to the king's problem." Daniel 2:19-23 (AMPC).

I just love how the Prophet Isaiah describes how our souls speak to God at night.

"The path of right-living people is level. The Leveler evens the road for the right-living. We're in no hurry, God. We're content to linger in the path sign-posted with your decisions. Through the night my soul longs for you. Deep from within me my spirit reaches out to you. When your decisions are on public display, everyone learns

how to live right. If the wicked are shown grace, they don't seem to get it. In the land of right living, they persist in wrong living, blind to the splendour of God." Isaiah 26:7-10 (MSG).

Having this type of relationship with God is not far-fetched at all, in fact it is incredibly close and possible for you right here right now. If this is the type of relationship you would want with Jesus, the Son of God then I invite you to say this prayer with me, from your heart.

Heavenly Father,

I come to you in prayer, recognizing my need for a Savior. I confess that I am a sinner and have fallen short of your glory. I believe that Jesus Christ is the Son of God and that He died on the cross for my sins. I believe that He rose again on the third day, conquering death and giving me the gift of eternal life.

Forgive me of my sins and come into my heart as my Lord and Savior. I surrender my life to you and ask that you guide me in your ways. Fill me with your Holy Spirit, that I may have the strength and courage to live for you. I renounce all wickedness from my life. I fill my life with the love and light of Jesus. I confess that you, Jesus, are the truth and the light.

I want to know you in a deeper more intimate way Lord, speak to me and reveal yourself to me in a supernatural way?

I want a Holy encounter with you. I want to hear your voice and see your work through my hands. Use me, Lord.

Thank you for your unconditional love and grace. I pray that I may grow in my faith and be a witness to your love and truth.

In Jesus' name, I pray.

Amen.

1.1 Spirit, Soul and Body

We are called to be creatures of balance. When God created the world with its weather patterns and cycles - light during the day and the moon to reflect the glory of the sun during night time. He established a flow that brought balance.

In the animal kingdom each carnivore received enough to survive. Each herbivore received enough vegetation to survive, and each insect was equipped with in-built instructions to aid the pollination process. All this was done to create balance, with one part not outweighing the other.

Human beings, God's masterpieces of creation, were made no differently. Having been created to function at their optimum when there is a balance. While comprising a body, soul, and spirit, where each part is important for the individual, the onus lies on everyone to find the balance to reach their fullest potential.

Science has shown that too much of anything can harm us. It is unfortunate to see that in the superficial world in which we live, the vast majority of people's focus is not necessarily on cultivating each aspect of their being, their soul and spirit. Instead, they focus on the external picture of what they perceive to be happiness- their bodies; resulting in disorder and ultimately chaos. Is it wrong to cultivate the body? Absolutely not!

As Apostle Paul says, we have been given these earthly tents that can be folded up at any time. It is our responsibility to take care of it. I was entertained for hours by the songs of Jan de Wet a South African gospel singer. I would listen to his albums one after the other as I lay on the carpet listening on CD Player. Jan de Wet En Die Loflaaities was some of my best friends. One of the songs I listened to often was "Weet jy nie jy is 'n tempel", translated as "Don't you know you're a temple?"

Don't you know, don't you know, you're a temple?
Don't you know, don't you know, you're a temple?
You are a temple of the Holy Spirit

Full of praise full of power full of joy
Full of praise full of power full of joy
Full of praise full of power full of joy
You are a temple of the Holy Spirit (Jan, n.d.)

As I am writing, I am singing along. What wonderful memories. The key is not to shame those who do cultivate their bodies, but to reveal that each part (body, spirit, and soul) makes them who they are and needs to be treated with an equal amount of respect. We need to be healthy and looked after. The Word of God says we need to prosper as our soul prospers.

When we look at humanity and the issues that plague us, it is plain to see that not enough people have seen the value in being **IN10TIONAL** about the state of their soul, leaving them unhappy, anxious, and depressed and in dire need of some tender loving care.

What is the soul?

The soul is one-third part off the triune being that consists of the body, the soul and the spirit. We say, we are spirit, living in a body that possesses a soul. The soul is attached to the spirit and not the body. The soul is the seat where a man or woman's mind, will, and emotions resides. The mind is our intellect. Our will is our passion and desire to create something and our emotions shows feeling. With each part of the soul explained briefly, one can clearly see that the soul is at the center of every decision, be it good or bad. When habits are formed, they are first conceived in the soul.

> >>>
> The soul is the seat where a man or woman's mind, will, and emotions resides.
> <<<

So how do we bring about the balance of the soul, you may ask? The answer is simple. In the same way, we set goals to reach fitness levels with regard to our bodies, which is similar to how we can set goals to our souls.

> >>>
> When habits are formed, they are first conceived in the soul.
> <<<

If this does not happen, we will soon be echoing the Psalmist in Psalm 42,

"Why are you in despair, O my soul? Why have you become restless and disquieted within me? Hope in God and wait expectantly for Him, for I shall yet praise Him, The help of my countenance and my God." Psalm 42:11 (AMP).

On a lazy Sunday afternoon, my family and I scrolled through the channels and came across a movie called 'Cowboys and Aliens'. The movie combines elements of the traditional western genre with science fiction and extraterrestrial themes. Not the kind of movie I would normally watch, but what caught my attention was the aliens who were living on earth while the people came from another world. How odd is that? The opposite of what we know, or is it?

The humans in the movie were from another planet. I realized when you are a child of God, you are from another "planet," and are simply passing through here. Even the Word says we are not of this world.

"I have given them your word. And the world hates them because they do not belong to the world, just as I do not belong to the world. I'm not asking you to take them out of the world, but to keep them safe from the evil one. They do not belong to this world any more than I do." John 17:14-16 (NLT).

We are citizens of Heaven, and not of the earth, and we are urged to live by the heavenly rules and not those of the earth. Our passports are stamped in Heaven as we travel through earth. As we live in expectation of the return of our Lord and Saviour.

"But our citizenship is in heaven. And we eagerly await a Saviour from there, the Lord Jesus Christ." Philippians 3:20 TPT).

The story is set in the late 19th century in the town of Absolution, Arizona Territory. The protagonist, Jake Lonergan (played by Daniel Craig), wakes up in the middle of the desert with no memory of his past and a strange metal device strapped to his wrist. As he makes his way to Absolution, he encounters hostile townsfolk and discovers he is a wanted outlaw.

However, the situation takes an unexpected turn when the town is attacked by an alien spacecraft. These technologically advanced extraterrestrials abduct several people, including the wife of Colonel Woodrow Dolarhyde (played by Harrison Ford), a wealthy and influential rancher. In the chaos, Lonergan's mysterious wrist device activates and proves to be a powerful weapon against the alien invaders.

As the story unfolds, secrets about Lonergan's past and the true nature of the alien invaders are revealed. They are the enemy of darkness. In the film, the humans were wearing strange metal devices strapped to their wrists. They were watches that connected them with 'their world'. I drew a comparison with a believer who came to earth with a powerful weapon strapped to his wrist; the Word of God. In our mouth is a two-edged sword of the Word.

"For the word of God is alive and powerful. It is sharper than the sharpest two-edged sword, cutting between soul and spirit, between joint and marrow. It exposes our innermost thoughts and desires." Hebrews 4:12 (NLT).

Part of their mission in the movie was that they had 'something' special to return to their world. So do we, souls for the Kingdom of God. They were only there because they were on a mission. When the mission is fulfilled they go home. As believers, we are also on a mission. Jesus told us *"But the one who endures to the end will be saved. And the Good News about the Kingdom will be preached throughout the whole world, so that all nations will hear it; and then the end will come."* Matthew 24:13-14 (NLT).

We are not of this world, and we are mission-orientated to bring souls to the Kingdom of God. We do not wear watches to connect with heaven, but we have the Holy Spirit to lead and guide our daily steps. Jesus also prays and intercedes on our behalf. And we do have a blueprint concerning our behavior on temporary earth.

"Don't copy the behavior and customs of this world, but let God transform you into a new person by changing the way you think. Then you will learn to know God's will for you, which is good and pleasing and perfect. Don't just pretend to love others. Really love them. Hate what is wrong. Hold tightly to what is good." Romans 12:2, 9 (NLT).

Peter also warns us in one of his letters. *"Beloved, I implore you as aliens and strangers and exiles [in this world] to abstain from the sensual urges (the evil desires, the passions of the flesh, your lower nature) that wage war against the soul."* (1 Peter 2:11 (PC).

How do we protect our hearts, and set goals for a healthy soul?

1.2 Goals for the Soul

How do you improve the health of your soul to prosper? It is after all what God wants for us, His will for us, to prosper not in just one thing but all things according to the Scriptures. John prays this earnest prayer for us:

"Beloved, I pray that in every way you may succeed and prosper and be in good health [physically], just as [I know] your soul prospers [spiritually]." 3 John 1:2 (AMP).

Therefore, it is time for us to look at a few ways to prosper our souls and grow spiritually.

- Spend time with God.
- Forgive people.
- Grow spiritually.
- Spend time with like-minded people.
- Share your faith with someone else.

1. Spending time with God

The most important goal for your soul is to spend time with the One who created you. Be it early in the morning or during the day, or even at night; your soul needs to feed off the presence of God. In Psalm 63:1. King David wrote: "My soul thirsts for you," revealing two things about the soul. The first is that it has the ability to become parched, dry, and thirsty. The second is the solution to quenching its thirst - with the presence of God.

> The most important goal for your soul is to spend time with the One whoe created you.

Set time apart for yourself during each day, become quiet, get a notebook. Have a pen ready and put worship music on. While you read the Word of God, ask the Holy Spirit to reveal the hidden mysteries and secrets of the Word to you. Worship God and tell Him how amazing He is. Show an attitude of thankfulness and instead of asking God for the next thing, thank Him for what you have. Pray, and confess the Scripture as this speaks life into any situation.

I apply the formula for prayer and spending time with the Word of God and building a relationship with Him through the examples given to us by the men of God in His Word.

The Message Translation of the Bible tells us how to enter joyfully into the presence of God by giving thanks. It teaches us how to spend time with God and gives us a glimpse of how to communicate with God. I believe it is no coincidence that the author of this Psalm is anonymous, God does nothing without reason, and I feel that this was written so any person could have written it and apply it to their lives.

Psalm 100:4-5 says, "Enter with the password: "Thank you!" Make yourselves at home, talking praise. Thank him. Worship him." To help us to understand that when we want to communicate with God, we need to have an attitude and exhibit thankfulness. I love how the Psalmist expresses himself by declaring, "Make yourself at home." To me, it says get comfortable, this might take you a while, do not rush your time with God. This is the reason why I say …

Find a quiet place. Get a pen and paper, and get ready to receive what God gives to you in these moments you spent with Him. The Scripture guides us as follows, "Thank Him. Worship Him." Each phrase is followed by a full stop, indicating first do the one and then the other. Thus, it entails a sequence of events to help us talk to God.

In the New Testament, Jesus also helps us to understand how to spend time with Him and how to pray; thereby, making this practical.

"But when you pray, go into your most private room, close the door and pray to your Father who is in secret, and your Father who sees [what is done] in secret will reward you." Matthew 6:6 (AMP)

Apostle Paul's letter to the Church in Philippi was a striking example of how to be thankful and grateful despite the circumstances. Even though he wrote to the Church from prison, the tone of the letter was joyful and full of hope and encouragement. It helps us to understand that Paul's relationship with Christ was grounded in the word and prayer. This indicates that the relationship equals favor and opens doors.

Paul gives us another formula for spending time with God in his letter:

"Do not be anxious or worried about anything, but in everything [every circumstance and situation] by prayer and petition with thanksgiving, continue to make your [specific] requests known to God. And the peace of God [that peace which reassures the heart, that peace] which transcends all understanding, [that peace which] stands guard over your hearts and your minds in Christ Jesus [is yours]." Philippians 4:6-7 (AMP).

He also tells us to speak to God through prayer and give thanks. Once again, praise and worship and an attitude of thankfulness are mentioned. This time, we turn our concerns into prayers.

Next, we continue to make our requests and petitions known to God. This gives us the assurance that we can and may ask God for the things we want and need. He tells us how to ask God for something in prayer by saying: Be specific and make your request known to God. You can remind God about the request and things asked for in prayer. Then you can receive the peace that God has heard your prayer and is working to answer it in His way. It always works out for your best.

From these examples, we can see a simple and practical way to help us enter into the presence of God and have two-way communication.

- Spend time with God in a quiet place where you are comfortable.
- Worship and praise Him by giving thanks and making His name great.
- Communicate with God, share your hearts' deepest desires, concerns, and thoughts with Him and receive the answer and comfort to your prayer.
- Take time to listen to what God is saying, do not do all the talking. Write it down in your notebook. When God speaks, make notes, and meditate about it.
- Receive from God what you need for the day.
- Read, study and meditate on the word of God daily.

We often hear we have to live with an attitude of gratitude, and this is why the statement rings true even today. When the people of Israel were delivered from the Egyptians, it did not take long for them to start murmur and complain. They stopped being thankful for what the Lord has done for them. During this time, the Israelites were wandering in the desert of Sin, which is between Elim and Sinai. Moses had just turned the bitter water at Marah into water for them to drink, when they grumbled about food. They sat around reminiscing about the past and the overflow of food and bread they had back in Egypt.

Do we not also behave like the Israelites? God comes through for us in a mighty way. The Red Sea is not even full yet, the miracle is still fresh?

Then we complain about our current situation. We reminisce about the past and the good old days, and how good things were. If only this, and if only that, are the thoughts which enter our minds.

Look how amazing God is despite their behavior, and even our own behavior. He then said to Moses: *"Behold, I will cause bread to rain from heaven for you; the people shall go out and gather a day's portion every day, so that I may test them [to determine] whether or not they will walk [obediently] in My instruction (law)."* Exodus 16:4 (AMP).

"So, in the evening, the quails came up and covered the camp, and in the morning, there was a blanket of dew around the camp. When the layer of dew evaporated, on the surface of the wilderness there was a fine, flake-like thing, as fine as frost on the ground. When the Israelites saw it, they said to one another: "What is it?" For they did not know what it was. And Moses said to them: "This is the bread which the LORD has given you to eat. This is what the LORD has commanded: 'Let every man gather as much of it as he needs. Take an omer for each person, according to the number of people each of you has in his tent.'"

"The Israelites did so, and some gathered much [of it] and some [only a] little. When they measured it with an omer, he who had gathered a large amount, had no excess, and he, who had gathered little, had no lack; every man gathered according to his need (family size). Moses said, "Let none of it be left [overnight] until [the next] morning." But they did not listen to Moses, and some left a supply of it until morning, and it bred worms and became foul and rotten, and Moses was angry with them. So they gathered it every morning, each as much as he needed, because when the sun was hot it melted." Exodus 16:13-21 (AMP).

Each family gathered manna according to their need. What is your need? What are your families' needs?

Each morning when we go into fellowship and conversation with God, He gives us new fresh manna for the day. Manna is a gift, and God has a gift for you to receive daily. New fresh manna from heaven awaits you every day from God. What do you need today? In John 6:48-51, Jesus compares Himself to manna. Christ is our daily bread that satisfies our eternal spiritual need. When we spend time with God, all our material and spiritual needs will be met.

2. Forgiving people

Unforgiveness is a merciless master who makes you buy into the lie that you would be better off living behind walls with a grudge. It does this with the intention of isolating and draining your soul of every good and enriching thing that comes your way. Relationships become strained, making the channel of giving and receiving difficult between people. Conversely, forgiveness is liberating, no longer allowing the hurts of others to determine how you live your own life. You should check your soul constantly for unforgiveness by observing your attitude around certain people. If you feel uneasy where there once was ease or are tempted to rejoice at their shortcomings, there may be a root of unforgiveness that needs to be addressed.

If you can just learn the lesson in the trial, you will make it through.

In high school, I randomly picked up a book by author Norman Vincent Peale. "The power of positive thinking" (Norman, 1998). It taught me that life comes with many challenges, but it remains our own choice how to respond to those challenges. Forgiveness for me is the same. It is a choice to work through something rather than to just get over something. We often say: "I'll just get over it," and then, not too long afterward, that same thing challenges you again, sometimes even with the same person. Until you really deal with the situation or person, it will always come back. Most of the time, unforgiveness entails unresolved conflict, feelings, or incidents.

When problems strike, even though we are doing the right thing, life can feel so unfair. Retrenchment, sickness, the loss of a loved one, theft, trauma and many other events can be real-life examples. Real life events with which we need to deal and work through and for which we forgive people.

You feel as if all doors are closing on you, you feel depressed, and all the opportunities are just gone. You lose your hope, joy and security. Just getting up in the morning is a challenge. You have a choice; either unforgiveness will deal with you, or you will deal with unforgiveness.

So many people regret the things they never did for a person or said to a person, because unforgiveness held them back. And when they wanted to act, it was too late. Disappointment lasts a moment, but regret lasts a lifetime. Unforgiveness holds you back from your promised future. Living a life of not carrying grudges and forgiving quickly, sets you free to accomplish God's plan for your life.

The word of God is extremely descriptive regarding how quick forgiveness is supposed to be and actually advises us to "drop the issue, let it go" in Mark 11:25.

"Whenever you stand praying, if you have anything against anyone, forgive him [drop the issue, let it go], so that your Father who is in heaven will also forgive you your transgressions and wrongdoings [against Him and others]." Mark 11:25 (AMP).

To drop something or letting it go happens almost instantly; you make a decision and then it drops vertically. Just like that.

In order for me to just get through the events life throws at me, I tell myself, "There is a lesson to learn in this. Not, someone wants to teach me a lesson." The quicker I learn the lesson, the quicker I move on. Changing my mindset from a victim mentality and taking responsibility for my actions helped me to cultivate a lifestyle of forgiveness.

Saying things such as, "Life is unfair, this should not have happened to me. I do not need this. Why me?" My friend, the fare is the price you pay for a train ticket. Life isn't going to treat you fair. Satan is the god of this world, and he has blinded the hearts and minds of unbelievers.

And all the things we say in hard pressing situations are signs of a victim-mentality. We should feel the emotions, work through the pain and loss, but from an overcomers-mentality. I believe forgiveness and accountability is the first step towards that overcomers-mentality.

What do you think will happen if you realise that there is something in this event that will strengthen your character and prepare you for bigger and better; next-level opportunities in life?

Like a bow and arrow, the things that feel as if they are pulling us back in life, or holding us back, are actually the things that propels us to shoot straight into our future. Now we can look at a drawback in life as preparation to the comeback in your life. For the future to power up and shoot further.

3. Growing spiritually

The spirit and soul are closely interlinked because our spiritual growth can improve the condition of our soul. The spirit looks the same as our physical bodies. The word refers to us as being created in God's image, meaning God is spirit, and so are we. Spiritual growth entails spending time in prayer, talking to God and listening to Him. If we are made in His image, and we are made the same, communication should be easy, right?

Reading the Bible to understand the mind of God and learn how we could allow His word to change our thoughts is a vital aspect of spiritual growth. Praise and worship, which changes the atmosphere around us and enhances our mood. It is also a tool that can help us with spiritual growth. Can you see how spiritual growth can influence your soul positively?

In Apostle John's third letter, he prays, *"Beloved, I pray that in every way you may succeed and prosper and be in good health [physically], just as [I know] your soul prospers [spiritually]"* 3 John 1:2 (AMP).

Let us look at prayer and how it can help our spiritual growth as well as the balance between our bodies and our souls. Our bodies are our most important communication tool. The words we speak entail the smallest part of communication because our non-verbal communication speaks much louder than words.

We have already mentioned that man consists of a spirit, soul and body and each of these parts serves a purpose. In the New Testament, we discover that our bodies are the temples of the Lord, made to honour him; we can do so through prayer and worship.

"Do you not know that your body is a temple of the Holy Spirit who is within you, whom you have [received as a gift] from God, and that you are not your own [property]? You were bought with a price [you were actually purchased with the precious blood of Jesus and made His own]. So then, honour and glorify God with your body" 1 Corinthians 6:19-20 (AMP).

When I pray, talk and communicate with God, I honor and glorify God with my body that He has gifted me. My grandmother was a great example of a praying woman; she used to talk to God all day long. Sometimes she talked, sometimes she sang to Him, and at other times she would pray and make her requests known to God, whether she was making supper, driving, in the church office, or in the garden - just everywhere she went and whatever she was doing.

Many times I would walk into a room, and she would be talking out loud. As a child, I would say: "You are getting old, Grandma; old people talk to themselves." I can still see that little smile on the side of her mouth as she looked at me over the stove. It was a kind of grin that said: "If you only knew." She treated Him like a person - like someone who was right there next to her. In fact, she shared her most intimate thoughts with Him. We can too.

> Talk out loud, whisper to Him, or even talk
> to Him in your mind as if He is right here
> next to you, because He is.

Talk out loud, whisper to Him, or even talk to Him in your mind as if He is right here next to you, because He is.

In a world filled with social media and posting, how do we stay on trend with heaven? I thought, "If Heaven was a social media platform and prayer was a way that we would post our thoughts and actions the same way we do on earth I would pray; Lord, help me to update my status to heaven rather than on earth? Help me to trend in the halls of Heaven rather than the halls of fame here on earth."

Posting is how we communicate with people. Praying is how we communicate with God. Jesus is the only follower I need. And the only one I need to follow. I want to post my thoughts, desires, and praises on His wall! May my status Glorify God today.

With prayer, I share and communicate the following to God:

- Share my revelations.
- Share my pictures (dreams, desires, vision).
- Share my thoughts.
- My ups and downs.
- My victories, my losses.
- My pure and impure thoughts.

Lord, help me to update my status to heaven so that my actions go viral on earth. Amen

> Lord, help me to update my status to Heaven
> so that my actions go viral on earth.

My status update is described as;
My current state of −
- Mind (Inner thoughts and feelings)
- Planned actions (Dreams and goals)
- A legal standing (Identity)
- Current position or location (Work-life and church)
- My opinions, convictions, and beliefs (Way of thinking)
- My high-ranking social status or position (Your position in Christ).

My status determines my current position!

Besides talking to God, how do you pray? Do you stand, or lie down. How do you communicate with God?

How do you talk to God, and what does the different positions mean when you pray? I used four different postures and laid out the meaning and explanation of each of them in order to help you understand how you can grow your spiritual life during prayer and supplication to God.

1. Bowing in prayer

When we bow down in our prayer time, while lowering our head, it symbolises a prayer of worship. We move into a position of lowering our head and body to show reverence and respect. Our arms are in an upright position to show surrender. Worship is a state, or posture, a feeling or expression of reverence and adoration for a deity, or a being with a divine status. A state of reverence, adoration, worship, devotion, praise, thanksgiving, praying and glorifying.

The stance we take is to bow down in honor and reverence for the King of Kings and the Lord of Lords expressing our love and adoration for Him with our bodies.

"O come, let us worship and bow down, Let us kneel before the LORD our Maker [in reverent praise and prayer]." Psalms 95:6 (AMP)

"The man bowed his head and worshipped the LORD." Genesis 24:26 (AMP).

"Moses bowed to the earth immediately and worshipped [the Lord]." Exodus 34:8 (AMP).

2. Kneeling in prayer

When we kneel in the presence of God, we strip ourselves of ourselves. We come before God in humbleness, and lay down our selfishness and ego. It becomes a moment of being real with God. We go down on our knees. We sometimes refer to someone on their knees as a person who is on the verge of giving up or at the end of their rope, a person desperate for change or an encounter. Being on our knees in prayer shows that we give full control over to the mercies of God. When we become quiet in the presence of God, we bring prayers of supplication to the Lord.

"When Solomon finished offering this entire prayer and supplication to the LORD, he arose from before the LORD's altar, where he had knelt down with his hands stretched toward heaven." 1 Kings 8:54 (AMP)

When I humble myself in the presence of God by kneeling:

- I become like clay in the Potter's hand that He can form and make according to His will.
- I become like a child who can look up in awe to my Heavenly Father. (Mathew 18:1-5)

- I choose to be a servant and not a slave. (Mark 10:42-45).
- I am set free from hurt, guilt, selfishness and hardheartedness in my life through repentance.
- It is a form of praise, thanksgiving and worship.
- I come to realise that it is not about me; it is about God and His Greatness.

"I have sworn [an oath] by Myself, The word is gone out of My mouth in right-eousness And shall not return, That to Me every knee shall bow, every tongue shall swear [allegiance]" Isaiah 45:23 (AMP).

"For this reason [grasping the greatness of this plan by which Jews and Gentiles are joined together in Christ] I bow my knees [in reverence] before the Father [of our Lord Jesus Christ]" Ephesians 3:14 (AMP).

When I kneel in prayer, I submit to the will of God for my life. I take up my position in Christ, I am freed from afflictions, and I acknowledge the Lordship of Jesus upon my life.

3. Praying on your face before God

Searching for the will of God for our life, is a lifelong journey, especially in times of crisis, in our lives and in the lives of others. We become aware of our weaknesses and shortcomings, and the greatness and strength of God are revealed.

"Then Moses and Aaron went from the presence of the assembly to the doorway of the Tent of Meeting (tabernacle) and fell on their faces [before the LORD in prayer]. Then the glory and brilliance of the LORD appeared to them." Numbers 20:6 (AMP).

The Glory of God can lift us out of circumstances and pull us out into victory and overcome our obstacles when we pray. This applies when we pray. We dwell in secret places, places of protection, breakthrough and the Glory of God.

> We dwell in secret places, places of protection, breakthrough and the Glory of God.

"He who dwells in the shelter of the Most High Will remain secure and rest in the shadow of the Almighty [whose power no enemy can withstand]. I will say of the LORD, "He is my refuge and my fortress, My God, in whom I trust [with great confidence, and on whom I rely]!" Psalms 91:1-2 (AMP).

When we are on our face before God, we show our total surrender to Him and His will in our lives. We wait upon Him to deliver, heal, protect, and set us free from ourselves and our circumstances. Our faces reveal our total surrender to God, but also our cry for help. We embrace the full surrender and obedience to Jesus. "Then Jesus said to his disciples, "If any of you wants to be my follower, you must give up your own way, take up your cross, and follow me." Matthew 16:24 (NLT).

"And after going a little farther, He fell face down and prayed, saying, "My Father, if it is possible [that is, consistent with Your will], let this cup pass from Me; yet not as I will, but as You will." Matthew 26:39 (AMP).

When I lie down on my face to pray, I surrender my life, my will and my emotions to God. His will for my life becomes evident, and the Gory of God comes upon me.

4. Standing in prayer

One of the most used postures in prayer is standing. Standing in prayer means action; it entails maintaining an upright position, supported by one's feet.

We pray in different ways while standing, such as:

- Standing with hands lifted high or with open arms.
- Standing with our head facing up or down.
- Standing with out-stretched arms.
- Standing with my hand on my heart.

When we stand, we also pray different types of prayers such as:

What King Solomon shows us in the book of 1 Kings 8:22.

"Then Solomon stood [in the courtyard] before the altar of the LORD in the presence of all the assembly of Israel and spread out his hands toward heaven." 1 Kings 8:22 AMP)

Jesus himself teaches us how to pray a powerful prayer of forgiveness when he left the city of Jerusalem.

"Whenever you stand praying, if you have anything against anyone, forgive him [drop the issue, let it go], so that your Father who is in heaven will also forgive you your transgressions and wrongdoings [against Him and others]" Mark 11:25 (AMP).

The habit of prayer alone will not bring spiritual growth; it not only empowers you, but also others. Praying is spending time with the word of God, reading and meditation a habit will bring growth to your spiritual life.

"But his delight is in the law of the LORD, And on His law [His precepts and teachings] he [habitually] meditates day and night. And he will be like a tree firmly planted [and fed] by streams of water, Which yields its fruit in its season; Its leaf does not wither; And in whatever he does, he prospers [and comes to maturity]." Psalms 1:2-3 (AMP).

Prayer and spending time with God does not only change our lives, but also the lives of people around us. We can pray for their salvation, health, prosperity and more; this, in turn, strengthens our faith and grows us spiritually at the same time.

We spend time with God through prayer and meditation. Hearing and reading the word of God, and praise and worship.

When I pray for my family and friends, I can see the works of God being administered in their lives. I witness the changes and breakthroughs through their answered prayers, and my spiritual life also grows. I grow in confidence in God, build faith and strength, as do my testimonies.

I thank God for their faith, spiritual growth, salvation, and daily encounters with the living God. I pray that my family and friends experience and express the power of God to spread the gospel through the way they live, the wisdom they receive and the manifested goodness of God which lead them in all they do.

"We give thanks to God, the Father of our Lord Jesus Christ, as we always pray for you, for we have heard of your faith in Christ Jesus [how you lean on Him with absolute confidence in His power, wisdom, and goodness], and of the [unselfish] love which you have for all the saints (God's people); because of the [confident] hope [of experiencing that] which is reserved and waiting for you in heaven. You previously heard of this hope in the message of truth, the gospel [regarding salvation], which has come to you. Indeed, just as in the whole world, the gospel is constantly bearing fruit and spreading [by God's power], just as it has been doing among you ever since the day you first heard of it and understood the grace of God in truth [becoming thoroughly and deeply acquainted with it]." Colossians 1:3-6 (AMP)

I thank God that they walk in the will and plan that He has for their lives daily. I declare that we are His workmanship and, therefore, we submit and accept His good and acceptable will for our lives. I ask the Holy Spirit to make us sensitive to hear His voice so that we do not wander off on our paths but stick to the one path where He goes before us to make all the crooked paths straight, the path planned and pre-destined for us even before we were born.

"Through our union with Christ, we too have been claimed by God as his own inheritance. Before we were even born, he gave us our destiny; that we would fulfil the plan of God who always accomplishes every purpose and plan in his heart." Ephesians 1:11 (TPT).

I thank God that no weapon formed against them will prosper, that even if they had to go through difficult situations, they will walk through it better on the other side according to Psalm 91. I thank God for protection and guidance over their life.

My grandmother prayed for each of us: children, grandchildren and great-grandchildren by name morning and night. One day, I ask her jokingly: "Why do you do that? Surely God knows who you are talking about. He made our family."

Her answer was as simple and sweet as always - full of wisdom, "God said, I have called you by name. You are mine. He formed you in your mother's womb. He knitted you together, you were made for His Glory. He is a God of detail and interested in small details.

> He is a God of detail and
> interested in small details.

When I pray for each one of you and I call you up by name I am simply reminding God of the promises that He has in store for you according to His plan. I remind Him that even if you might be going through different hardships and troubles as other family members. He promised He will be with you, and you will not be overwhelmed, that you will not be burned. He will make it all work out well, despite your current circumstances. Your name is precious to God, it will not be ruined, or your reputation ruined. I remind Him of His word for each one of you, and, therefore, I know you are protected, loved and prospering."

For my friends I also pray for a good character, good morals and success in all that they set out to achieve according to Colossians 1:10.

"So that you will walk in a manner worthy of the Lord [displaying admirable character, moral courage, and personal integrity], to [fully] please Him in all things, bearing fruit in every good work and steadily growing in the knowledge of God [with deeper faith, clearer insight and fervent love for His precepts]." Colossians 1:10 (AMP).

Praying for friends and family brings me to my next point.

1. Spending time with like-minded people

The familiar saying that birds of a feather flock together should be your truth. My mom still says today, and there is not a better way of saying it than in Afrikaans, *"Meng jou met die semels dan vreet die varke jou op."* A simple way of saying "Do not be deceived:

"Bad company corrupts good morals." 1 Corinthians 15:33 (AMP).

Choose your friends and also your circles wisely. You will become like them and be associated with them.

** In English, people sometimes refer to the same saying as, "One bad apple spoils the rest."*

As your soul begins to gain healthy habits, sustaining that way of life would require (as sung by the Beatles) that you get by with a little help from your friends. True friends should encourage and uplift you, but should also guide you when you veer off the chosen path.

I always say a true friend knows the lyrics to your song, and when times are tough, and you forget your own words, they are able to sing the words back at you.

Do you have those kinds of people around you? The ones who love you all the time, not just sometimes. People who stick closer to you than a brother. In addition, the one who strengthens you in the workplace, has your back and holds the ladder for your success. Do you still have your old friends, the ones with whom you grew up?

What role do all of these people play in your life? Do they make you excel in life or do they drag you down?

Not all people are your friends; I understand the professional boundaries and the people I call my tribe. You need companionship, love, and support of that one person you call your husband or wife, and I realised I needed a best friend, who, for me, is Jesus.

Each of them plays a different role in your life. Therefore maintaining old, new, and future friendships and relationships are important. How to maintain them in a healthy way entails applying boundaries using the 5 - **S** - Rule.

- **S** et boundaries. Ooh, that's a hard one, yes, I did say in a healthy way.
- **S** tay in contact.
- **S** pend time on quality conversations, empower and encourage each other.
- **S** how a lot of love and pay attention to detail.
- **S** hare successes and pray for losses.

I have seen it time and time again; I know I am ready to move to the next chapter in my life when God brings people from my past back into my life and introduces them to my present. I assess why they are here, what chapter I am closing and what new chapter is opening.

That does not mean I write those people off; it is a simple wink from God telling me, "Get ready".

You are moving from one point to another. Sometimes it is spiritual; at other times it is in my career and, at times, it is in my personal life. Who have you met up with lately?

2. Sharing your faith with someone else

Lastly, share your faith, share your God story. This brings a two-fold reward. What it does for others is, it allows them to join in the soul **IN10TIONALLY** while, re-enforcing and validating what you believe. Sharing your faith with someone else is like exercising a muscle; the more you do it, the stronger it becomes and the better you get at it. Therefore, share your faith with someone you know, in a faith group, or with a complete stranger

1.3 IN10TIONAL Thinking

Being **IN10TIONAL** in your soul means setting objectives. In doing so, you commit to cultivating one of the most important components that make up who you are. Just remember that Rome was not built in a day, so be patient with yourself and take your time with each goal. As time goes on, you will find that it will get easier to prioritize your soul health.

I encourage you right now to take a deep breath, hold it for four seconds and breathe out, three times. Every time you do this, think about how blessed you are to be alive, be determined to rejoice in gratefulness today and be glad in it. Release all the negative emotions and be **IN10TIONAL** about your soul. Now give thanks in one of the new ways in which you learn to express the emotions of your soul.

I would encourage you to become part of a good Bible-based church that can walk the road with you and teach and encourage you as you grow. Read the Word daily, remain in prayer and surround yourself with like-minded faith-building believers.

Once again, stop for a moment and evaluate yourself by asking these questions. Write them down and review them every year. With the right decisions and people surrounding us, we can embark on a very successful and prosperous journey of **IN10TIONALITY**.

- Who are the people who surround you?
- Who is your tribe?
- Do you have people who stick to you closer than a brother or sister?
- Who strengthens you in the workplace, has your back and holds the ladder for your success?
- Do you still have your old friends with whom you grew up?
- Do you still cultivate those relationships?
- What role do all of these people play in your life?
- Do the people around you make you excel in life or do they drag you down?
- Who should change?
- Who should you let go of?
- Who should you have more off?
- Who should you be more like?

Ps Lillian van der Westhuizen always comforts me with the words, "Forgive quickly and love deeply." When you are ready to take the next step in your spiritual journey and spend time with God. Forgive people. Grow spiritually. Spend time with like-minded people. And share your faith with someone else. Pray this prayer with me:

Dear Heavenly Father,

I come before You with a humble heart, seeking a deeper and more intentional relationship with You. I recognize that prayer, worship, and fasting are powerful means through which I can draw closer to Your presence, understanding, and guidance. Today, I offer this prayer as a declaration of my sincere desire to strengthen our connection.

Lord, I ask for Your wisdom and discernment to prioritize and invest my time in prayer. Help me to carve out dedicated moments each day to enter into communion with You. May my prayers be genuine, heartfelt, and filled with gratitude for Your blessings, as well as an expression of my needs, hopes, and concerns. Teach me to listen attentively to Your still, small voice and to surrender my will to Yours.

Father, I long to experience deeper worship in Your presence. Open my eyes to the beauty of Your creation, the majesty of Your character, and the wonder of Your love. Let my worship be sincere, not merely in words or rituals, but in spirit and truth. Help me to surrender my whole being to You, offering my praises, adoration, and surrendering my ambitions, fears, and weaknesses at Your feet.

In seeking a more intentional relationship with You, I understand the significance of fasting. Give me the strength and discipline to deny my fleshly desires for a season, that I may focus my attention on You. As I abstain from certain foods or activities, I pray that my physical hunger will be a reminder of my spiritual hunger for You. Purify my heart, Lord, and create in me a hunger and thirst for righteousness.

Lord, I acknowledge that my relationship with You is a journey, and I am imperfect. I may stumble and fall, but I trust in Your grace and forgiveness. Help me to learn from my mistakes, grow in faith, and continually strive to deepen my connection with You.

May this prayer be a starting point, a turning point in my pursuit of a more intentional relationship with You. Grant me the discipline, passion, and perseverance to commit myself to prayer, worship, and fasting. Let these acts of devotion become a wellspring of spiritual renewal, guidance, and transformation in my life.

I offer this prayer in the name of Jesus, who showed us the way to a deeper relationship with You.

Amen.

Chapter II

IN10TIONALITY - Personal Heavenly Encounters

"My Father's house has many dwelling places. If it were otherwise, I would tell you plainly, because I go to prepare a place for you. And when everything is ready, I will come back and take you to myself so that you will be where I am. And you already know the way to the place where I'm going." John 14:2-4 (TPT).

In 2009, I got a disturbing phone call from Dubai who told me that my mother just had a stroke. It was very serious and we must pray for her life. What they didn't know at the time was that I had already had an awful feeling and I knew that I had to intercede for a family member. As I was praying fervently, I sensed in my spirit that I was indeed praying for my mom. It was already more than one hour of intense warfare when the phone call came through.

When I received that phone call it was just confirmation. I knew that if God would give me an assignment and burden for prayer then there is hope and I must push through in prayer. About half an hour after I received a call, I prevailed in prayer and suddenly the peace of God came upon me. I knew she was going to be okay.

A very similar situation happened on my 21st birthday in April. We were away in Limpopo on our game farm where my family and some close friends were gathered to celebrate. At around midday my grandmother went to lie on the bed to rest. I remember my aunt's expression when she heard that my grandmother wanted to lie down. "She never lies down, what is wrong?" she said. They went to see if she was okay and she was not.

The next moment, she was rushed to the hospital in Bela Bela. She was having a heart attack. They phoned the hospital in advance and arranged for a doctor and a helicopter to take her to the correct hospital with the best care at her age. She arrived in time and the rest was unknown to me.

At that point of my life it was very difficult for me to express emotion. It was way too much emotion and my heart was overwhelmed with fear. I felt feelings I had never felt before. This was my favorite person in the whole world and the shock was just too great. This was supposed to be a celebration.

At the same time the waiting just became too long. Time felt like it hardly ticked over. I went to the bathroom and sat on the toilet lid and I prayed. It wasn't about the place, but it was about having a place that was secluded and where I could actually just be alone with God. I mean no one would just walk into the bathroom. It was private.

I asked God to heal her, to make sure that she is fine, to give her a long life, to give her plenty of time with us, to heal her heart, to make everything right. I pleaded with God in that moment for health and healing! As I was sitting there, the same peace of God came upon me and I just knew that she was going to be 100% fine.

I went to sit on the veranda and waited for the news to come. It was good news. She was stable and she was going to be okay.

As I was praying for my mother that day with her stroke, the same peace that came upon me when my gran had had a heart attack, came upon me again. I knew that she is going to be fine. I knew the feeling of peace, I knew how the love of God felt. I knew the Healer. My grandmother lived many more years after that. She was 100% fine after her heart attack.

My mom, on the other hand, went to heaven that day. My mom also came back that very same day. Just like the Holy Spirit said to me it would be. This is her encounter and what she experienced in heaven.

While she was on her way to the hospital in the ambulance. She could vaguely remember the people telling her to hold on, stay awake, stay with us. Actually, she did not have the power to hold on or stay awake, or the energy for that matter to stay with anyone.

On the other hand, she felt how she travelled very quickly to which she knew was Heaven. No one told her it is what she described as an inner knowing. No one spoke to her but she knew.

I call it, a heavenly knowing. A kind of peace indescribable overcame her. In a time like this you just have an inkling, a knowing not known to a natural man but a knowing only understood by your spiritual man, even when you do not know why you know.

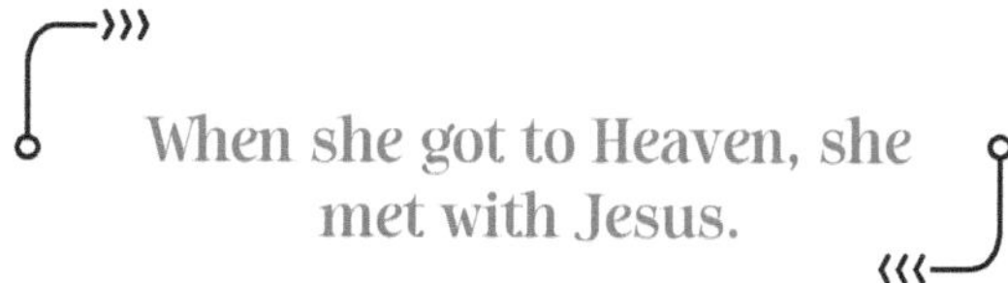

As a child, I imagined you walk into Heaven and Jesus is sitting behind a big brown desk, with a gold trim. The Book of Life is open before Him with a gold pen and a feather on it. Ready to read you your fate and all you did wrong in your life. Then if you did more right then wrong, you are allowed into heaven. If you were a good person. But no, not the real version of Jesus. He is gentle, loving, kind, and full of compassion. Being a good person won't get you into heaven only salvation gets you into Heaven.

In the book of Revelation, John, the author of Revelation, saw a vision of Jesus in which he described His appearance, saying, "His head and his hairs were white like wool, as white as snow; and his eyes were as a flame of fire."

"His head and his hair were white like wool—white as glistening snow. And his eyes were like flames of fire! His feet were gleaming like bright metal, as though they were glowing in a fire, and his voice was like the roar of many rushing waters. In his right hand he held seven stars, and out of his mouth was a sharp, double-edged sword. And his face was shining like the brightness of the blinding sun! When I saw him, I fell down at his feet as good as dead, but he laid his right hand on me and I heard his reassuring voice saying: Don't yield to fear. I am the Beginning and I am the End, the Living One! I was dead, but now look—I am alive forever and ever. And I hold the keys that unlock death and the unseen world." Revelation 1:14-18(TPT)

The fiery eyes of Jesus in this vision are a symbol of His divine judgment and power. Fire often represents purification, testing, and judgment, and the image of Jesus with fiery eyes may indicate that He is all-knowing and able to see into the hearts of people. In other words, nothing is hidden from Him, and He knows the true nature of every person.

The main focus of this vision is not on Jesus' physical appearance but on His divine authority, power, and sovereignty over all things.

My mother never saw His face but was in His Holy presence, with peace and a joy never experienced before. She truly met her Maker, but also her Healer, Jehovah Rapha. She met Yahweh that day. Moses also never saw the face of the Lord on the mountain and God kept him hidden in the crevice of the rock. The Lord said to Moses:

"No one may see me and live." Exodus 33:19-23

They walked in Heaven and He showed my mother her home or dwelling place, the one He is preparing for her. From her mouth to God's ears, as we like to say. The way that He knows her intimately and the way that He knows what she likes was one of the most comforting things that she could ever experience.

Do I think we will all have our own homes in Heaven? I mean why not. Knowing God, there will be more than enough to go around. I also believe the Bible speaks about a dwelling place. Not just like the house we live in here on earth. But He is saying Heaven in all its Glory will be our dwelling place. Sometimes because of our own limited understanding, we compare things spoken of in the Word of God to what we know here on Earth. We won't need to sleep or rest in Heaven so why would we need a physical house? The whole of Heaven is our home.

Do I believe there will be actual houses in Heaven? I do yes, I just do not think they will serve the same purpose as here on Earth. We won't need safety or shelter in Heaven. I do think there will be structures, better and more magnificent than anything we have seen here on Earth. The houses and structures will be absolutely magical and they will look like mansions and there will be more than enough dwelling places for everyone.

The scripture that refers to our home in Heaven that God is preparing for us is found in John 14:2-4, where Jesus is speaking to His disciples before His crucifixion. He says, *"In My Father's house are many mansions; if it were not so, I would have told you. I go to prepare a place for you. And if I go and prepare a place for you, I will come again and receive you to Myself; that where I am, there you may be also. And where I go you know, and the way you know."*

The word "mansion" is not actually found in the original Greek or Hebrew texts of the Bible. It is a word that was used in some older English translations to translate the Greek word "monē" in John 14:2.

"Monē" literally means "abiding place" or "dwelling place," and it is used to describe the place that Jesus is preparing for His disciples in Heaven. The place He is preparing for you and me. In more recent English translations of the Bible, the word "rooms" or "dwelling places" is used instead of "mansion" to convey the meaning of "monē."

While "mansion" is not a direct translation of the Greek or Hebrew word, it is an older English rendering of the concept of the "abiding place" or "dwelling place" that Jesus spoke of. This passage teaches us that Heaven is a real place, and that Jesus is preparing a place for His bride to dwell with Him there. It also reveals Jesus' promise to return and take us to be with Him in that place.

The concept of our eternal home in Heaven is also mentioned in other parts of the New Testament, such as 2 Corinthians 5:1-2, where the apostle Paul writes, *"For we know that if the earthly tent we live in is destroyed, we have a building from God, an eternal house in heaven, not built by human hands. Meanwhile, we groan, longing to be clothed instead with our heavenly dwelling."*

The way The Passion translation describes this passage, colors an even clearer picture of what to expect from our eternal home, what to look forward to and also the coming of Jesus and the marriage supper of the Lamb.

"We are convinced that even if these bodies we live in are folded up at death like tents, we will still have a God-built home that no human hands have built, which will last forever in the heavenly realm. We inwardly sigh as we live in these physical "tents," longing to put on a new body for our life in heaven, in the belief that once we put on our new "clothing" we won't find ourselves "naked." So, while living in this "tent," we groan under its burden, not because we want to die but because we want these new bodies. We crave for all that is mortal to be swallowed up by eternal life. And this is no empty hope, for God himself is the one who has prepared us for this wonderful destiny. And to confirm this promise, he has given us the Holy Spirit, like an engagement ring, as a guarantee. That's why we're always full of courage. Even while we're at home in the body, we're homesick to be with the Master— for we live by faith, not by what we see with our eyes. We live with a joyful confidence, yet at the same time we take delight in the thought of leaving our bodies behind to be at home with the Lord." 2 Corinthians 5:1-8(TPT).

The Bible teaches that our home in Heaven is a place of everlasting joy, peace, and fellowship with God and His people. While we may not fully understand what it will be like, we can have confidence in Jesus' promise that He is preparing a place for us, and that we will be with Him forever with our new and improved Heavenly bodies.

When I do something special for my children, my youngest daughter would turn to me so innocently with a big smile full of appreciation and say: "It is because you know me so well mommy."

I think that I know how my mother felt that day in Heaven, it is the love of the Father. "It is because You know me so well Daddy." He knew what she liked, and it was beautiful. Just the way she always imagined, but better. It was better than what she could ever, ever imagine.

Heaven includes all our desires and even the ones we did not even know we had, but our Daddy knows exactly what we like, even when we do not know. He was the one who knitted us together in our mother's womb. He knows our every breath and our every desire. He knows us so intimately. As she stood there and took in the breath of heaven, the splendor and the beauty, time stood completely still.

> He knows our every breath and our every desire. He knows us so intimately.

"O Lord, You have searched me and known me. You know my sitting down and my rising up; You understand my thought afar off. You comprehend my path and my lying down, And are acquainted with all my ways. For there is not a word on my tongue, But behold, O Lord, You know it altogether. You have hedged me behind and before, And laid Your hand upon me. Such knowledge is too wonderful for me; It is high, I cannot attain it. Where can I go from Your Spirit? Or where can I flee from Your presence? If I ascend into heaven, You are there; If I make my bed in hell, behold, You are there. If I take the wings of the morning, And dwell in the uttermost parts of the sea, Even there Your hand shall lead me, And Your right hand shall hold me. For You formed my inward parts; You covered me in my mother's womb. I will praise You, for I am fearfully and wonderfully made; Marvelous are Your works, And that my soul knows very well. My frame was not hidden from You, When I was made in secret, And skillfully wrought in the lowest parts of the earth. Your eyes saw my substance, being yet unformed. And in Your book they all were written, The days fashioned for me, When as yet there were none of hem. How precious also are Your thoughts to me, O God! How great is the sum of them! If I should count them,

they would be more in number than the sand; When I awake, I am still with You."
Psalms 139:1-10, 13-18 (NKJV).

Now and then my mother still heard the faint voices of the medical
personnel asking her to hold on. She felt cold, but she was already in
Heaven and she was walking with Jesus on the green pastures. Then
God spoke and said to her, "You have to go back, it is not yet your
appointed time. You still have work to do."

She woke up later that day in the hospital. She was alive and well. A
road to recovery laid ahead. Her journey to healing was longer than
expected. Yet over time she fully recovered. She had that encounter to
hold on to for the rest of her earthly life, and the promise of a long,
long life to come.

I love reading books about Heaven. I have been reading them since I
was a little girl. This story of my mom reminded me of a book I read,
"Heaven – An unexpected journey". I mean none of us ever expects
to visit Heaven. When we go we are going for eternity.

2.1 Look up! Jesus is coming

Look up, Jesus is coming in the clouds. It is no conspiracy that the big
day of the return of Jesus is soon. On the day of Jesus's return, many
will suddenly be caught up in the clouds. The day will start like any
other, but end in a remarkable way.

The Word of God teaches us that it will be like the days of Noah and
Lot when Jesus returns. When the Pharisees demanded Jesus to tell
them when the Kingdom of God would come, He answered them,
*"Just as it was in the days of Noah, so also will it be in the days of the Son of
Man. People were eating, drinking, marrying and being given in marriage up to the
day Noah entered the ark. Then the flood came and destroyed them all."*

"It was the same in the days of Lot. People were eating and drinking, buying and selling, planting and building - but the day Lot left Sodom, fire and sulpher rained down from heaven and destroyed them all."

Luke 21:8-36 gives a detailed account of the coming day of the Lord in the words of Jesus. Jesus tells us what will be happening on the great day and also how we, as children of God, should be expectant and at peace.

In fact we should rejoice in these difficult times, because the day of our redemption is drawing near. When speaking about the end times, many people get gripped by fear. That is not Jesus's intention. He is the God of peace. He tells us what to expect so that we are not afraid. He expects the exact opposite from us – to become excited for His return. He is so serious about us getting excited. He is waiting for us in Heaven with a reward. The crown of righteousness. Imagine walking into Heaven and receiving a crown.

There are many rewards and crowns awaiting us in Heaven. In 2 Timothy Apostle Paul encourages us with the words,

"Now there is in store for me the crown of righteousness, which the Lord, the righteous Judge, will award to me on that day - and not only to me, but also to all who have longed for His appearing." 2 Timothy 4 : 8 (NIV).

The Crowns we can look forward to receiving in Heaven:

- **The Crown of Righteousness:** Referred to in 2 Timothy 4:8. This biblical passage promises the bestowal of the crown to those who hold a deep love for and eagerly anticipate the Second Coming of Christ. These devoted Christians seek intimate communion with God, reflecting their profound spiritual yearning and devotion.

- **The Incorruptible Crown:** This is also referred to as the Imperishable Crown, as found in the biblical passage 1 Corinthians 9:25. The Incorruptible Crown is reserved for individuals who exemplify qualities of self-denial and perseverance, making it a symbol of enduring dedication and unwavering commitment. The denial and discipline of things of the flesh, the practice of disciplining our bodies with the correct food, exercise, and even sexual desires. All the good healthy **IN10TIONAL** habits.

- **The Crown of Rejoicing** is alternatively referred to as the Crown of Exultation or the Crown of Auxiliary. This extraordinary crown finds its origins in the biblical passages of 1 Thessalonians 2:19 and Philippians 4:1, wherein it is described as a reward for those who actively participate in evangelizing individuals outside the Christian Church.

- **Crown of Life, known as the Martyr's Crown:** Is found in biblical passages such as James 1:12 and Revelation 2:10. This symbolic honor is granted to those who demonstrate unwavering perseverance in the face of adversity and trials. The significance of the Crown of Life is highlighted when Jesus addresses the Church in Smyrna, urging them not to fear the impending suffering. Instead, he encourages them to remain faithful, even in the face of death, promising the bestowal of the revered Crown of Life as a reward for their steadfastness. This biblical truth serves as a powerful reminder of the strength and resilience required to endure hardships and stay faithful to one's beliefs.

- **The Crown of Glory,** as mentioned in 1 Peter 5:4. This crown is given to leaders and shepherds of the flock who set a virtuous example for others to follow. The Crown of Glory stands as a testament to the dedicated service and exemplary conduct of Elders, Pastors, and Shephards, honoring their commitment to nurturing the spiritual well-being of their members and inspiring others to lead lives of faith and compassion. Do you sometimes ask in difficult situations, "Why me God?" God brings life and life in abundance; the devil stole from you. Not God. God is faithful and just and He will one day reward you in Heaven. Hold On! Persevere until the end.

How you live now matters!

It matters now and it will matter for eternity to come. My spiritual Father Apostle Nicky always say that earth is our training ground for one day in Heaven. It reminds me of an athlete. Apostle Paul also likes to talk about and use examples of athletes and the race we run here on earth. No professional athlete starts training in game season. They train months and even years before. As children of God, we train for years to become efficient and operate with excellence in all we do. We must be ready, as the Word says, in and out of season.

Take a cyclist, the total training duration for a professional cyclist preparing for a big race can range from 6 to 9 months, depending on their team's training philosophy and how they structure their season.

Training typically includes a combination of the following aspects:

1. Base Training:

Cyclists begin with a foundation-building phase, focusing on long, steady rides at a moderate intensity. This helps improve endurance and aerobic capacity.

The same for us when we get saved. We build our foundation on the Rock that is Jesus so that our foundation is strong and won't be washed away when the storm of life come. We do not build on sand. We also do not store up our treasures on earth, we store them in Heaven. We build endurance through patience, and increase our capacity by being rooted and grounded in the Word.

2. Intensity Training:

As the race approaches, cyclists incorporate interval training and high-intensity efforts to improve their power output and ability to sustain intense efforts.

We also go through times of intense trails and turbulence ... intense times of testing increases as breakthrough approaches. By pressing in through prayer and applying our faith, this increase the amount of supernatural power we are able to put out. Thus increasing our endurance.

3. Climbing Practice:

Since races features challenging mountain stages, cyclists specifically train for climbing to develop the strength and technique required for the climbs.

And the more difficult the season in your life is, the harder the climb. The more important it is for you to push through. Apostle Paul relates back to our self-discipline in 1 Corinthians 9. He says that everyone is competing with strict training. You do not get a crown when you come last or if you run your race aimlessly, or doing air boxing. We do so with passion, power and purpose. Plan your race well, with discipline and excitement for what lies ahead.

4. Time Trials:

Time trials are crucial stages in a preparation for race day. Cyclists work on their time trial skills, optimizing aerodynamics and pacing for these individual efforts against the clock.

We are also working against the clock. We plan with precision and execute our defined well trained skills. This gets used in how to spread the Gospel of Jesus before His soon coming return. We are on a time trial preparing for the great race day. We need to be dynamic, making impact and keep the pace to get the message out of salvation and the return of Jesus.

5. Group Riding:

Cyclists also practice riding in groups (pelotons) to learn the dynamics of drafting, conserving energy, and maneuvering in the pack.

Just like the body of Christ we cannot operate without a limb. We need the full body to operate and conserve our energy while moving the pack along steadily. It is not about one person, but how we can operate as a team.

6. Recovery:

Adequate rest and recovery is vital during training to allow the body to adapt and avoid overtraining.

A good friend of mine always says that ministry is a marathon and we need to pace ourselves so that we do not burn out. She could not be more spot on. Just like God told us to rest on the sabbath or the seventh day, so should we as the body of Christ also rest to recover.

A word of warning.

Avoid over training to avoid burnout. That is how we lose many people in the body of Christ. They get burdened and burnt out and then leave their faith race because they were over training.

I like how Mark Hitchcock puts this race we are in. "The earth is our training time for reigning time."

Until then, Jesus tells us what will happen next; *"There will be signs in the sun, moon and stars. On the earth, nations will be in anguish and perplexity at the roaring and tossing of the sea. People will faint from terror, apprehensive of what is coming on the world, for the heavenly bodies will be shaken.*

At that time they will see the Son of Man coming in a cloud with power and great glory. When these things begin to take place, stand up and lift up your heads, because your redemption is drawing near."

He told them this parable: *"Look at the fig tree and all the trees. When they sprout leaves, you can see for yourselves and know that summer is near. Even so, when you see these things happening, you know that the kingdom of God is near.*

"Truly I tell you, this generation will certainly not pass away until all these things have happened. Heaven and earth will pass away, but my words will never pass

away. "Be careful, or your hearts will be weighed down with carousing, drunkenness and the anxieties of life, and that day will close on you suddenly like a trap. For it will come on all those who live on the face of the whole earth. Be always on the watch, and pray that you may be able to escape all that is about to happen, and that you may be able to stand before the Son of Man." Luke 21:25-36 (NIV)

How to live in the times we find ourselves in right now:

1. Do not be afraid.
2. Stand up for what you believe in.
3. Get your loved ones saved.
4. Lift your head, have hope and excitement for the return of Jesus.
5. Be watchful at all times.
6. Pray always.
7. Keep your heart clean and pure.
8. Guard your heart from the anxieties of this world.
9. Spread the gospel.
10. Stand on the word of God.

You are part of the generation that will not pass away. You got an upgraded ticket. You are missing start, passing by jail and the grave and going straight to Heaven. If you are saved and a child of God, you won't be on earth to see the tribulation. God will snatch you away just in the nick of time. That is something to celebrate!

Once we have been caught up in the clouds, we will attend the marriage supper of the Lamb, meet our loved ones, and be with Jesus for eternity.

No more sorrow, no more pain.

"Heaven – An unexpected journey" written by Jim Woodford, writes about his experience with Heaven. His subtitle powerfully reads – "One Man's Experience with Heaven, Angels, and the Afterlife." The book is a personal account of Jim's near-death experience, in which he claims to have been transported to Heaven and experienced a glimpse of the afterlife.

In the book, Jim recounts his story of being clinically dead for a short period of time after a severe heart attack, during which he claims to have encountered angels and experienced the beauty and peace of Heaven. He also shares how his experience transformed his life and deepened his faith in God.

I believe the reason so many accounts of Heaven is recorded is so that the children of God can come back and share the stories hope, beauty and splendor with us still here on earth. To lift our faith and expectation of Heaven. We are living in the end times and the coming of Jesus is closer than ever.

Like Paul prayed for his friend Simon Peter in the face of adversity. I also pray that your faith may not fail.

This prayer occurred during the last supper, where Jesus had just predicted Peter's denial of Him. In Luke 22:31-32, Jesus says to Peter: *"Simon, Simon, Satan has asked to sift all of you as wheat. But I have prayed for you, Simon, that your faith may not fail. And when you have turned back, strengthen your brothers."*

In this passage, Jesus tells Peter that Satan wants to "sift" him, or test him, like wheat. But Jesus assures Peter that He has prayed for him, that his faith may not fail. This prayer demonstrates Jesus' concern for Peter's spiritual wellbeing and His desire for him to remain faithful, even in the face of difficult circumstances.

The fact that Jesus prays for Peter's faith not to fail, rather than praying that Peter not deny Him, is significant. It shows that Jesus is concerned with Peter's inner spiritual state, rather than just his outward behavior. It was truly a situation of "if looks could kill". Jesus knew that Peter will fail Him, but He also knew that Peter's faith will ultimately be restored and strengthened.

Jesus knows how hard life is here on earth. He shared it with us for 33 years. He knows daily the trials and tribulations we face and He knows that the end is drawing near. Yet He is still concerned just as with Peter for our spiritual wellbeing. Therefore, He is interested more in what the state of our heart looks like than the state of our reputation.

David, a man after God's own heart was not so because of his deeds. He was a murderer. I believe he was a man after God's own heart because of the pureness of heart, love, and deep devotion that He showed towards God.

Throughout his life, David demonstrated a heart that was open to God's will and that sought after God's heart.

- **He was faithful:** Despite facing many challenges and difficulties in his life, David remained faithful to God. He always turned to God in times of trouble and sought His guidance and wisdom. He trusted in God's promises and believed in His goodness and faithfulness.

- **He worshipped God with sincerity:** David was known for his heartfelt and passionate worship of God. He wrote many psalms expressing his love and adoration for God, and he often danced and sang before the Lord with great joy and enthusiasm. To me King David is one of the Bible's most famous poets. An example, that no matter your title or reputation you can worship God with all your heart and soul.

- **He repented of his sins:** David was not a perfect man, and he made mistakes and committed sin. However, when he sinned, he acknowledged his wrongdoing and repented before God. Repent means making a 180° turn in behavior. He was quick to confess his sins and seek God's forgiveness, and he was willing to accept the consequences of his actions by living a life pleasing to God.

- **He had a desire to please God:** David's ultimate desire was to please God and to do His will. He was not motivated by his own selfish desires or ambitions but sought to follow God's plan for his life.

- **He trusted in God's grace:** David knew that he was not deserving of God's love and mercy, but he trusted in God's grace to forgive and restore him. He recognized that it was only through God's mercy and grace that he could be called a man after God's own heart.

Are you a man or woman after God's heart? I believe I am a product of God's grace.

No matter what you have done in your life, when you truly repent and turn toward God. He is faithful and just to forgive you.

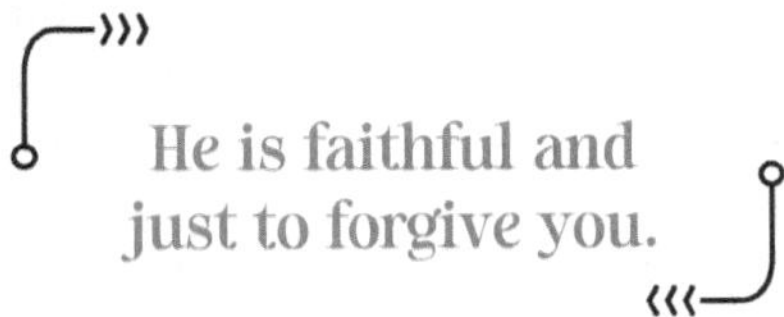

The end is drawing near very quickly and Jesus can come back at any minute. Nothing more needs to happen for Him to come back. You are also a product of God's grace. Like David make sure you live a life of obedience, faithfulness, prayer, worship and repentance.

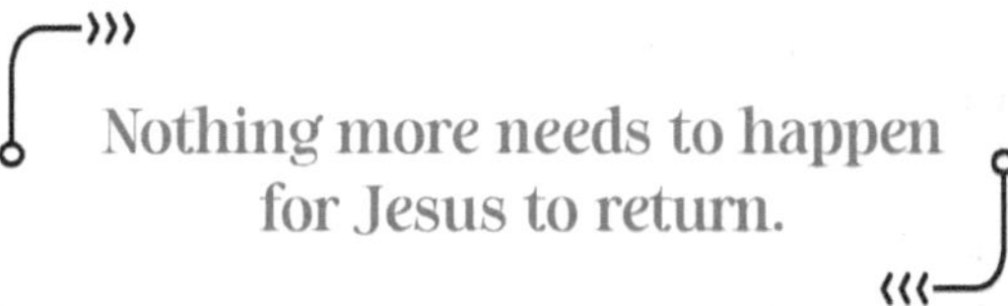

"Now when these things begin to occur, look up and lift up your heads, because your redemption (deliverance) is drawing near." Luke21:28 (AMPC).

This verse is a call to hope and encouragement in the midst of difficult and uncertain times. Jesus is reminding His disciples that even though there may be trials and tribulations on earth, they can trust that God's redemption is coming and that they will ultimately be saved. By lifting up our heads, we are symbolically demonstrating our faith in God's promises and our readiness to receive His redemption.

This word of God also emphasizes the importance of staying alert and watchful in the face of adversity. Jesus goes on to say in Luke 21:34-36:

"Be careful, or your hearts will be weighed down with carousing, drunkenness and the anxieties of life, and that day will close on you suddenly like a trap. For it will come on all those who live on the face of the whole earth. Be always on the watch, and pray that you may be able to escape all that is about to happen, and that you may be able to stand before the Son of Man."

In these verses, Jesus is urging us to remain vigilant and prayerful, so that we will be prepared to receive His redemption when He comes to snatch us up to Heaven to be with Him in the twinkling of an eye.

Jesus is coming soon and He is taking His bride, with him to Heaven for the celebration of a lifetime. *"For the Lord Himself will descend from heaven with a loud cry of summons, with the shout of an archangel, and with the blast of the trumpet of God. And those who have departed this life in Christ will rise first. Then we, the living ones who remain [on the earth], shall simultaneously be caught up along with [the resurrected dead] in the clouds to meet the Lord in the air; and so always (through the eternity of the eternities) we shall be with the Lord! Therefore comfort and encourage one another with these words.* ” 1 Thessalonians 4:16-18 (AMPC).

Just as Jim Woodford had an experience of being with Jesus in Heaven, even just for a moment, so will we experience Heaven and the presence of Jesus for eternity.

Jim explains the sounds of Heaven as "beautiful music that is alive with light, color, and fragrance." He goes on to say that the music was not just audible, but could also be seen and felt. He describes it as a "complete sensory experience," with the music flowing through every part of his being and bringing a sense of joy and peace.

Heaven to Jim was filled with "light, colors, and a sense of infinite space." He notes that everything in Heaven seems to radiate with light and color, giving it a vibrant and otherworldly appearance. He also describes the people he saw in Heaven as being "perfect and beautiful," with an inner radiance that was reflected in their appearance.

He writes about how Heaven seemed to be a place of perfect peace, with no pain, suffering, or conflict. A place of total acceptance and love, where everyone was welcomed and embraced. He notes that he felt a deep sense of belonging and connection while in Heaven, and that he never wanted to leave. In Heaven you never want to leave.

Oh, what a day that will be when we will all be with Jesus in Heaven. After his experience, Jim was revived and eventually regained consciousness, but his physical recovery was slow and difficult.

Jim experienced a number of physical and emotional challenges in the aftermath of his near-death experience. He struggled with intense pain, weakness, and fatigue, and had difficulty communicating with his doctors and loved ones about his experience. He also grappled with the intense emotions that came with his experience, including a deep longing to return to Heaven.

How can he not have this longing? He has seen the other side. His earthly tent was almost folded up like Apostle Paul described. He had a perfect body and had to return to earth to his not so perfect and frail earthly suit.

Despite these challenges, Jim also notes that his experience had a profound impact on his life and his faith. He became more focused on helping others and sharing his message of hope and faith, and he started to live his life with a greater sense of purpose and meaning.

When looking at these accounts of Heaven I can't help to wonder about what King David said in Psalm 8:4-5.

"What is man that You are mindful of him, and the son of [earthborn] man that You care for him? Yet You have made him but a little lower than God [or heavenly beings], and You have crowned him with glory and honor." Psalm 8:4-5 (AMPC).

David is believed to have written this psalm as a reflection on the greatness of God and the place of human beings within His creation. The psalm is often seen as a declaration of God's glory and sovereignty, and a celebration of the beauty and wonder of His creation.

That's exactly how I see these encounters with Heaven also. A declaration of God's glory and sovereignty and a glimpse of what we can expect in our eternal life hereafter.

Encounters with Heaven is a declaration of God's glory and sovereignty and a glimpse of what we can expect in our eternal life hereafter.

2.2 What does Heaven look like?

What does Heaven look like for us who has not visited it yet? The Bible describes Heaven as:

- **A place of perfect beauty and holiness.** In the book of Revelation, for example, John the Apostle describes seeing a vision of the "New Jerusalem" descending from Heaven, a city of pure gold with gates of pearl and streets of transparent glass (Revelation 21:1-21). The city is described as being lit by the glory of God, and there is no need for a sun or moon because God's light shines upon it.

- **A place of perfect peace and rest.** In Revelation 21:4, it says that God "will wipe every tear from their eyes. There will be no more death or mourning or crying or pain, for the old order of things has passed away." This passage suggests that in Heaven, all our sorrows and sufferings will be lifted, and we will experience a sense of deep peace and contentment. Like Jim, we would never want to leave.

- **A place of fellowship and communion with God and with one another.** In 1 Corinthians 13:12, Paul writes, "For now we see only a reflection as in a mirror; then we shall see face to face. Now I know in part; then I shall know fully, even as I am fully known." This passage suggests that in Heaven, we will have a deeper and more intimate knowledge of God and of one another, and we will be able to experience a sense of love and community that is impossible to achieve on earth.

The descriptions of Heaven are designed to inspire hope and faith in

God's promise of eternal life. While we may not know exactly what Heaven will be like with our limited human understanding. Until then we can trust that it will be a place of perfect beauty, peace, and fellowship with God and that we will experience a profound sense of joy and contentment in His presence.

> The descriptions of Heaven are designed to inspire hope and faith in God's promise of eternal live.

I was around the age of 13 when I read the book "A Divine Revelation of Heaven & Hell" by Mary K. Baxter and T. L. Lowery. (T.L Lowery, n.d.). Kids watched horror movies back then, so I figured this would be ok too. My word, how this book changed my life, and literary put the fear of God in me. In a good way.

Mary K. Baxter wrote "A Divine Revelation of Heaven & Hell" to share her experience of a series of visions she had over a 30-day period in 1976. During this time she claims to have been taken on a guided tour of both heaven and hell by Jesus Christ. In her visions, she describes in detail the sights, sounds, and experiences of both places, as well as the messages she received from Jesus during her journey.

According to Baxter, she wrote the book to share her experience with others and to help them gain a deeper understanding of the afterlife. The reality of heaven and hell, and the importance of accepting Jesus Christ as their personal savior. Baxter believes that her experience was a divine revelation from God, and she hopes that her book will inspire others to seek a personal relationship with Jesus and to prepare for eternal life in Heaven.

Since its publication, "A Divine Revelation of Heaven & Hell" has become a popular book within certain Christian circles, and its detailed descriptions of heaven and hell have been both praised and criticized by various religious groups. Nonetheless, Baxter's book has had a significant impact on many readers, who have been inspired by her vision and message.

Mary Baxter describes her vision of heaven as a place of incredible beauty, peace, and joy. Similar to the experiences that Jim and my mother had. She writes that she saw streets of gold, gates of pearl, and a river of life that flowed through the center of the city. She also saw many mansions and heard the voices of angels singing praises to God.

Baxter describes the throne room of God as a place of immense glory and power, with lightning and thunder emanating from the throne. She writes that she saw the Lamb of God, Jesus Christ, sitting at the right hand of God the Father, surrounded by angels and elders who were bowing down and worshiping Him.

She described the people in heaven as being in perfect health and having glorified bodies that do not age or experience pain. She writes that she saw people from all nations and tongues, united in worship and love for God.

Over the years many books of unique encounters have been released with many of the experiences overlapping. This gives me great hope! I do have an encounter with my name on. I just have to be hungry for the presence of God to receive this.

She described the places in heaven she visited as:

The City:

- The city of Heaven is incredibly beautiful, with streets of pure gold and gates of pearl.

- The city is surrounded by a high wall with twelve gates, each gate made of a single pearl.
- The city is lit by the glory of God, and there is no need for the sun or moon.
- The river of life flows through the center of the city, and the tree of life grows on either side of the river.
- The mansions of heaven are individually designed, with unique features and colors.
- The mansions are made of pure gold and are very large, with many rooms.

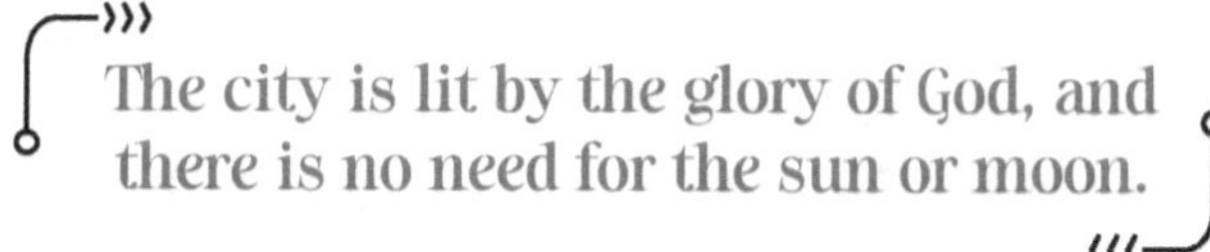

The Throne Room:

- The throne room of God is a place of incredible power and glory.
- The throne of God is surrounded by lightning and thunder, and the presence of God is overwhelming.
- The Lamb of God, Jesus Christ, sits at the right hand of God the Father, and angels and elders worship Him.
- The elders wear white robes and have crowns of gold on their heads.
- The four living creatures, who represent the characteristics of God, worship God day and night and night and day.

"The air around the throne was filled with baby cherubim, singing and kissing the Lord upon His face, His hands and His feet. The song they sang was "Holy, holy, holy is the Lord God Almighty" The cherubim had tongues of fire sitting on their heads and on the tips of each tiny wing. The motion of their wings seemed synchronized with the movement of the power and glory of the Lord." (T.L Lowery, n.d.)

The People:

- The people of Heaven are in perfect health and have glorified bodies that do not age or experience pain.
- People from all nations and tongues are in heaven, united in worship and love for God.
- There is no sickness, death, or sorrow in heaven.
- The people of Heaven are constantly worshiping God and giving Him glory.
- The children in Heaven are cared for by angels and have a special place in the heart of God.

Other Features:

- There are many angels in Heaven, serving God and ministering to the people.
- The book of life is kept in Heaven, and the names of those who have accepted Jesus Christ as their savior are written in it.
- The marriage supper of the Lamb will take place in Heaven, where the bride of Christ (the church) is united with the bridegroom (Jesus).
- There are many different kinds of flowers and trees in Heaven, and the air is filled with the fragrance of their beauty.
- The love of God permeates every aspect of Heaven and is felt by everyone who is there.

"As the angel and I approached two giant gates in a huge wall, we saw two exceptionally large angels with swords. They were about fifty feet tall, and their hair was spun gold. The gates were so high I could not see the tops of them. They were the most beautiful works of art I have ever seen.

They were hand-carved, with intricate folds, drapes, layers and carvings, and were studded with pearls, diamonds, rubies, sapphires and other gems. Everything on the gates was in perfect balance, and the gates opened outward. An angel with a book in his hand came out from behind the gates. After checking the book, the angel nodded, confirming that I could enter." Said Mary.

Mary K. Baxter describes the sounds and colors of Heaven as being unlike anything she had ever experienced on earth.

- The colors in Heaven are brighter and more vibrant than any colors on earth.
- The streets of gold shine with a brilliant, golden light.
- The gates of pearl are iridescent and change colors depending on the angle of the light.
- The mansions are adorned with colors that are indescribable, with colors that change and blend together in ways that are impossible to describe.

> The colors in Heaven are brighter and more vibrant than any colors on earth

The music in Heaven is indescribable and fills the air with joy and peace. The angels sing praises to God with beautiful, harmonious voices. The sound of the river of life is soothing and calming, and its gentle flow can be heard throughout the city. The sound of people worshiping God with one voice is overwhelming, and the power of their worship can be felt in every corner of heaven.

Mary Baxter also describes a kind of "color-sound" relationship in Heaven, where colors and sounds are interrelated and blended together in a way that is difficult to describe. For example, she describes how the colors of the mansions in Heaven seem to emit sounds that blend together in a beautiful symphony of color and sound.

Another account of Heaven was written by Randy Alcorn in his book "Heaven". His book is a comprehensive exploration of what the Bible teaches about the afterlife and the nature of heaven.

Randy Alcorn's book "Heaven" (Alcorn, 2004) is not based on a personal vision or experience, but rather on his extensive research of the Bible and other theological works. The book is a comprehensive exploration of the biblical teachings on the nature of Heaven and the afterlife, and Alcorn draws upon a wide range of sources to create a detailed and compelling picture of what Heaven may be like.

Alcorn's approach is to carefully examine what the Bible teaches about Heaven and to extrapolate from that to create a vision or picture for us, of what it might be like. He uses scripture as his primary source, but also draws on the writings of many Christian theologians and thinkers throughout history to gain a deeper understanding of the topic.

Here are some of the key elements of Alcorn's depiction of Heaven:

The New Earth:

- Alcorn believes that Heaven will be located on a new, physical Earth that has been restored to its original perfection.
- The New Earth will be a place of incredible beauty, with vibrant colors, beautiful landscapes, and perfect weather.
- The New Earth will be a place where people can enjoy physical activities like eating, drinking, and exploring.

"Who are the people of the new heaven and new earth? They are the resurrected people of God, those who belong to Christ and have been saved by grace through faith. They are the redeemed of all ages, from all nations, tribes, peoples, and languages."

Will you be one of them?

The City:

- The city of Heaven, the New Jerusalem, is a place of incredible beauty, with streets of pure gold and walls adorned with precious stones.
- The city is designed to be a place of community, with many different dwelling places where people can live and interact with one another.
- The city is lit by the glory of God, and there is no need for the sun or moon.

"We will know and recognize each other in Heaven. We will be able to have meaningful conversations with those who have gone before us, including our loved ones. We will not only recognize those we knew on earth but also those we didn't know, including Old Testament saints, apostles, and martyrs."

The People:

- People in Heaven will have glorified bodies that are perfect and free from all sin and disease.
- The people of Heaven will experience incredible joy and fulfillment as they worship God and serve Him in various ways.
- Relationships between people will be characterized by love, respect, and unity.

"We will have new, glorified bodies in Heaven. These bodies will be free from the effects of sin and death, and they will never grow old or wear out. Our eternal bodies will perfectly reflect our eternal identity in Christ, and we will be able to serve Him and worship Him without hindrance."

Other Features:

- In Heaven people will be able to see and interact with loved ones who have passed away.
- There will be no death, pain, or suffering in heaven.
- People will be able to experience God's presence in a way that is impossible on earth.
- There will be many different activities and pursuits in heaven, including worship, work, and leisure.

"We will have perfect relationships in Heaven. Our relationships will not be hindered by sin, selfishness, or pride. We will love one another perfectly, and there will be no envy, jealousy, or strife. We will have a deep sense of unity and purpose in Christ."

Overall, Randy Alcorn's description of Heaven is one that emphasizes the continuity between this life and the next, as well as the incredible beauty and joy that await those who put their faith in Jesus Christ.

Another example and there are many more, is "Heavenly Rewards" from Mark Hitchcock (Hitchcock, 2018). In his book, he explains that heaven is a real place, and that it is a place of incredible beauty and joy.

"In Heaven, we will be part of a great multitude from every nation, tribe, people, and language, worshiping together around the throne of God. We will have a sense of unity and community that transcends all earthly barriers."

He draws heavily on biblical teachings to describe the nature of Heaven, including the fact that it is a place where there is no sin or sorrow, and where believers will be able to experience the fullness of God's love and presence.

"In Heaven, we will be reunited with loved ones who have gone before us. Our relationships with them will be deeper and more fulfilling than we ever experienced on earth. We will also have new relationships with believers from every nation, tribe, and language who will become part of our heavenly family."

Hitchcock also explores the concept of the New Jerusalem, the city that is described in the book of Revelation, and he explains how this city is a symbol of the incredible beauty and perfection of heaven.

"The Church is referred to as the Bride of Christ in the New Testament. In Heaven, we will be united with Christ, our Bridegroom, in a way that is beyond our comprehension. Our relationship with Him will be more intimate than we can ever imagine."

Although each of the three writers - Mary K. Baxter, Randy Alcorn, and Mark Hitchcock - offers a unique perspective on what Heaven is like, there are some commonalities in their descriptions:

- **Heaven is a real and tangible place:** Heaven is not an abstract concept or a metaphor, but a literal and physical place and something for all believers to look forward to.

- **There is no sin or sorrow in Heaven:** Heaven is described as a place where there is no suffering, pain, or evil. Instead, it is a place of perfect peace, joy, and love.

- **The presence of God is central:** The most important

aspect of Heaven is being in the presence of God. We will live in Glory! They describe Heaven as a place where believers can experience the fullness of God's love, glory, and majesty.

- **There is a sense of community and fellowship:** Heaven is a place where believers will be reunited with loved ones who have gone before them, and where they will experience a deep sense of belonging and fellowship with other believers.

- **A place of beauty and wonder:** Heaven is described as a place of incredible beauty and wonder, with sights, sounds, and experiences that are beyond what we can imagine or know on earth today.

While there are certainly differences in the details of each writer's description of Heaven, these commonalities suggest that there is a shared understanding among Christians of what Heaven is like, based on the teachings of the Bible.

The book and movie "90 Minutes and Heaven" touched me in the deepest way. "90 Minutes in Heaven" written by Don Piper. The book recounts Don Piper's personal experience of a near-death experience and his subsequent recovery. Don Piper, a Baptist minister, was involved in a severe car accident that left him trapped in his crushed vehicle for 90 minutes. During this time, he was declared dead by paramedics. However, despite the grim circumstances, Piper claims to have experienced a glimpse of Heaven during those 90 minutes before being revived by a passing pastor who prayed over him.

"God told him to pray for a dead man. As bizarre as that seemed to him, Dick had no doubt that the Holy Spirit was prompting him to act. I'd like to pray for the man in the red car," Dick finally said to the officer.

'Like I said, he's dead."
"I know this sounds strange, but I want to pray for him anyway."

The officer stared at him a long time before he finally said.
"Well, you know, if that's what you want to do, go ahead, but
I've got to tell you it's an awful sight. He's dead, and it's really
a mess under the tarp. Blood and glass are everywhere, and the
body's all mangled."

Dick, then in his forties, said, "I was a medic in Vietnam, so the
idea of blood doesn't bother me."

"I have to warn you-" The man stopped, shrugged, and said,
"Do what you want, but I'll tell you that you haven't seen any-
body this bad."

"Thanks," Dick said and walked to the tarp-covered car.

From the pictures of that smashed-down car, it's almost impossible to believe, but somehow Dick actually crawled into the
trunk of my Ford. It had been a hatchback, but that part of
the car had been severed. I was still covered by the tarp, which
he didn't remove, so it was extremely dark inside the car. Dick
crept in behind me, leaned over the backseat, and put his hand
on my right shoulder. He began praying for me. As he said later,
"I felt compelled to pray. I didn't know who the man was or
whether he was a believer. I knew only that God told me I had
to pray for him."

As Dick prayed, he became quite emotional and broke down
and cried several times. Then he sang. Dick had an excellent
voice and often sang publicly. He paused several times to sing a
hymn and then went back to prayer.

Not only did Dick believe God had called him to pray for me but he prayed quite specifically that I would be delivered from unseen injuries, meaning brain and internal injuries.

This sounds strange, because Dick knew I was dead. Not only had the police officer told him but he also had checked for a pulse. He had no idea why he prayed as he did, except God told him to. He didn't pray for the injuries he could see, only for the healing of internal damage. He said he prayed the most passionate, fervent, emotional prayer of his life. As I would later learn, Dick was a highly emotional man anyway.

Then he began to sing again. "O what peace we often forfeit, O what needless pain we bear, all because we do not carry everything to God in prayer!"

> "O what peace we often forfeit, O what needless pain we bare, all because we do not carry everything to God in prayer!"

The only thing I personally know for certain about the entire event is that as he sang the blessed old hymn "What a Friend We Have in Jesus, I began to sing with him.

In that first moment of consciousness, I was aware of two things. First, I was singing a different kind of singing than the cones of heaven- I heard my own voice and then became aware of someone else singing.

The second thing I was aware of was that someone clutched my hand. It was a strong, powerful touch and the first physical sensation I experienced with my return to earthly life.

More than a year would lapse before I understood the significance of that hand clasping mine. What a miracle from Heaven. (Piper, 2004)

Piper details his journey through the physical and emotional challenges of recovery, as well as his struggle to reconcile his earthly existence with the heavenly encounter he had. The book delves into themes of faith, spirituality, and the afterlife, as Piper grapples with his own beliefs and those of the people around him.

Both the book and the movie offer a portrayal of one man's encounter with mortality, his heavenly experience, and his journey back to life and faith. The story has resonated with many readers and viewers, sparking discussions about the nature of life, death, and the mysteries of the afterlife.

2.3 Visions from Heaven

Some of the accounts from Heaven was recorded as visions that men and woman of God had and not actual visitations. Some of the examples and accounts recorded was actual visitations to Heaven or hell. Mary K. Baxter often describes her experience as visions, or revelation even though her soul was instantly taken out of her body.

"Instantly, my soul was taken out of my body. I went with Jesus up out of my room and into the sky. I knew all that was going on about me. I saw my husband and children asleep in our home below".

There is so much more to Heaven than what we can even think or imagine. We do have limited knowledge here on earth but we will know in full what we only know now in part. Yet we have facets on earth where we can tap into the Heavenly power to aid us with our journey. Visions are one of them.

When we think of the word vision three things come to mind. The vision we have with our eyes to see. A vision or a carefully curated plan we have laid out or thirdly a spiritual vision. The Bible is full of divinely inspired visions from Heaven. Visions occur at night, during prayer or worship and even when some people are wide awake.

Prophet Isaiah saw a powerful vision when King Uzziah died. "It was in the year King Uzziah died that I saw the Lord. He was sitting on a lofty throne, and the train of his robe filled the Temple. Attending him were mighty seraphim, each having six wings. With two wings they covered their faces, with two they covered their feet, and with two they flew. They were calling out to each other, "Holy, holy, holy is the Lord of Heaven's Armies! The whole earth is filled with his glory!"" Isaiah 6:1-3(NLT).

Daniel was also known for his visions. Visions are often hard to understand and interpret and require deep spiritual discernment and understanding. Sometimes often long periods of prayer and fasting.

There are also several other individuals in the Bible who had visions of Heaven like;

- **Ezekiel:-** In the book of Ezekiel, the prophet has a vision of God's throne in Heaven, surrounded by living creatures and angels. Ezekiel 1:1-28; Ezekiel 10:1-22

- **Isaiah:-** In Isaiah's vision, he sees the Lord sitting on a throne in Heaven, and is visited by seraphim who praise God and cleanse his lips with a coal from the altar. Isaiah 6:1-13

- **John:-** In the book of Revelation, John has a series of visions of Heaven, including seeing the Throne of God, the Lamb of God, and the New Jerusalem. Revelation 4:1-11; Revelation 5:1-14; Revelation 21:1-27

- **Stephen:-** Just before he was stoned to death, Stephen had a vision of Jesus standing at the right hand of God in Heaven. Acts 7:54-60

- **Paul:-** In 2 Corinthians 12, Paul describes being caught up to the third Heaven, where he heard things that he was not permitted to share. 2 Corinthians 12:1-10

In the book Visions from Heaven: "Visitations to My Father's Chamber" - Wendy Alec (Alec, 2012), one of the owners of God.TV shared her personal experiences of heavenly visions and encounters with God. She felt a strong calling from God to share her experiences with others and encourage them to seek a deeper relationship with God.

During the writing of the book, Alec was going through a difficult time which left her feeling broken and alone. However, she also experienced a powerful sense of God's presence and love during this time, which she describes in the book as a transformative experience that brought healing and restoration to her life. The book is a testimony to her personal journey and a reflection of her deep faith in God.

Her vision of restoration after trauma, rejection and abandonment touched me deeply, she wrote:

> "It was my birthday. It was actually my fifty-third birthday. I was in Jerusalem, Israel, filming for TV. Now - two years later - my physical body was already in a restoration process and I wanted to spend my birthday with my Heavenly Father. We'd had a long day of filming in our TV studios and it must have been around two in the morning, the time when often I am with 'Daddy.' Lately, my visits with 'Daddy' had taken place in three distinct places. I would find myself in the Throne Room, in a vast meadow, or in what seemed to be one of the Father's chambers, which seemed like an intimate library.

Whenever I visit him in this chamber, I call it 'My Father's Chamber.' I find myself sitting on His lap and I seem to be snuggling into His chest. In front of us is a huge desk; sometimes it appears to be an altar of some kind. Many times when I am there, there is a large open book on the table in front of us, which He explained to me is my personal Book of Life, and from which He often explains many things to me. I never see much further into the rest of the Chamber.

One particular visit, I had picked bunches of flowers for my beautiful Heavenly Father and one bunch of roses that I had given Him instantly became embedded in the left-hand wall of this chamber – it was incredible – they were living, breathing flowers decorating His wall – like living floral wallpaper. Exquisite, beautiful.

The second place where I have found myself often recently is **THE MEADOW**. It is a vast, brightly green meadow filled with the most incredible array of flowers. To my far left, far off, is my earthly father's own garden. My earthly father is often painting using an easel. Sometimes he is playing the violin. To my far right is the Heavenly Father's own personal rose garden. Oh, how incredible! He walks in His heavenly garden like He used to walk with Adam and Eve and watches as I play in the meadow. But today, on my birthday, I found myself in 'My Father's Chamber.'

I had such an excitement in my spirit as I visited Him this evening. Sometimes when I visit Him there, I seem to be a small child of around four or five, but today I felt I was around nineteen, it seemed - a princess coming of age. "Daddy, Daddy! It's my birthday!" I cuddled into Him. I was excited, for I knew somehow that my Daddy had a gift for me. I was right. There, on the table in front of us, was a large box, beautifully wrapped in the palest aquamarine, my favorite color in the entire world, and it had a beautiful, pale pink bow around it. Diamonds glistened from the center of the bow.

"Unwrap it." I could literally hear that gorgeous 'twinkle' in His voice. I slid off His lap. Suddenly, I was standing on the far side of His chamber and walking towards Him – walking through the thick, thick presence of His glory. Saturated in His presence. Hardly able to walk toward Him because of the sheer weight of the Glory that emanated from Him. With one foot before the other, I walked towards His table. I carefully untied the pink bow and then removed the wrapping. I lifted the lid and gasped. Inside the box, in beautiful pale aqua tissue paper, lay the most exquisite tiara.

It was silver, with diamonds and pale aquamarine stones. I lifted it up with both hands and carefully slipped it on my head, but something hard seemed to be in the way. Softly, I ran my fingers over small fragments of glass protruding from my head. I gasped in shock, looking back to my Father.

I had not noticed them before, yet, instantly I knew what the glass fragments were. "They are trauma, Daddy, aren't they?" The Father smiled gently and nodded.

"Up until now, beloved, they were so deeply embedded in your soul, that they were not externally visible. But now, your mind is healing from the long season of sickness and trauma and they are being exposed." I nodded. I knew that this was indeed the truth. I looked back down into the box and slowly lifted away the second layer of tissue paper. I gasped. There lay a pale blue dress in the exact shade of robin's egg blue that I loved so much. I held it up and instantly I was wearing it. It was so utterly beautiful.

"Thank you, Daddy! Thank you. It's beautiful!" Then I looked down and saw there was a huge seeping bloodstain over my heart. I looked up in horror at my Heavenly Father. "It is the wound of abandonment," He said softly. "When you were sick you experienced deep wounds of abandonment. You did not understand why such a thing could have happened to you. And so you felt unprotected."

The Father closed His eyes as though in great agony of soul. "You thought I failed to protect you."

I stood silent before Him. For I knew it was all true. Although my spirit always knew otherwise, my heart had been so intensely assailed by the enemy, that indeed I felt during the worst, most awful physical suffering that my Heavenly Father had abandoned me. "But you understand more now."

"Yes," I whispered.

"My child, beloved child of My heart. "I watched you. Crying for you. Yearning for you. Yet knowing that eventually you would return. In your most intense suffering, although you were not aware, I never left your side."

The Father picked up the most exquisitely cut glass canister filled to the brim with a liquid. "These are your tears that you shed during your time of intense trial." He picked up another much, much larger canister. "And, these are the tears that I shed. For you." And the Father lifted the canister of His tears and poured them over the blood seeping from my heart. Instantly the blood stopped flowing and a great comfort washed over my heart.

"I will never abandon you. There is much, much more that I have yet to share with you, about the great sifting of the saints. But your heart is not yet ready." He smiled tenderly at me. "There is another present." I looked into the box. There was more tissue paper. Slowly I lifted it up. "Oh!" This was the present of all presents. It was a pen. It looked like a fountain pen. I delicately picked it up and walked over and handed it to the Father.

I wanted Him to keep it for me. "Watch." The Father picked it up, opened it and wrote. Immediately blood and fire flowed from the pen. "This is your pen, beloved. "When you write, you will write by the shed blood of My Son and by the fire of My Holy Spirit. Without it, your words hold no power to change lives. With it, beloved child – a great impartation of My love, a great healing shall flow from the pages you write into the hearts and minds of those who read."

He laid it tenderly on His table. "I shall keep it for you here. Never write without coming here first and picking up the pen from Me." I looked longingly at Him. "I will, Daddy.

Daddy, you are so beautiful," I whispered. "You are so beautiful, My beloved child." And once again, like a little child, I jumped on the Father's lap and snuggled into His chest. "Tell My children," the Father's voice was filled with tenderness, "Tell My sons and daughters how I yearn for them; how I long for their fellowship. That I will never, never abandon them." I yawned. I was now tired. "Of course, I will, Daddy." And I fell asleep in my beautiful Father's everlasting arms. (Alec, 2012).

How beautiful is this vision of Heaven? The Glory of the Father and the relationship that he longs to have with each one of his beloved children. Visions are spirit birthed where dreams are more from the realm of the soul where our mind and our emotions are in control. Visions are much deeper manifestations of the power of God.

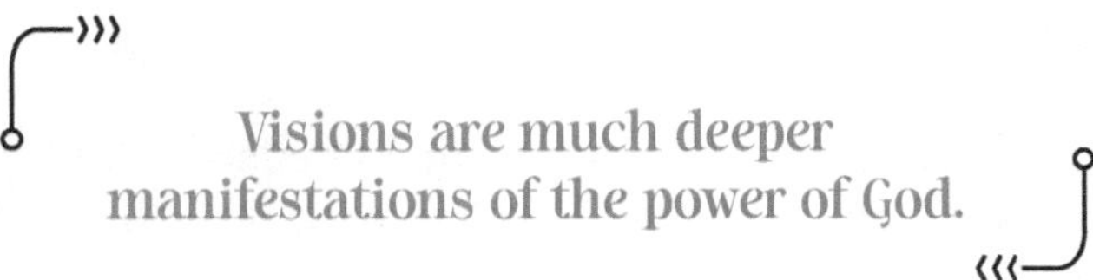

Spiritual visions are important to people, particularly to those who believe in a higher power or divine being, for several reasons:

1. Guidance and Direction:

Visions can provide people with guidance and direction for their lives. They may receive insights into their purpose, their calling, or the steps they need to take to achieve their goals. Or even for the body of Christ. These always need to be submitted and laid under the authority of the Spiritual Father of the Church they belong to. My spiritual father. Apostle Nicky van der Westhuizen always says:- "In order to have authority you have to submit under authority." So in order for these powerful visions of God to be carried out with authority it needs to be submitted to spiritual authority in the house of God."

2. Encouragement:

Visions can also provide people with encouragement, hope, and comfort during difficult times. They may receive a message of reassurance that they are not alone and that things will get better.

3. Spiritual Growth:

Visions can lead to spiritual growth and transformation. They may reveal areas of a person's life where they need to change or grow, or they may provide a deeper understanding of spiritual truths and concepts. They may also serve as life-altering encounters with the supernatural power of God.

4. Confirmation:

Visions can serve as a confirmation of one's beliefs or faith. They may provide a sense of confirmation that a person is on the right path or that they are living according to God's will.

In Greek, the word for "vision" is "ὅραμα" (horama), which can be translated as "a sight, a spectacle, or a vision". In the New Testament, the word is used to refer to divine visions or revelations, such as the vision of Jesus on the Mount of Transfiguration (Matthew 17:9) or the vision of a man from Macedonia that prompted Paul to go there and preach the gospel (Acts 16:9-10).

In Hebrew, the word for "vision" is "חָזוֹן" (chazon), which can be translated as "a vision, a revelation, or a prophecy". In the Old Testament, the word is used to refer to divine visions or revelations, such as the vision of Ezekiel (Ezekiel 1:1) or the vision of Isaiah in the Temple (Isaiah 6:1-13).

The concept of vision in both Greek and Hebrew is closely associated with divine communication, revelation, and guidance. It is often used to refer to supernatural experiences in which God communicates with his people, either through dreams, visions, or other means.

These visions may be prophetic in nature, providing insights into the future, or they may be personal, providing guidance or encouragement to an individual. The concept of vision is central to many religious traditions and plays an important role in the spiritual lives of believers.

Visions may be prophetic in nature, providing insights into the future, or personal, providing guidance or encouragement to an individual.

2.4 How does hell look like?

Well, I probably should not have read that book at such a young age but it provoked something inside of me, a curiosity, love and longing to understand more of these supernatural things. The good part of the supernatural not the demonic. These books opened my heart and imagination to what can be if I do live a Holy and righteous life. If hell is such an awful place why would people want to go there?

Mary K. Baxter describes hell as a place of darkness, fire, and torment.

1. A place of darkness:

Hell is a place where there is no light, only darkness. The complete opposite of Heaven. It is so dark that you cannot even see your hand in front of your face. It is a never ending darkness.

A deep darkness descended on us, and with the darkness came a smell so horrible it took my breath away. Along the sides of this tunnel were living forms embedded in the walls. Dark gray in color, the forms moved and cried out to us as we passed. I knew without being told that they were evil. (T.L Lowery, n.d.)

The forms could move but were still attached to the walls. A horrible smell came from them, and they screeched at us with the most awful cries. I felt an invisible, evil force moving inside the tunnels.

At times in the darkness, I could make out the forms. A dirty fog covered most of them. "Lord, what are these?" I asked as I held on tightly to Jesus' hand. He said, "These are evil spirits ready to be spewed out on the earth when Satan gives the orders."

2. A place of fire:

A place of unquenchable fire. Mary pleads that the flames are everywhere, and that they are so intense that they burn but never consume. She also describes the heat as being unbearable. The smell of demons and rotting flesh is overwhelming.

> The smell of demons and rotting flesh is overwhelming

"In the next pit was a very small-framed woman who looked to be about eighty years old. I can't say how I knew her age, but I did. The skin was removed from her bones by the continual flame, only the bones remained with a dirty-mist soul inside. I watched as the fire burned her. Soon there were only the bones and the worms crawling inside which the fire could not burn.

I looked back at the woman. Her cries were so sad. As I watched her, she put her bony hands together, as if in prayer. I couldn't help crying. I was in a spirit form, and I was crying. I knew that people in hell felt all these things, too.

Jesus knew my thoughts. "Yes, child," He said, "they do. When people come here, they have the same feelings and thoughts as when they were on earth. They remember their families and friends and all the times they had a chance to repent but refused to do so. Memory is always with them. If only they had believed the Gospel and repented before it was too late." (T.L Lowery, n.d.)

3. A place of torment:

In hell there are demons who torment and torture the souls of the damned. She describes people being stabbed, beaten, and tortured in a variety of ways. Torture that will never ever stop, the pain that can never go away, being completely engulfed in flames burning the flesh straight of your body. All your senses work in hell in fact they are intensified, you hear the torment smell, the burning flesh and see the devastation, demons and torture.

> "Oh, yes, I had all my senses. I could hear, smell, see, feel and even taste the evil in this place. If anything, my senses had become more sensitive, and the odor and filth almost made me sick."

In the next pit was a woman on her knees, as if looking for something. Her skeletal form also was full of holes. Her bones were showing through, and her torn dress was on fire. Her head was bald, and there were only holes where her eyes and nose were supposed to be. A small fire was burning around her feet where she was kneeling, and she clawed the sides of the brimstone pit.

The fire clung to her hands, and dead flesh kept falling off as she dug. Tremendous sobs shook her. "O Lord, O Lord," she cried, "want out." As we watched, she finally got to the top of the pit with her feet. I thought she was going to get out when a large demon with great wings that seemed to be broken at the top and hung down his sides ran to her. His color was brownish-black, and he had hair all over his large form.

His eyes were set far back into his head, and he was about the size of a large grizzly bear. The demon rushed up to the woman and pushed her very hard backward into the pit and fire.

I watched in horror as she fell. I felt so sorry for her. I wanted to take her into my arms and hold her, to ask God to heal her and take her out of there.

His color was brownish-black, and he had hair all over his large form. His eyes were set far back into his head, and he was about the size of a large grizzly bear. The demon rushed up to the woman and pushed her very hard backward into the pit and fire. I watched in horror as she fell.

Jesus knew my thoughts and said:- "My child, judgment has been set. God has spoken. Even when she was a child, I called and called her to repent and to serve Me. When she was sixteen years old, I came to her and said, 'I love you. Give your life to Me, and come follow Me, for I have called you for a special purpose.' I called her all her life, but she would not listen. She said, 'Someday I will serve You. I have no time for You now. No time, no time, I have my life of fun. No time, no time to serve You, Jesus. Tomorrow I will.' Tomorrow never came, for she waited too long."

The woman cried out to Jesus, "My soul is truly in torment. There is no way out. I know that I wanted the world instead of You, Lord. I wanted riches, fame and fortune, and I got it. I could buy anything I wanted; I was my own boss. I was the prettiest, best-dressed woman of my time. And I had riches, fame and fortune, but I found I could not take them with me in death. O Lord, hell is horrible.

I have no rest day or night. I am always in pain and torment. Help me, Lord," she cried.

The woman looked up at Jesus so longingly and said, "My sweet Lord, if only I had listened to you!" (T.L Lowery, n.d.)

4. A place of hopelessness:

Baxter emphasizes that in hell, there is no hope of escape or relief. The suffering is eternal, and there is no way out. Jesus cannot help you in hell. Hell is too late.

"With sorrow, Jesus and I walked on to the next pit. The back-slidden preacher was still cursing and angry at Jesus. As we walked past the pits of fire, the hands of the lost reached out to Jesus, and in pleading voices they called out to Him for mercy.

Their bony hands and arms were gray-black from the burning-no live flesh or blood, no organs, only death and dying. Inside myself I was crying, O earth, repent. If you don't, you'll come here. Stop before it is t oo late.

We stopped at another pit. I felt such pity for all of them and such sorrow that I was physically weak and could hardly stand. Great sobs shook me.

"Jesus, I hurt so much inside," I said.

From the pit a woman's voice spoke to Jesus. She stood in the center of the flames, and they covered her whole body. Her bones were full of worms and dead flesh. As the flames flickered up around her, she raised her hands towards Jesus, crying, 'Let me out of here. I will give You my heart now, Jesus. I will tell others about Your forgiveness.

I will witness for You. I beg You, please let me out!' Jesus said, "My Word is true, and it declares that all must repent and turn from their sins and ask Me to come into their lives if they are to escape this place.

The woman asked, "Lord, is there no way out of here?"

Jesus spoke very softly. "Woman," He said, "you were given many opportunities to repent, but you hardened your heart and would not. And you knew My Word said that all whoremongers will have their part in the lake of fire." (T.L Lowery, n.d.)

5. A place of separation from God:

The worst part of hell is the complete separation from God. She says that the souls in hell are cut off from any hope of salvation or redemption, and are doomed to an eternity of suffering and separation from God.

"I had no sleep, no rest, no food and no water. I had a great hunger and was thirstier than I could ever remember being in all my life. I was so tired and so sleepy but the pain went on and on. Each time the jaws opened they dumped another load of lost humanity into hell, I wondered if anyone I knew was among them. Would they bring my husband here?" (T.L Lowery, n.d.).

In hell, I emphasize, souls are completely separated from God and there is no hope of escape or relief. When you get to hell there is no more turning back. It is too late. If you are reading this there is still time to repent and turn your life and heart to Jesus.

One of the most touching and emotional things she wrote about in her revelations, was that she saw her mother in hell being tormented by demons and flames. She stated that her mother was not a believer in Jesus Christ, and thus did not accept salvation during her life. Would you like to see your mother in a place like this? Oh Lord no, we need to pray for our families.

Bill Wiese's account of his "23 Minutes In Hell" is the story of his visitation to hell. He told to have had a near-death experience where he was transported to hell and spent 23 minutes in that place of torment. In the book, Wiese describes the horrifying sights, sounds, and sensations he experienced during his time in hell, including the intense heat, the overwhelming stench, and the screams of the damned. He also shares how his experience changed his life and strengthened his faith in God. His descriptions are an eye-opener to anyone who thought hell is not a real place.

> In The Dungeon of Lost Souls Bill describes how he saw souls of people suffering in torment in various levels of hell, including a dark dungeon where souls were being tormented by demons. He gives a choking visual explanation of how he was taken to the bottomless pit where he saw demons torturing souls. Even in The Abyss; he saw fallen angels being tormented. Also he himself was tormented by demons who used various methods of torture, including piercing him with hooks and crushing him with heavy weights. Bill explains the stench in hell, "It was unbearable and overwhelming, like a mixture of burning sulfur and rotting flesh." The sound of agonizing screams tortured his soul for months, they were the most chilling and disturbing sounds he had ever heard. Combined with the overwhelming sense of fear was indescribable. Fear consumed him during his

time in hell he felt a sense of hopelessness and despair, knowing that there was no way out and that he was there for eternity. (Wiese, 2006).

No person should ever feel like this or have to go through this kind of pain and suffering. Think about your family, your children, your loved ones. Are they saved and will their home one day be in Heaven. The time is almost up.

It is time we build ourselves up in prayer. Stay in the love of God so we can join Jesus in heaven very soon. Help those around you who doubt and save their lives through salvation in Jesus Christ. Keep them from the eternal flames of hell.

It is time we build ourselves up in prayer. Stay in the love of God so we can join Jesus in heaven very soon.

"But you, beloved, building yourselves up in your most holy faith and praying in the Holy Spirit, keep yourselves in the love of God, waiting for the mercy of our Lord Jesus Christ that leads to eternal life. And have mercy on those who doubt; save others by snatching them out of the fire; to others show mercy with fear, hating even the garment stained by the flesh." Jude 1:20-23(ESV).

> It is time we build ourselves up in prayer. Stay in the love of God so we can join Jesus in heaven very soon.

2.5 The Four Distinct Realms of Hell: A Journey Through the Afterlife

Don't worry. I do not have a personal testimony on hell. That would have been hot off the press.

In the realm of eschatology, various religious traditions offer unique perspectives on the nature of hell. Within Christian theology, four distinct types of hell can be discerned, each with its own purpose and inhabitants.

1. Hades

The first realm serves as a temporary holding place for departed souls, as mentioned in Luke 16:3 and Revelation 20:14. Here, the lost souls await final judgment, reflecting upon their earthly actions.

In the Gospel of Luke, Chapter 16, Jesus tells a parable that includes a story involving two characters: a rich man, and a beggar named Lazarus.

According to the story, the rich man lived a life of luxury, indulging in fine clothing and abundant feasts. At his gate, lay a poor beggar named Lazarus, who was covered in sores and longed to eat the scraps that fell from the rich man's table.

As the narrative unfolds, both the rich man and Lazarus die. Lazarus, the beggar, is carried by angels to the "bosom of Abraham," a place of honor and comfort. In contrast, the rich man finds himself in Hades, the realm of the dead, where he experiences torment and anguish.

From Hades, the rich man looks up and sees Abraham and Lazarus in a far-off place of paradise. In his distress, he calls out to Abraham, pleading for mercy and relief. He asks Abraham to send Lazarus to dip the tip of his finger in water and cool the rich man's tongue, as he is tormented by the flames.

Abraham responds, explaining that a great chasm separates them and that no one can cross over from one side to the other. Abraham also reminds the rich man of his earthly life, where he enjoyed wealth and abundance while ignoring the suffering of Lazarus.

The rich man, realizing the irreversible nature of his situation, requests that Lazarus be sent back to warn his family about the torment of Hades, hoping to prevent them from ending up in the same place. Abraham, however, tells him that his family has the teachings of Moses and the prophets and should heed their words.

Hell truly is a point of no return, a place, an anguish, torment and eternal regret you can't escape. No relief and no more chances to turn your life around.

The parable concludes with Abraham stating that even if someone were to rise from the dead and speak to the rich man's family, they still might not believe or change their ways.

2. Gehenna

Also known as the lake of fire or the second death, stands as the second realm. It is an eternal abode characterized by unquenchable flames, where the wicked face everlasting torment and separation from the divine.

Spending eternity without Jesus? Unthinkable. The world we live in is hard and painful enough, but not even a drop in the ocean of the horrors of hell. Going to a place where the suffering is all you have. No! You still have time, and it is running out fast.

The term "Gehenna" is primarily mentioned in the New Testament, particularly in the teachings of Jesus.

In Matthew 5:22: Jesus warns about the consequences of anger and insults, stating that anyone who insults their brother is liable to judgment and Gehenna.

"But I say to you that everyone who continues to be angry with his brother or harbors malice (enmity of heart) against him, shall be liable to and unable to escape the punishment imposed by the court; and whoever speaks contemptuously and insultingly to his brother, shall be liable to and unable to escape the punishment imposed by the Sanhedrin. And whoever says, You cursed fool! [You empty-headed idiot!] shall be liable to and unable to escape the hell (Gehenna) of fire." Matthew 5:22 (AMPC)

In Matthew 5:29-30: In these verses, Jesus speaks metaphorically, advising his followers to take extreme measures to avoid sin. He mentions that it is better to lose a body part and enter life than to have the whole body be thrown into Gehenna.

"If your right eye serves as a trap to ensnare you, or is an occasion for you to stumble and sin, pluck it out and throw it away. It is better that you lose one of your members than that your whole body be cast into hell (Gehenna)." Matthew 5:29 (AMPC)

In Matthew 10:28: Jesus reassures his disciples about their fears, stating that they should not fear those who can kill the body but cannot kill the soul. Instead, they should fear God, who has the power to destroy both body and soul in Gehenna.

"And do not be afraid of those who kill the body but cannot kill the soul; but rather be afraid of Him who can destroy both soul and body in hell (Gehenna)." Matthew 10:28 (AMPC)

In Mark 9:43-48: In this passage, Jesus emphasizes the severity of sin and the importance of radical action to avoid it. He describes Gehenna as a place of unquenchable fire, where their worm does not die.

"And if your hand puts a stumbling block before you and causes you to sin, cut it off! It is more profitable and wholesome for you to go into life [that is really worthwhile] maimed, than with two hands to go to hell (Gehenna), into the fire that cannot be put out. And if your foot is a cause of stumbling and sin to you, cut it off! It is more profitable and wholesome for you to enter into life [that is really worthwhile] crippled than, having two feet, to be cast into hell (Gehenna). And if your eye causes you to stumble and sin, pluck it out! It is more profitable and wholesome for you to enter the kingdom of God with one eye than with two eyes to be thrown into hell (Gehenna)."
Mark 9:43, 45, 47(AMPC)

These passages highlight Jesus' teachings about the consequences of sin and the seriousness of Gehenna as a place of judgment and punishment.

There are bigger things than life right here, right now. Deeper things than what we see. Eternity awaits us, make sure yours is not spent in Gehenna.

There are bigger things than life right here, right now. Deeper things than what we see.

3. Abyss

The third realm, the abyss serves as a prison for fallen angels, shackling them for their rebellion and transgressions. Satan is also a fallen angel. It represents a place of darkness and confinement, reserved for supernatural beings.

Jesus encounters a man possessed by demons. The demons beg Jesus not to send them into the abyss or the bottomless pit. "And they begged [Jesus] not to command them to depart into the Abyss (bottomless pit). [Rev. 9:1.]" Luke 8:31 AMPC).

In Revelation 9:1-2 This passage describes the opening of the fifth seal, and it mentions a star that fell from heaven to the earth, opening the abyss and releasing smoke and locusts.

"THEN THE fifth angel blew [his] trumpet, and I saw a star that had fallen from the sky to the earth; and to the angel was given the key of the shaft of the Abyss (the bottomless pit). He opened the long shaft of the Abyss (the bottomless pit), and smoke like the smoke of a huge furnace puffed out of the long shaft, so that the sun and the atmosphere were darkened by the smoke from the long shaft. [Gen. 19:28; Exod. 19:18; Joel 2:10.] Then out of the smoke locusts came forth on the earth, and such power was granted them as the power the earth's scorpions have. [Exod. 10: 12-15.]" Revelation 9:13 (AMPC).

Apostle John envisions an angel binding Satan and casting him into the abyss for a thousand years during the millennial reign.

4. Tartarus

Lastly, Tartarus, mentioned in 2 Peter chapter 2, constitutes a specific area within the abyss, reserved for the confinement of particularly wicked entities. It represents the deepest depths of punishment and retribution.

"For if Elohim did not spare the messengers who sinned, but sent them to Tartaros, and delivered them into chains of darkness, to be kept for judgment." (2 Peter)2:4 (TS2009).

These four distinct realms of hell offer a glimpse into the multifaceted nature of the afterlife. They serve as reminders of the consequences of our actions during our life on earth as well as the eternal ramifications they may hold.

As we ponder the mysteries beyond this mortal coil, understanding spiritual truths helps to deepen our understanding of the complex tapestry of belief and spirituality.

Remember, the supernatural realm is more real than the natural realm.

2.6 IN10TIONAL Thinking

In this chapter the difference between Heaven and hell is evident.
I don't think you get two things more opposite. Jesus gave us free will,
meaning we can choose where we want to end up. He trusts us with that
decision and He shows us both sides of the coin. He also trusts you with
your decision about your future. Maybe this prayer is not for you and you
are saved, but a friend or family member you know, is not yet.

Now you can share the truth with them and help them find their way into
Heaven.

When engaging in discussions about faith and salvation with a friend,
it's important to approach the conversation with sensitivity, respect, and
a genuine desire to understand their beliefs. Rather than asking direct
yes-or-no questions, consider asking open-ended questions that invite
thoughtful reflection and discussion.

- **What does your faith mean to you?** This question allows your
  friend to express their personal understanding and significance of
  their faith. It opens up an opportunity for them to share their
  beliefs, experiences, and the role their faith plays in their life.

- **How has your relationship with God influenced your life?**
  By asking this question, you invite your friend to reflect on how
  their faith has impacted their attitudes, decisions, and actions. It
  encourages them to share personal experiences and testimonies
  that may offer insights into their spiritual journey.

- **What are your beliefs about salvation and how does
  one attain it?** This question prompts your friend to share their
  understanding of salvation and the means by which they believe
  it is obtained. It can lead to a deeper discussion about their faith

perspective and allow for comparisons and contrasts with your own beliefs, fostering mutual understanding.

- **Can you share a time when you experienced a sense of God's presence or grace in your life?** By asking this question, you create an opportunity for your friend to recount a personal experience that may have deepened their faith or provided them with a sense of assurance. It invites them to reflect on specific moments where they felt a connection to the divine.

Remember, the goal of these questions is to foster dialogue, gain understanding, and encourage mutual growth by means of salvation. Be attentive, listen actively, and respond with empathy to create a safe and respectful environment for open discussion.

How can you love, support and encourage other believers, that has already made this decision to follow Jesus?

- **Pray for one another:** Regularly pray for your family, friends, and fellow believers, that God will strengthen them in their faith and give them the grace to persevere until the end.

- **Share words of encouragement:** Speak kind words and uplift messages to others, reminding them of God's love and the hope that we have in Christ.

- **Attend church together:** Regularly attend church services and gatherings with other believers, as this can be a source of fellowship, support, and encouragement.

- **Share testimonies:** Share your personal testimonies of how God has worked in your life, as this can inspire and encourage others to trust in God and His faithfulness.

- **Read and study the Bible together:** Encourage others to read and study the Bible with you, as this can deepen your understanding of God's Word and strengthen your faith.

- **Offer practical help:** Offer practical help to others, such as providing meals, running errands, or offering a listening ear when they need to talk.

- **Be patient and compassionate:** Show patience and compassion towards others, especially those who may be struggling or going through difficult times

During my studies, a line from a first year subject stuck with me. "If you had to die today, do you know with certainty that you will open your eyes in Heaven?"

That is a BIG deal!

Today I ask you the same question. If you had to die today, do you know with certainty that you will open your eyes in Heaven?

> If you had to die today, do you know with certainty that you will open your eyes in Heaven?

Repentance means making a complete change of direction in your life with your mind, heart, and attitude. Repentance also means to change the ways you used to do things.

Be **IN10TIONAL** with eternity. If the words on these pages and accounts from Heaven and hell made you rethink your actions, and made you want to live the life God has ordained for you, then now is the time to turn back and repent.

Pray and confess this prayer out loud with me:

Lord Jesus, I realize that I have been living a life that is not pleasing to you. I confess my sins to you and ask for your forgiveness. I repent of my wicked ways and ask that you cleanse me of all unrighteousness. I renounce the devil and all his works and declare that I belong to you.

I ask that you cover me with the blood of Jesus and that you wash away all my sins. I submit myself to you, Lord, and ask that you take control of my life. I surrender my will to yours and ask that you guide me in the path of righteousness. I declare Ephesians 2:10 over my life. I am God's masterpiece and I will walk in the will and plan that He has for my life.

Thank you for your mercy and your grace. Thank you for your love that never fails. I declare today that I am a child of God and that I am saved by your grace. In Jesus Name.

Amen.

Just making a confession will not get you a free ticket into Heaven. Neither if you attend church Sunday by Sunday. Also not if your parents serve God.

Only a devoted, surrendered and **IN10TIONAL** life for Jesus Christ will get you to Heaven to spend eternity with the King of Kings.

Chapter III

ANGELS

"And these signs will follow those who believe: In My name they will cast out demons; they will speak with new tongues; they will take up serpents; and if they drink anything deadly, it will by no means hurt them; they will lay hands on the sick, and they will recover." Mark 16:17-18(NKJV).

The activities of angels and demons are more real than the person next to you right now. More real than the person in the room with you or the house next door. More real than most people know.

The word supernatural means: attributed to some force beyond scientific understanding or the laws of nature or "a supernatural being." This includes all Godly and ungodly manifestations like angels and demons. The good and the bad. The question is; who's side you are on?

It is stated, the super above the natural that we see, feel and touch. Signs miracles and wonders are part of the supernatural. When we say something is supernatural, it means that it is connected to a power or force that goes beyond what science can explain or usual laws of nature.

> The supernatural is; the super above the natural that we see, feel and touch.

When we talk about a supernatural being like an angel or demon, we mean a being that has abilities or qualities that are beyond what we see in the natural world. Anything labeled as supernatural is something extraordinary and beyond our normal understanding of how things work.

The devil has distorted the meaning of the supernatural and many people believe the supernatural is zombies, demon manifestations and the occult, etc. It is part of the supernatural, but not all of it. It was what the devil wanted people to believe. There is so much more! And they are good not evil.

When we experience and see the manifested presence of God, miracles happen, healing happens, and deliverance takes place. The supernatural is being displayed. We had been created to have divine encounters with the Lord, to dwell in the realm of the supernatural, and to bask in the glory of God. Our very existence is woven to thrive within His presence. Devine encounters with God include healing, raising from the dead, deliverance, miracles, signs and wonders.

As a child of God, it should be natural to do supernatural miracles, signs and wonders on earth. We do so in the name of Jesus. *"And these signs will follow those who believe: In My name they will cast out demons; they will speak with new tongues; they will take up serpents; and if they drink anything deadly, it will by no means hurt them; they will lay hands on the sick, and they will recover.*" Mark 16:17-18 (NKJV).

In the book of Mark, 19 miracles are recorded, he writes about the divine supernatural power of God demonstrated on earth.

- Eight Healing miracles were recorded.
- Five Miracles that show the power of Jesus over nature.
- Four Miracles showed God's power over demons.
- Two Miracles showed Jesus's power over death. (Thompson Frank Charles, 2005, p. 1665)

Matthew writes about how Jesus summoned the disciples for impartation. Impartation had to take place for them to have the authority to cast out demons and heal the sick. *"Jesus called his twelve disciples together and gave them authority to cast out evil spirits and to heal every kind of disease and illness."* Matthew 10:1 (NLT)

Today we are the disciples of men and therefore God has given us the authority to cast out demons and heal the sick. Just like the disciples in the New Testament. We have an instruction from Heaven to operate in the supernatural power of God imparted to us.

> Today we are the disciples of men and therefore God has given us the authority to cast out demons and heal the sick.

The supernatural is natural. The Bible is supernatural. How could we remove the supernatural from the pages of the Bible? It is not possible. For the very essence of creation itself was birthed through the supernatural. From feeding multitudes with scarce resources to sealing the mouths of fierce lions. The Bible is replete with accounts of extraordinary events that defy natural laws.

My spiritual father, Apostle Nicky van der Westhuizen, uses the example of when the sun stood still. Just imagine the enormity of it. The Earth had to cease its rotation, the oceans held back their waves, and even celestial bodies such as the Sun, Moon, Mars, and Pluto halted their movements. All of this was orchestrated so that Joshua could triumph over his adversaries. To me, this act clearly demonstrates the supernatural in its purest form.

God split open the seas. He protected Daniel from the mouths of hungry lions. Healed the woman with the issue of blood after 12 years, made the lame walk ... the blind see. He raised Lazarus, one of his close friends, from the dead after four days. Jesus himself was raised from the dead after three days and then went up to Heaven to sit at the right hand of God. You are not tripping! Twilight the movie has nothing on the Bible.

God is supernatural. He made you to do the same. He gave us a promise that we would do the same as what He had done and more so.

"I tell you the truth, anyone who believes in me will do the same works I have done, and even greater works, because I am going to be with the Father." John 14:12 (NLT).

God is currently extending the time for individuals on earth. There is a tangible presence of His divine intervention, as He adds moments and opportunities to the lives of people. Do not waste the super that is being added to your natural. Seeing these manifestations of the goodness, mercy and grace of God daily affirms that He continues to work in supernatural ways even in our present age.

> Do not waste the super that is
> being added to your natural.

Apostle Nicky is the forerunner of the supernatural movement. His mandate is to demonstrate the supernatural power of God to this generation. He explains the presence of God and the supernatural in the simplest manner to bring understanding.

The supernatural is comparable to a fish removed from its natural habitat. If you take a fish out of the water, he will die. Nothing else has to be done. The fish being removed from its natural habitat will cause death.

Similarly, if we choose to live outside the presence of God, spiritual death awaits us, and this will lead to natural death in due time. In the same way as a fish, nothing else needs to be done by anyone else for death to come to man when he is removed from his natural habitat. The presence of God.

When God informed Adam that he would experience death, it was because he had strayed from God's divine presence.

Although it took 900+ years for the ultimate outcome to manifest, and Adam to die. Adam's separation from the glory of God gradually led to his demise without anyone else having to intervene.

Stepping away from the presence of God initiates a process of decay and deterioration. It is in that state of spiritual disconnection that all aspects of life start to crumble and lose their vibrancy.

How do you remain saturated in the presence of God? How do I have an encounter with God? You have to become hungry for God.

What is the first thing you lose when you are sick? You lose your appetite and you don't want to eat. You just want chicken soup. When you lose your hunger in the Spirit, it's like you're not hungry for the presence of God.

You are sick in the spiritual realm. (Van der Westhuizen, 2016)

The best way to fight the natural aging process of our bodies is to stay in the presence of God. The presence of God heals our bodies, restores our souls and refreshes our minds. It also delivers people from demons.

The presence of God heals our bodies, restores our souls and refreshes our minds.

The devil and his demons cannot stand the presence of God so they flee or manifest.

The supernatural is real, and so are the activities of angels and demons. God uses angels to administer tasks here on earth. Because they are supernatural beings, they can travel between heaven and earth. The seen and unseen.

The Hebrew word for angel is "mal'akh" (מַלְאָךְ). The literal translation of "mal'akh" is "messenger" or "one who is sent." In the Hebrew Bible (Old Testament), the term "mal'akh" is used to refer to both heavenly messengers (angels) and human messengers.

The word "mal'akh" is derived from the Hebrew root "l-'-k" (כ‏-‏א‏-‏ל), which carries the meaning of sending or dispatching. It signifies the role of angels as divine emissaries sent by God to deliver messages, fulfil tasks, and carry out His will.

In the biblical context, angels are often described as intermediaries between God and humanity. They serve as messengers, protectors, and agents of God's divine intervention in the world. The term "mal'akh" emphasizes their function as messengers who carry out specific assignments on behalf of God.

They are being sent or dispatched to deliver a divinely sent word or action from God.

3.1 The Purpose of Angels

Angels serve various purposes and fulfil different roles.

Purposes and roles of angels as mentioned in the Bible:

1. Messengers of God

Angels are often depicted as messengers of God, delivering His messages and carrying out His commands. For example, the angel Gabriel was sent to deliver important announcements to individuals like Mary (Luke 1:26-38) and Zechariah (Luke 1:11-20).

"In the sixth month of Elizabeth's pregnancy, God sent the angel Gabriel to Nazareth, a village in Galilee, to a virgin named Mary. She was engaged to be married to a man named Joseph, a descendant of King David. Gabriel appeared to her and said, "Greetings, favored woman! The Lord is with you!" Confused and disturbed, Mary tried to think what the angel could mean. "Don't be afraid, Mary," the angel told her, "for you have found favor with God! You will conceive and give birth to a son, and you will name him Jesus. He will be very great and will be called the Son of the Most High. The Lord God will give him the throne of his ancestor David. And he will reign over Israel forever; his Kingdom will never end!" Mary asked the angel, "But how can this happen? I am a virgin." The angel replied, "The Holy Spirit will come upon you, and the power of the Most High will overshadow you. So the baby to be born will be holy, and he will be called the Son of God. What's more, your relative Elizabeth has become pregnant in her old age! People used to say she was barren, but she has conceived a son and is now in her sixth month. Mary responded, "I am the Lord's servant. May everything you have said about me come true." And then the angel left her." Luke 1:26-36, 38 (NLT).

"While Zechariah was in the sanctuary, an angel of the Lord appeared to him, standing to the right of the incense altar. Zechariah was shaken and overwhelmed with fear when he saw him. But the angel said, "Don't be afraid, Zechariah! God has heard your prayer. Your wife, Elizabeth, will give you a son, and you are to name him John. You will have great joy and gladness, and many will rejoice at his birth, for he will be great in the eyes of the Lord. He must never touch wine or other alcoholic drinks. He will be filled with the Holy Spirit, even before his birth. And he will turn many Israelites to the Lord their God. He will be a man with the spirit and power of Elijah. He will prepare the people for the coming of the Lord. He will turn the hearts of the fathers to their children, and he will cause those who are rebellious to accept the wisdom of the godly." Zechariah said to the angel, "How can I be sure this will happen? I'm an old man now, and my wife is also well along in years." Then the angel said, "I am Gabriel! I stand in the very presence of God. It was he who sent me to bring you this good news! But now, since you didn't believe what I said, you will be silent and unable to speak until the child is born. For my words will certainly be fulfilled at the proper time.""" Luke 1:11-20 (NLT).

2. Worship and Praise

Angels are worshiping and praising God. They are described as surrounding the throne of God, offering continual worship and adoration.

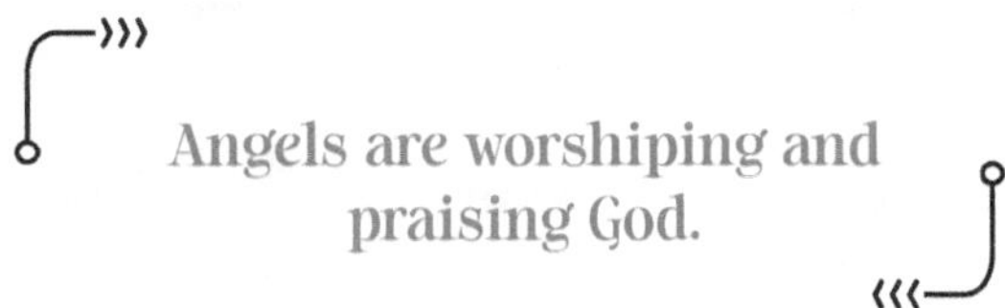

"Then I looked again, and I heard the voices of thousands and millions of angels around the throne and of the living beings and the elders. And they sang in a mighty chorus: "Worthy is the Lamb who was slaughtered— to receive power and riches and wisdom and strength and honor and glory and blessing."" Revelation 5:11-12(NLT).

3. Guardians and Protectors

Angels are sometimes portrayed as guardians and protectors. They watch over and help God's people. In Psalm 91:11-12, it says, *"For he will command his angels concerning you to guard you in all your ways. On their hands, they will bear you up, lest you strike your foot against a stone."*

In the book of Daniel he said, *"My God sent his angel to shut the lions' mouths so that they would not hurt me, for I have been found innocent in his sight. And I have not wronged you, Your Majesty."* Daniel 6:22 (NLT).

4. Protectors of children

When Jesus answered the questions of who is the greatest in the Kingdom he said, "these little ones." With this we know that from a young age God assigns angels to our lives that are constantly in the presence of God. I believe those angels travel in between heaven and earth to bring forth destinies that God has placed on people.

"Beware that you don't look down on any of these little ones. For I tell you that in heaven their angels are always in the presence of my heavenly Father." Matthew 18:10 (NLT).

5. Executors of God's Judgment

Angels can be involved in executing God's judgment upon individuals or nations. In the Old Testament, angels were sometimes sent to bring destruction or carry out God's justice, such as the angels who were sent to destroy Sodom and Gomorrah (Genesis 19:1-29).

"That evening the two angels came to the entrance of the city of Sodom. Lot was sitting there, and when he saw them, he stood up to meet them. Then he welcomed them and bowed with his face to the ground. "My Lords," he said, "come to my home to wash your feet, and be my guests for the night. You may then get up early in the morning and be on your way again."

"Oh no," they replied. "We'll just spend the night out here in the city square." But Lot insisted, so at last they went home with him. Lot prepared a feast for them, complete with fresh bread made without yeast, and they ate. But before they retired for the night, all the men of Sodom, young and old, came from all over the city and surrounded the house.

They shouted to Lot, "Where are the men who came to spend the night with you? Bring them out to us so we can have sex with them!" So Lot stepped outside to talk to them, shutting the door behind him.

"Please, my brothers," he begged, "don't do such a wicked thing. Look, I have two virgin daughters. Let me bring them out to you, and you can do with them as you wish. But please, leave these men alone, for they are my guests and are under my protection."

"*Stand back!*" *they shouted. "This fellow came to town as an outsider, and now he's acting like our judge! We'll treat you far worse than those other men!" And they lunged toward Lot to break down the door. But the two angels reached out, pulled Lot into the house, and bolted the door. Then they blinded all the men, young and old, who were at the door of the house, so they gave up trying to get inside.*

Meanwhile, the angels questioned Lot. "Do you have any other relatives here in the city?" they asked. "Get them out of this place — your sons-in-law, sons, daughters, or anyone else. For we are about to destroy this city completely. The outcry against this place is so great it has reached the Lord, and he has sent us to destroy it."

So Lot rushed out to tell his daughters' fiancés, "Quick, get out of the city! The Lord is about to destroy it." But the young men thought he was only joking. At dawn the next morning the angels became insistent.

"Hurry," they said to Lot. "Take your wife and your two daughters who are here. Get out right now, or you will be swept away in the destruction of the city!"

When Lot still hesitated, the angels seized his hand and the hands of his wife and two daughters and rushed them to safety outside the city, for the Lord was merciful. When they were safely out of the city, one of the angels ordered, "Run for your lives! And don't look back or stop anywhere in the valley! Escape to the mountains, or you will be swept away!"

"Oh no, my Lord!" Lot begged. "You have been so gracious to me and saved my life, and you have shown such great kindness. But I cannot go to the mountains. Disaster would catch up to me there, and I would soon die. See, there is a small village nearby. Please let me go there instead; don't you see how small it is? Then my life will be saved."

"All right," the angel said, "I will grant your request. I will not destroy the little village. But hurry! Escape to it, for I can do nothing until you arrive there." (This explains why that village was known as Zoar, which means "little place.")

Lot reached the village just as the sun was rising over the horizon. Then the Lord rained down fire and burning sulfur from the sky on Sodom and Gomorrah. He utterly destroyed them, along with the other cities and villages of the plain, wiping out all the people and every bit of vegetation. But Lot's wife looked back as she was following behind him, and she turned into a pillar of salt.

Abraham got up early that morning and hurried out to the place where he had stood in the Lord's presence. He looked out across the plain toward Sodom and Gomorrah and watched as columns of smoke rose from the cities like smoke from a furnace.

But God had listened to Abraham's request and kept Lot safe, removing him from the disaster that engulfed the cities on the plain." Genesis 19:1-29 (NLT).

6. Angels of Salvation

I often get the question - can I have more than one angel assigned to my life? Yes, you can. When we get saved and give our hearts fully to Jesus, more angels get sent to us to care for us in times of need and help us to fulfill the purposes of God for our life.

When you commit your life to Christ, you position yourself for angelic activity in your life. We never seek out or worship angels, but they are sent to us from Heaven to interact with and help us with day-to-day life.

"And God never said to any of the angels, "Sit in the place of honor at my right hand until I humble your enemies, making them a footstool under your feet." Therefore, angels are only servants — spirits sent to care for people who will inherit salvation." Hebrews 1:13-14 (NLT)

The Parable of the Lost coin is found in Luke 15:8-10, where Jesus tells a story to illustrate a spiritual truth.

In the parable, Jesus speaks of a woman who has ten silver coins and loses one of them. She lights a lamp, sweeps the house diligently, and searches carefully until she finds the lost coin. When she finds it, she calls her friends and neighbors together and says, "Rejoice with me, for I have found the coin that I had lost."

This parable is part of a series of parables in Luke 15 that highlight the theme of lost things being found and the subsequent rejoicing. It is often interpreted as a representation of God's relentless love and pursuit of lost sinners.

In this parable, the woman symbolizes God, while the lost coin represents a person who is spiritually lost or separated from God. The woman's diligent search for the lost coin reflects God's active and persistent seeking of those who are lost.

The lighting of the lamp and sweeping of the house can be seen as symbolic actions that represent the illumination and cleansing of our hearts that comes with the discovery of God's truth and salvation.

The climax of the parable is the celebration that takes place when the lost coin is found. The woman calls her friends and neighbors to rejoice with her. This emphasizes the joy and celebration in heaven when a lost soul repents and turns to God. The parable highlights the value that God places on each individual and His desire to see them restored to a relationship with Him.

The mention of the angels in heaven celebrating, conveys the significance when someone accepts salvation and turns to God. It illustrates the joy and rejoicing that takes place in the spiritual realm when a person's soul is saved. The parable reminds us of the immense love and grace of God, who actively seeks the lost and rejoices when they are found.

7. Spiritual Warfare

Angels are associated with spiritual warfare against the forces of evil. The archangel Michael, for example, is described as a powerful warrior against Satan and his demonic forces (Daniel 10:13, Jude 1:9, Revelation 12:7).

> Angels fight in spiritual warfare against the forces of evil.

The spiritual realm operates with different rankings therefore we need to know who we are up against in to know what weapons to use. That is why the Word of God urges us to put on the full armor of God in Ephesians 6.

"Put on the complete armor of Elohim, for you to have power to stand against the schemes of the devil. Because we do not wrestle against flesh and blood, but against principalities, against authorities, against the world-rulers of the darkness of this age, against spiritual matters of wickedness in the heavenlies." Ephesians 6:11-12 (TS2009).

The good news is, Heaven also has ranking and we can call on God and His angels to fight on our behalf. Just like they did for Daniel when the prince of Persia blocked his breakthrough;

"But for twenty-one days the spirit prince of the kingdom of Persia blocked my way. Then Michael, one of the archangels, came to help me, and I left him there with the spirit prince of the kingdom of Persia." Daniel 10:13 (NLT)

8. Angels of prosperity

Angels of prosperity are for us to command to bring prosperity to our lives. As per God's will for our lives to prosper. Angels are our helpers that go beyond space, time and matter.

Scripture speaks about God's desire for His people to prosper. It's important to understand that prosperity, according to biblical teachings, encompasses more than just material wealth. It includes spiritual abundance, emotional well-being, and relational blessings. With the help of angels we can command these blessings to be a part of our lives according to God's will.

- *"For I know the plans I have for you," declares the Lord, "plans to prosper you and not to harm you, plans to give you hope and a future."* Jeremiah 29:11 (NIV).

- *"The LORD God of heaven, which took me from my father's house, and from the land of my kindred, and which spake unto me, and that sware unto me, saying, Unto thy seed will I give this land; he shall send his angel before thee, and thou shalt take a wife unto my son from thence."* Genesis 24:7 (KJV).
- *"And he said, I am Abraham's servant. And the LORD hath blessed my master greatly; and he is become great: and he hath given him flocks, and herds, and silver, and gold, and menservants, and maidservants, and camels, and asses."* Genesis 24:34-35 (KJV).
- *"And he said unto me, The LORD, before whom I walk, will send his angel with thee, and prosper thy way; and thou shalt take a wife for my son of my kindred, and of my father's house:"* Genesis 24:40 (KJV).

- *"May those who delight in my vindication shout for joy and gladness; may they always say, "The Lord be exalted, who delights in the well-being of his servant.""* Psalm 35:27 (NIV).

- *"Dear friend, I pray that you may enjoy good health and that all may go well with you, even as your soul is getting along well."* 3 John 1:2 (NIV).

- *"But remember the Lord your God, for it is he who gives you the ability to produce wealth, and so confirms his covenant, which he swore to your ancestors, as it is today."* Deuteronomy 8:18 (NIV).

These verses highlight God's desire for His people to experience well-being and abundance in various areas of life.

However, it's important to approach prosperity in a balanced way, understanding that it is not solely about amassing material wealth but also about aligning our lives with God's purposes, seeking His kingdom, and finding fulfilment in Him.

The opposite is also true. Remember demons are fallen angels. This is why there are demons of poverty that need to be cast out of people. Their assignment is to keep people poor and broke.

Be aware.

9. Ministry and Assistance to Believers

Angels can minister to and provide assistance to believers. They can offer guidance, protection, and encouragement. In Hebrews 1:14, it says, "Are not all angels ministering spirits sent to serve those who will inherit salvation?"

It's important to note that the primary purpose of angels is to serve and glorify God. They carry out His will and fulfil their roles as directed by God.

3.2 Angelic Encounter

As a child, I was very fortunate to spend a lot of time with my grandmother. She is still today the closest thing to heaven I have ever experienced. On one of those days, we were sitting down and listened to all kinds of music all day long, just experiencing the presence of God.

I remember lying in that lounge flat on my back, and there was always the presence of Angels around me. I would lie there for hours and never feel alone, I would go through one record after the other listening to all the various kinds of music, and I loved every second.

My grandmother would be on the other side of the room, busy with lunch or supper, while I was enjoying the music. Today I still love listening to records and all kinds of music. I remember one particular day she walked into the lounge where I was lying and listening to music. I asked her, out of the blue like only a child can do, why did you start working at the Church? I remember the expression on her face changing drastically, as if she at that point in time realized… it is time.

She sat down on the white and blue patterned sofa, and I sat at her feet. She started telling me.

"A couple of years ago, the Minister of our Church where I was serving, kept on asking me to come and work for the Church. There was an open position, but I just wasn't ready. "I was still working with your grandfather, and I had a lot of things on my agenda. So, time passed by, and I never applied."

"The one morning at around 1:00 am your grandfather headed out to one of the mines he was working at."

"Around 02:30 in the morning I heard a rattle outside my room, in this very same lounge where we are sitting in now, and I got up to go and see."

"Maybe your grandfather forgot something, and he came back to get it," she said. I was in shock. I couldn't believe what my grandmother was telling me. To me, it sounded like the start of a horror movie. She was woman alone on a 2,5 hectare small holdings in the middle of the night. The nearest town was about 30km away, so no one to come out and help her.

If you hear these kind of noises, you run! You never go out and see who is there. If you have watched any horror movies before, you know what is about to happen.

Nonetheless, this brave woman unlocked the gate to her bedroom and went straight into the living room. The same living room we are now sitting in and she is telling me the story.

She told me: "Turn around. You see where the round dining table is now? On your right you see the cupboard where I put the snacks and the tablecloths?

"Yes Ouma," I nodded suspiciously.

"That is where it happened."

Now I was even more unsure of what on earth this middle-of-the-night story Ouma is telling me, has got to do with my previous question to her about why she started at church. She used to tell me many stories and fables, and I knew a lesson was coming, but was not ready for this one.

"As I entered the room, the room filled up with a bright light. It was the brightest light I have ever seen in my life, a light that shined with glorious colors. It filled up the entire room. The atmosphere of Heaven filled the room. I do not know how I knew, but I knew." Ouma pointed and said: "There … right there between the cupboard and the table, stood a very tall angel. Right in front of me."

She told me the story again like it was playing out in front of her. With tears in her gentle blue eyes she said, "He stood right through the roof. Dressed in white, with gold colors swirling all around him. Soft feathers covered the powerful large white and golden wings."

My heart felt like bursting. As young as I was, I felt the presence of God in the room as she told me her story. I knew the feeling well, because I felt that before when I was about 4 years old.

Her words echoing through my ears - "A giant, massive, larger than life angel extending high into the ceiling stood in front of her. He looked like he was taller than the ceiling and that there was at that moment no ceiling at all."

"Ouma!" I remember yelling. "Were you not scared?"

"At first I got a fright, and tried to reason with what was happening, but at the same time I felt the peace of God upon and around me like never before. The presence of God flooded the room and the light of the angel lit up every corner of this living room."

She paused; took a deep breath like she was reliving that moment once again. Even where I was sitting by her feet, I could feel the tangible presence of God.

Then the angel spoke with a loud and authoritative voice, "I have a message for you from God."

God said, "You are not doing enough for me."

I gasped loudly! "And then Ouma, what did you say?"

"Nothing, all of a sudden the light dimmed, and everything went dark again. I was by myself. It was very quiet, but Peace and Love stayed with me. I knew I was not alone. My heart was filled with astonishment and the love of God, but I knew there was work to do."

"What did you do then? What did you feel?" I had so many questions.

"I went back to bed, but couldn't sleep. The first thing the next morning I phoned the minister of my church. I asked him whether the position was still available?"

His reply was subtle, "I've been waiting for your call."

The rest is history and for more than 20 years she worked and served the Kingdom of God through that same church.

What a beautiful legacy left for us as children and grandchildren. She was an example of how to serve Jesus with all your heart. She taught us all how to read and pray the Word of God. I never knew her any other way but as a God-fearing woman of God, a teacher of the Word and a true prayer warrior. I remember how she used to read the Bible to me and my sister whilst the morning weather played softly in the background. It is how I knew it was 10 minutes before we had to leave for school. An impartation of 10 minutes lasted a lifetime.

This chapter is dedicated to my grandmother whom I miss dearly and think about daily.

Anet de Koker: 18 May 1938 – 20 May 2018.

3.3 Types of Angels

We deal with angels daily and throughout our day. They even keep an eye out for us while we sleep. They are messengers of God. They administer miracles and protection for the children of God. The person I have learned most about angels, is angel expert Joshua Mills, who said: "There are over 394 scriptures on angels in the Bible."

They are strong, fierce, and lit up by the power and strength of God.

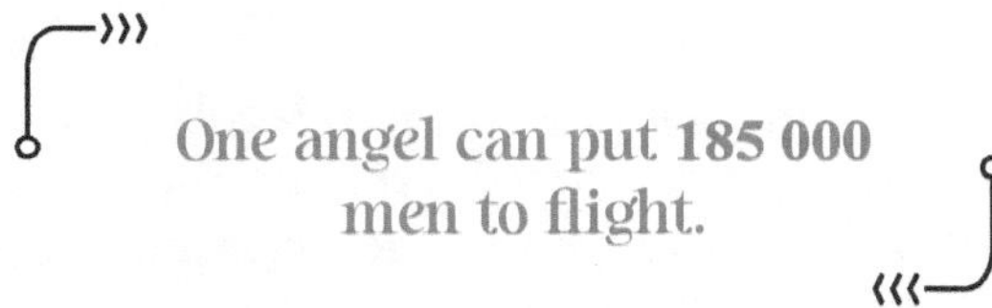

Many people are fearful of angelic activity because it has been perverted over decades of false teaching. If it is in the parameters of the Word of God, angelic activity is a supernatural sign and wonder displaying the Glory of Heaven. It is one of the signs that connects heaven to earth.

Angels are seen in two ways, with our naked eye or with our spiritual eye in the form of a dream or vision. Different angels are assigned to various assignments over people. My favourite angel account in the Bible is the account of Jacob. Genesis 28:12 recounts a significant event in the life of Jacob, one of the patriarchs of Israel.

Jacob, the son of Isaac and grandson of Abraham, was on a journey from his homeland to Haran. He left Beersheba and set out on his way, traveling alone. As nightfall approached, Jacob found a suitable place to rest for the night and slept there.

Using a stone as a pillow, Jacob lay down and drifted off. During his slumber, he had a profound dream — a dream that would forever shape his life. In the dream, he saw a ladder or staircase that reached Heaven. The top of the ladder extended into the heavens, and angels of God were ascending and descending on it.

As Jacob watched the angelic beings moving between heaven and earth, he witnessed a divine presence standing above the ladder. God spoke to Jacob in the dream, reiterating the promises He had made to Abraham and Isaac. He assured Jacob of His continuous presence and blessings, promising to give him the land he was lying on, and to be with him wherever he went.

Overwhelmed by the significant encounter, Jacob awoke from his sleep and realized that he had experienced a remarkable encounter with the divine. Filled with awe and reverence, he declared:- "Surely the Lord is in this place, and I did not know it!"

In the morning, Jacob rose early and took the stone that had served as his pillow. He set it up as a memorial pillar, and poured oil over of it. He named the place Bethel, which means "House of God." He recognized it as a sacred location where he had encountered the presence of God.

Jacob made a vow … promising that if God would protect and guide him on his journey, provide him with food, clothing, and a safe return to his father's house, then the Lord would be his God. He committed to offering a tithe, giving a tenth of all he possessed, as an act of worship and gratitude to God.

With this profound experience and newfound commitment to God, Jacob continued his journey to Haran, carrying with him the assurance of God's presence and blessings. The encounter at Bethel marked a turning point in Jacob's life, setting the stage for his future encounters with God and his eventual transformation into the patriarch Israel.

3.4 Examples of angels mentioned in the Bible:

1. Seraphim

Seraphim is mentioned in Isaiah 6:2-6. They are described as having six wings and flying. They are seen surrounding the throne of God, praising and worshipping Him.

"Above Him seraphim (heavenly beings) stood; each one had six wings: with two wings he covered his face, with two wings he covered his feet, and with two wings he flew. And one called out to another, saying, "Holy, Holy, Holy is the Lord of hosts; The whole earth is filled with His glory."" Isaiah 6 : 2 - 3 (AMP).

In Greek, the word for Seraphim is "Seraphim" (Σεραφείμ). The term "Seraphim" is derived from the Hebrew word "saraph" (שָׂרָף) which means "burning ones" or "fiery ones."

In theological contexts, the Seraphim are often associated with a high order of celestial beings or angels. In the book of Isaiah, chapter 6, verse 2, they are depicted as attending to the presence of God in the heavenly realm. They are portrayed as having six wings – two covering their faces, two covering their feet, and two used for flying.

The word "Seraphim" highlights the burning nature of these angelic beings. It can suggest their association with intense radiance, holiness, and purification. In the Bible the Seraphim reverence and worship of God is depicted, with serving wings as a symbol of their readiness to fulfill divine commands. Their posture represents humility and awe in the presence of the Almighty.

It's worth noting that the concept of Seraphim is primarily found within biblical and religious literature, and their precise nature and function are not extensively elaborated upon in the Bible. The term

"Seraphim" has become an important part of theological and artistic traditions, symbolizing the heavenly beings that surround the throne of God and partake in divine worship.

2. Cherubim

Cherubim is mentioned throughout the Bible, including Genesis 3:24 and Exodus 25:18-22. They are often depicted as angelic beings guarding the presence of God, and they are associated with wisdom and knowledge.

"So God drove the man out; and at the east of the Garden of Eden, He [permanently] stationed the cherubim and the sword with the flashing blade which turned round and round [in every direction] to protect and guard the way (entrance, access) to the tree of life." Genesis 3:24 (AMP).

"You shall make two cherubim (winged angelic figures) of [solid] hammered gold at the two ends of the mercy seat. Make one cherub at each end, making the cherubim of one piece with the mercy seat at its two ends. The cherubim shall have their wings spread upward, covering the mercy seat with their wings and facing each other. The faces of the cherubim are to be looking downward toward the mercy seat. You shall put the mercy seat on the top of the ark, and in the ark you shall put the Testimony which I will give you. There I will meet with you; from above the mercy seat, from between the two cherubim which are on the ark of the Testimony, I will speak [intimately] with you regarding every commandment that I will give you for the Israelites." Exodus 25:18-22 (AMP).

In Greek, the word for Cherubim is "Cheroubim" (Χερουβείμ). The term "Cheroubim" is derived from the Hebrew word "keruvim" (מִיבוּרְכ) and is used to refer to a particular order of celestial beings or angels.

Cherubim is mentioned in various contexts, particularly in the books of Genesis and Exodus. They are depicted as powerful and majestic creatures associated with the presence of God. Cherubim are often described as having multiple wings and unique forms, such as having the face of a lion, an ox, an eagle, or a human.

The exact meaning of the word "Cheroubim" is not specified in the biblical text, but it is believed to be derived from a root word that means "to be near" or "to guard." This suggests that Cherubim may be associated with guarding or protecting sacred spaces or objects.

I believe I am sacred to God.

In early 2023, I received a word from the Lord through a prophet. It had not been the first prophecy where the person who prophesies sees an angel at exactly the same place. An angel of protection and an assignment to make sure I accomplish what God's purpose and plan is for my life.

He said:- "Stand up again. You feel the left side of your body is all hot. Feel it now. More so than the right side. Do you feel it?

Tell me if it's true. You know why? It's actually heating up. Warmer. You feel it. You know why?

Because I see an angel right behind her on the left-hand side of the body. You can ask her. Her whole body is all warm on the left-hand side. More so than the right. Now that angel is touching you.

Now feel it.

Feel it even more. He's touching you. I see he's protecting your back. I see he's protecting you. His sword is in his hand and he's protecting you.

Things have tried to derail certain projects in your life. God is putting an end to that derailment. There will be no more confusion. There will be no more derailment. It will be established that God what which God has purposed." (Prophet Didier Tison)

In theological and artistic traditions, Cherubim are often depicted as angelic guardians or attendants surrounding the throne of God. They are beings of great wisdom and holiness, carrying out divine tasks and serving as intermediaries between heaven and earth.

I believe a Cherubim has been assigned to my life. I have seen him, felt him, and experienced him. My is my helping hand from heaven to operate in the supernatural power of God for the Glory for God.

3. Archangels

In Christian theology, Archangels are considered being high-ranking angels with significant roles and responsibilities. While the Bible does not explicitly provide a list of Archangels or define their specific names, there are references to certain angelic beings who being Archangels based on their roles and prominence.

In Greek, the word for archangels is "Archangelos" (Αρχάγγελος). The term "Archangelos" is derived from two Greek words: "arche" meaning "chief" or "principal", and "angelos' meaning "messenger" or "angel." Thus, the term "Archangelos" can be translated as "chief messenger" or "principal angel".

Archangels are high-ranking angels. While the Bible names two archangels, Michael and Gabriel, the term "archangel" implies that there may be other angels of high rank.

Michael, whose name means "Who is like God?" Michael is described as a powerful spiritual warrior and defender, associated with leading the angelic forces against evil powers. He is often regarded as the chief or prince of the heavenly host. He is often associated with protection and warfare.

Other Archangels, although not named in the Bible, are mentioned in various religious and apocryphal texts, such as Gabriel and Raphael.

Gabriel is known as a messenger and is often associated with delivering important announcements. Gabriel is known as a messenger of God, delivering important announcements and revelations, including the Annunciation to Mary.

Raphael is often associated with healing and protection. Where Raphael is associated with healing. The name Raphael is derived from the Hebrew root word "rapha" (אָפָר), which means "healing" or "to heal."

4. Angels

The general term "angel" refers to the heavenly beings created by God. They are messengers of God and carry out His commands. Angels are often seen as intermediaries between God and humans, delivering messages, providing guidance, and offering protection.

5. Fallen Angels

The Bible also mentions angels who have rebelled against God and fallen from their heavenly positions. The most notable fallen angel is Satan (also referred to as Lucifer), who led a rebellion against God. Other fallen angels are mentioned in Jude 1:6 and 2 Peter 2:4.

"And angels who did not keep their own designated place of power, but abandoned their proper dwelling place, [these] He has kept in eternal chains under [the thick gloom of utter] darkness for the judgment of the great day," Jude 1:6 (AMP).

"For if God did not [even] spare angels that sinned, but threw them into hell and sent them to pits of gloom to be kept [there] for judgment;" 2 Peter 2:4(AMP).

3.5 IN10TIONAL Thinking

Angels are a helping hand for us here on earth in times of salvation, celebration, trouble, sickness and communication with God. I will give you various prayers to activate the angelic activity over your life. Some prayers are for right now and others you might need in the future during sickness or difficult times. Refer back to them when you need to.

> Angels are a helping hand for us here on earth in times of salvation, celebration, trouble, sickness and communication with God.

1. Prayer for activating angelic activity over your life:

Heavenly Father,

I recognize your power and authority over all creation. I thank you for your promise in Psalm 91:11-12, which says, "For he will command his angels concerning you to guard you in all your ways. On their hands they will bear you up, lest you strike your foot against a stone." I believe in the truth of your Word, and in faith for the activation of angelic activity in my life.

Father, I ask that you dispatch your angels to surround me and my loved ones. According to Hebrews 1:14, I know that angels are ministering spirits sent to serve those who will inherit salvation. I invite their presence and assistance in my life. Let them encamp around me, shielding me from danger and thwarting the schemes of the enemy.

Lord, I pray that your angels will go before me, preparing the way and removing any obstacles that may hinder my progress. As it says in Exodus 23:20, "Behold, I send an angel before you to guard you on the way and to bring you to the place that I have prepared." Guide my steps and lead me along the path of righteousness.

I ask for increased angelic activity in my life, both seen and unseen. I pray that your angels will fight on my behalf in the spiritual realm, as described in Daniel 10:12-13. Strengthen them in their battle against the forces of darkness that seek to hinder me. Let them wage war against every spiritual opposition and bring victory in every area of my life.

Father, grant me the spiritual discernment to recognize the presence and work of your angels. Open my eyes to see the heavenly realm and the angelic hosts that surround me. Help me to cooperate with them and align my life with your purposes.

I commit myself to walk in obedience to your Word and to follow the leading of your Holy Spirit. I repent of any sins or actions that may hinder the ministry of your angels in my life. I surrender myself to you completely, inviting your angels to fulfill their assignments in accordance with your perfect will.
Thank you, Lord, for the assurance that your angels are with me. I trust in your faithfulness and provision. I declare that angelic activity is activated over my life, and I am grateful for the protection, guidance, and assistance they bring.

In Jesus' name, I pray.

Amen.

2. Prayer for activating angels of prosperity over your life:

Heavenly Father,

I thank you for your promises in your Word regarding prosperity and abundance. In Deuteronomy 8:18, you declare that it is You who gives the power to create wealth. I humbly ask for the activation of angels of prosperity in my life, according to your will.

Lord, I ask that you dispatch your angels of prosperity to go before me and open doors of opportunity. As it is written in Psalm 37:23, "The steps of a man are established by the Lord, when he delights in his way." I pray that your angels will guide my steps, leading me to the right paths and connecting me with the right people and resources for financial increase.

Father, I command your angels to intervene in my financial affairs. According to Philippians 4:19, you promise to supply all my needs according to your riches in glory. I pray that your angels will bring forth divine provision and abundance into my life. Let them bring favor, increase, and multiplication in my finances.

I renounce any mindset of lack or poverty and choose to align my thoughts and beliefs with your Word. Help me to be a good steward of the resources you bless me with. Give me wisdom to make sound financial decisions and the discipline to manage my finances in a way that honors you.

Lord, I pray that your angels will guard and protect my financial endeavors. Protect me from deceit, fraud, and any schemes of the enemy that seek to hinder my prosperity. Let your angels be a shield around me, keeping me safe from financial harm.

I commit to using the resources and blessings you provide for the advancement of your kingdom and the well-being of others. Help me to be generous and to sow into good works that bring glory to your name.

Thank you, Lord, for your faithfulness and your desire for my prosperity. I trust in your provision and believe that as I activate the angels of prosperity in my life through prayer, you will bring forth abundance and increase. May your name be glorified through my financial blessings.

In Jesus' name, I pray.

Amen.

3. Prayer for activating angels of supernatural protection, deliverance and victory over your life:

Heavenly Father,

I come before you in the name of Jesus, acknowledging your power and authority over all the forces of darkness. I thank you for your promises in your Word regarding supernatural protection, deliverance, and victory. In Psalm 91:11-12, you declare that you will command your angels to guard us in all our ways. I humbly ask for the activation of angels of supernatural protection, deliverance, and victory in my life, according to your will.

Lord, I pray that you dispatch your mighty angels to encamp around me and my loved ones. I invite their presence and their supernatural protection to surround us. As it is written in 2 Kings 6:16, "Do not be afraid, for those who are with us are more than those who are with them." I declare that your angelic hosts are greater in number and strength than any adversary we may face.

Father, I ask for the intervention of your angels in every area of my life that needs deliverance. Set me free from every bondage, oppression, and stronghold that the enemy has established. According to Psalm 34:7, "The angel of the Lord encamps around those who fear him and delivers them." I believe that your angels will bring deliverance and break every chain in my life.

I pray for supernatural victory in every spiritual battle I face. As it is written in 1 Corinthians 15:57, "But thanks be to God, who gives us the victory through our Lord Jesus Christ." I declare that with the assistance of your angels, I am more than a conqueror in Christ Jesus. Let your angels fight on my behalf and bring forth triumph in every situation.

Father, I ask for discernment; to recognize the presence and work of your angels. Open my spiritual eyes to see the supernatural realm and the angelic hosts that are assigned to protect and deliver me. Help me to cooperate with them and align my life with your purposes.

I commit myself to walk in obedience to your Word and to follow the leading of your Holy Spirit. I renounce every form of darkness and sin that may hinder the ministry of your angels in my life. I surrender myself to you completely, inviting your angels to fulfil their assignments in accordance with your perfect will.

Thank you, Lord, for the assurance that your angels are with me. I trust in your supernatural protection, deliverance, and victory. I declare that the angels of supernatural protection, deliverance, and victory are activated over my life, and I am grateful for the peace and security they bring.

In Jesus' name, I pray.

Amen.

4. Prayer for activating angels of healing over your life:

Heavenly Father,

I come before you in the name of Jesus, believing in your power to heal and restore. I thank you for your promises in your Word regarding healing and the ministry of angels. In Psalm 103:3, You declare You forgive all our sins and heal all our diseases. I humbly ask for the activation of angels of healing in my life, according to your will.

Lord, I pray that you dispatch your angels of healing to minister to every area of my body, soul, and spirit that needs healing. I invite their presence and their supernatural touch to bring forth restoration and wholeness. As it is written in Exodus 23:20, "See, I am sending an angel ahead of you to guard you along the way and to bring you to the place I have prepared." I believe that your healing angels will guide me to the place of divine health.

Father, I ask for the intervention of your angels in every aspect of my health. Whether it be physical, emotional, or mental, I trust in your healing power. According to Matthew 8:17, Jesus took our infirmities and carried our diseases. I declare that by His stripes, I am healed. Let your angels release the healing virtue of Jesus into my body and bring about complete restoration.

I pray for supernatural wisdom and discernment regarding my health. Help me to make wise choices and seek appropriate medical care when needed. Guide me to the right treatments, therapies, and professionals who can assist in my healing journey. I trust in your divine guidance and provision.

Father, I surrender myself completely to you and your healing plan for my life. I renounce any unbelief, fear, or doubt that may hinder the manifestation of your healing power. I choose to stand on the truth of your Word and believe that your angels are working on my behalf.

I commit myself to live a lifestyle that promotes health and well-being. Help me to take care of my body, mind, and spirit, honoring you with my choices and actions. Give me the strength and discipline to implement healthy habits and make positive changes.

Thank you, Lord, for the ministry of angels and their role in bringing healing. I trust in your supernatural healing power and believe that as I activate the angels of healing in my life through prayer, I will experience your divine restoration.

In Jesus' name, I pray.

Amen.

5. Prayer for activating angels of breakthrough over your life:

Heavenly Father,

I come before you in the name of Jesus, recognizing your power and authority to bring breakthrough in every area of my life. I thank you for your promises in your Word regarding breakthrough and the ministry of angels. In Psalm 34:7, it is written, "The angel of the Lord encamps around those who fear him, and he delivers them." I humbly ask for the activation of angels of breakthrough in my life, according to your will.

Lord, I pray that you dispatch your angels of breakthrough to go before me and make a way where there seems to be no way. I invite their presence and their supernatural assistance in breaking down barriers, removing obstacles, and opening doors of opportunity. As it is written in Isaiah 45:2, "I will go before you and level the mountains; I will break down gates of bronze and cut through bars of iron." I believe that your angels will go before me and bring about breakthrough in every area of my life.

Father, I ask for the intervention of your angels in my circumstances. Whether it be financial breakthrough, breakthrough in relationships, breakthrough in career or ministry, or any other area of need, I trust in your ability to bring about breakthrough. According to Philippians 4:19, you promise to supply all my needs according to your riches in glory. I declare that your angels are at work, aligning circumstances and bringing forth the breakthrough I need.

I pray for supernatural wisdom and discernment to recognize the opportunities and doors of breakthrough that you open. Help me to walk in faith and step into the divine opportunities you present. Guide me in making wise decisions and taking the necessary actions to cooperate with your plans for breakthrough.

Father, I surrender myself completely to you and your timing. I renounce impatience, doubt, and discouragement that may hinder the manifestation of breakthrough. I choose to trust in your perfect timing and believe that your angels are working on my behalf.

I commit myself to seek your Kingdom first and align my life with your purposes. Help me to walk in obedience to your Word and follow the leading of your Holy Spirit. Give me the courage and perseverance to press on, knowing that breakthrough is on the horizon.

Thank you, Lord, for the ministry of angels and their role in bringing breakthrough. I trust in your supernatural power and believe that as I activate the angels of breakthrough in my life through prayer, I will experience your divine intervention.

In Jesus' name, I pray.

Amen.

6. Prayer for activating angels of revival over your life:

Heavenly Father,

I come before you in the name of Jesus, longing for a fresh outpouring of your Spirit and a revival in my life. I thank you for your promises in your Word regarding revival and the ministry of angels. In Psalm 85:6, it is written, "Will you not revive us again, that your people may rejoice in you?" I humbly ask for the activation of angels of revival in my life, according to your will.

Lord, I pray that you release your angels of revival to bring a mighty awakening in my heart and in the hearts of your people. I invite their presence and their supernatural touch to ignite a passion for you and a hunger for your presence. As it is written in Acts 3:19, "Repent, then, and turn to God, so that your sins may be wiped out, that times of refreshing may come from the Lord." I believe that your angels of revival will usher in times of refreshment and renewal.

Father, I ask for the intervention of your angels in my spiritual life. I long for a deeper relationship with you, a greater intimacy, and a fervent love for your Word. I pray that your angels will stir up a hunger for prayer, worship, and the study of your Word. Let them ignite a fire in my heart that cannot be quenched, and let revival flow from within me to those around me.

I pray for a revival of repentance and surrender. Help me to examine my heart and to turn away from any sin or hindrance that may be hindering your work in my life. Create in me a clean heart, O God, and renew a steadfast spirit within me. Use your angels of revival to convict, heal, and restore.

Father, I surrender myself completely to you and your work of revival. I renounce complacency, apathy, and lukewarmness that may hinder the movement of your Spirit. I choose to seek you with all my heart, to humble myself before you, and to allow your Spirit to have full control. I believe that your angels are at work, bringing a revival that will transform lives and bring glory to your name.

I commit myself to be a vessel of revival and to share your love and truth with those around me. Help me to be a catalyst for revival in my family, my community, and beyond. Empower me with boldness and anointing to proclaim the Gospel and to lead others to a personal encounter with you.

Thank you, Lord, for the ministry of angels and their role in bringing revival. I trust in your supernatural power and believe that as I activate the angels of revival in my life through prayer, I will experience a mighty outpouring of your Spirit.

In Jesus' name, I pray.

Amen.

7. Prayer for activating angels of prayer over your life:

Heavenly Father,

I come before you in the name of Jesus, recognizing the power of prayer and the ministry of angels in the spiritual realm. I thank you for your promises in your Word regarding prayer and the assistance of angels. In Psalm 34:15, it is written, "The eyes of the Lord are toward the righteous and his ears toward their cry." I humbly ask for the activation of angels of prayer in my life, according to your will.

Lord, I pray that You release your angels of prayer to surround me and empower me in my prayer life. I invite their presence and their supernatural assistance to intercede on my behalf. As it is written in Romans 8:26, "Likewise the Spirit helps us in our weakness. For we do not know what to pray for as we ought, but the Spirit himself intercedes for us with groanings too deep for words." As you intercede on my behalf Jesus, I believe it will bring forth breakthrough in my prayers.

Father, I ask for the intervention of your angels to strengthen and guide me in my prayer life. Help me to align my prayers with your will and to pray according to your Word. Let your angels prompt me in prayer, leading me to pray for the things that are in your heart. I pray that they will surround me with a heavenly atmosphere of prayer, increasing my faith and fervency.

I pray for a greater sensitivity to the leading of your Spirit in prayer. Open my spiritual eyes and ears to discern your voice and to pray in alignment with your purposes. Let your angels minister to me as I pray, bringing encouragement, revelation, and spiritual breakthrough. I trust that they will assist me in overcoming distractions, discouragement, and spiritual warfare that may hinder my prayer life.

Father, I surrender myself completely to you and your work through prayer. I renounce any complacency, distraction, or lack of discipline that may hinder my prayer life. I choose to prioritize prayer and seek your face with persistence and faith. I believe that your angels are at work, partnering with me in prayer and bringing about your divine purposes.

I commit myself to a lifestyle of prayer and intercession. Help me to pray without ceasing, to pray for others, and to stand in the gap for those in need. Use me as an instrument of your love and mercy, as I lift my voice in prayer and seek your kingdom first.

Thank you, Lord, for the ministry of angels and their role in empowering my prayer life. I trust in your supernatural power and believe that as I activate the angels of prayer through prayer, I will experience a deeper intimacy with you and see the manifestation of your answers.

In Jesus' name, I pray. Amen.

8. Prayer for activating angels over your life for a specific assignment:

Heavenly Father,

I come before you in the name of Jesus, recognizing the power and ministry of angels in carrying out specific assignments according to your will. I thank You for your promises in your Word regarding the assistance of angels in fulfilling your purposes. In Psalm 91:11-12, it is written, "He will command his angels concerning you to guard you in all your ways. On their hands they will bear you up, lest you strike your foot against a stone." I command for the activation of angels over my life for the specific assignment I am called to, according to your divine plan.

Lord, I pray that You release your angels to surround me and empower me for the specific assignment You have for my life. I invite their presence and their supernatural assistance in carrying out your purposes. As it is written in Hebrews 1:14, "Are they not all ministering spirits sent out to serve for the sake of those who are to inherit salvation?" I believe that your angels are ready to minister and support me in fulfilling my calling.

Father, I ask for the intervention of your angels in every aspect of my assignment. Guide them and direct them as they go before me and prepare the way. Let them bring divine protection, wisdom, and provision as I step into the assignment you have ordained for me. I pray that your angels will fight on my behalf, standing against every obstacle, opposition, and spiritual attack that may come my way.

I pray for a greater sensitivity to the leading of your Spirit in carrying out my assignment. Open my spiritual eyes and ears to discern your guidance and the promptings of your angels. Let them provide divine insight, strategies, and supernatural favor in every step I take. I trust that they will bring divine connections, divine appointments, and divine opportunities aligned with your purpose.

Father, I surrender myself completely to you and your work in and through me. I yield to your timing and guidance, knowing that your angels are at work to fulfil your perfect plan. I renounce any fear, doubt, or self-reliance that may hinder the assignment you have for me. I choose to walk in faith, trusting in your supernatural provision and empowerment.

I commit myself to faithfully follow your leading and to be obedient to your voice. Help me to stay aligned with your Word and to seek your face in every decision and action. Use your angels to assist me in accomplishing the specific assignment you have entrusted to me.

Thank you, Lord, for the ministry of angels and their role in fulfilling your purposes in my life. I trust in your supernatural power and believe that as I activate the angels for my specific assignment through prayer and obedience, I will see the manifestation of your glory and the fulfillment of your plan.

In Jesus' name, I pray.

Amen.

Chapter IV

DEMONS

"For I am convinced [and continue to be convinced — beyond any doubt] that neither death, nor life, nor angels, nor principalities, nor things present and threatening, nor things to come, nor powers, nor height, nor depth, nor any other created thing, will be able to separate us from the [unlimited] love of God, which is in Christ Jesus our Lord." Romans 8:38-39AMP.

4.1 Types of Demons

In Hebrew, the word for demon is "shed" (שֵׁד). The term "shed" is often translated as "demon" or "evil spirit" in English. It refers to malevolent supernatural beings or spirits that are considered opposing to God and engage in harmful or deceptive actions.

In the Hebrew Bible (Old Testament), "shed" is mentioned in various contexts, often associated with idolatry and practices of pagan worship. It is used to describe entities that are believed to possess individuals or cause afflictions. The term can also be used metaphorically to represent destructive forces or influences.

The Bible mentions various evil spirits or entities, referred to as demons. The focus of the Bible is primarily on the relationship between God and humanity, the message of salvation, and the power of Jesus Christ to overcome evil. As mentioned in Revelation 12:11.

"They conquered him completely through the blood of the Lamb and the powerful word of his testimony. They triumphed because they did not love and cling to their own lives, even when faced with death." Revelation 12:11 (TPT).

While specific types of demons are not explicitly listed in the Bible, there are descriptions and encounters with demonic entities that can be found.

Here are some examples:

- **Unclean spirits:** This term is used in the New Testament to refer to demonic entities. They are mentioned in various instances, such as in Mark 1:23-26 and Luke 8:2. The term "unclean" suggests their impure or wicked nature.

- **Legion:** In Mark 5:1-20 and Luke 8:26-39, there is an account of a demon-possessed man who referred to himself as Legion because he was possessed by many demons. This suggests that multiple demons can be present within a single individual.

- **Deceitful spirits:** In 1 Timothy 4:1, it speaks of "deceitful spirits" or "seducing spirits" that lead people astray from the faith.

- **Satan and his demons:** While not explicitly categorized as demons, Satan (also known as the devil). Satan is often depicted as the leader or ruler of demons, seeking to deceive and destroy humanity. The Word of God explains that satan is the ruler of this World.

- **Fallen angels:** Fallen angels are malevolent spiritual beings. They rebelled against God and oppose His purposes.

> Satan is leader or ruler of demons, seeking to deceive and destroy humanity.

"In the same way, there were heavenly messengers in rebellion who went outside their rightful domain of authority and abandoned their appointed realms. God bound them in everlasting chains and is keeping them in the dark abyss of the netherworld until the judgment of the great day." Jude (Judah) 1:6 (TPT).

"Now, don't forget, God had no pity for the angels when they sinned but threw them into the lowest, darkest dungeon of gloom and locked them in chains, where they are firmly held until the judgment of torment." 2 Peter 2:4 (TPT).

It's important to approach discussions of demons with caution and focus on the biblical teachings about resisting evil and finding refuge and protection in God. The Bible emphasizes the power and authority of Jesus Christ over all evil spirits, providing hope and deliverance from their influence.

Demons are on assignment from the devil. The same way angels are on assignment from God. We can invite them into our lives the same way we can invite angels into our lives. The difference is life and death. Demons are on assignment from the devil. The same way angels are on assignment from God.

4.2 Demon Possession

Demons can take hold of and possess unbelievers and also up to a certain extent a believer. Making it clear that a demon cannot possess a born-again child of God. The devil can use his demons to take authority over a believer or unbeliever only where they give him the right to enter.

You give demons a right to enter by sin. Demon possession does not happen overnight it happens gradually the more you allow the devil a foothold over your life. The word warns us that God's people perish because of a lack of knowledge in Hosea 4:6. Therefore we need to equip ourselves with knowledge to overcome.

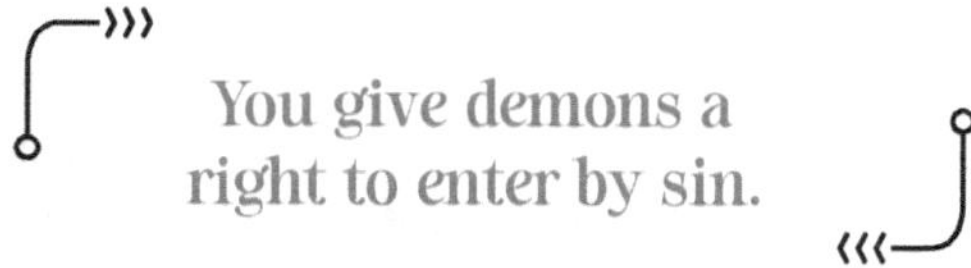

Demon possession can be broken down into three simple steps that the devil uses to take hold over our life.

1. First is oppression,
2. Second is obsession,
3. Third is possession.

What are the ways we allow the devil a foothold in our lives?

- Sin.
- Backsliding.
- Stagnation.
- Wrong choices and lifestyles.
- Laziness and lifelessness.
- Depression and Anxiety.

- Addiction to Alcohol, Nicotine, Vaping and Drugs.
- Molestation.
- Homosexuality.
- Abuse.
- Disobedience.
- Trauma, Shock and Fear.
- Separation from the presence of God and more.

All sin was not because of our wrong choices, but because of the wrong choices of others. These wrong choices impact our lives in a profound and traumatic way. It remains our responsibility to be set free from trauma and the sins of others in our past.

Sin separates us from God and we need to repent and turn back to God. Then leave your old life and lifestyles behind and be in one heart and mind with God.

Some sins enter our lives through the sins of others. A baby can be oppressed in a mother's womb because of the choices of that mother.

> A baby can be oppressed in a mother's womb because of the choices of that mother.

Physical abuse is a sin committed by another person but oppresses the person being abused. The same for sexual and emotional abuse. Homosexuality often occurs with people who have been sexually, mentally, or physically abused by someone of the opposite sex.

These sins cause trauma, shock, depression and fear, with far more long lasting trauma responses. Through sin, sin is being put on people because of the wrong choices of the person committing the sin. It oppresses the person being abused and makes them think and believe that they are not worthy of love from others. Worthy of God's love or worthy of the natural way of receiving love, that is man or woman. They lose their identity in Christ which causes them to lose their identity entirely.

The further we move away from God and the more we sin. The closer we walk to the devil and his demons, the more we become oppressed. The more sin the more you open the door for demon oppression. Oppression leads to obsession that leads to full on demon possession.

> The further we move away from God, the more we sin.

1. Demon Oppression

How does a person know that they are being oppressed?

- When you become so heavy in your spirit that you cannot carry the load in your life anymore
- You become disconnected.
- You will feel depressed and have stagnated in your walk with God.
- You don't hear the voice of God anymore.
- You feel your prayers are hitting the ceiling.
- You have a blank look on your face and no feelings are expressed anymore. Either it hurts too much, or you are just not interested.
- You just do not see the point in life anymore.

The devil is oppressing you. It is time for you to be set free. If you can relate and feel this way pray this prayer with me to renounce the devil and his plans over your life, and be set free. At this stage you can still do self-deliverance.

> Oppression leads to obsession
> that leads to full on demon
> possession.

Heavenly Father,

I come before Your presence with a heavy heart and a burdened spirit. I confess that I have been oppressed by the enemy, and I am unable to carry the load in my life alone anymore. I feel the weight of depression and stagnation in my walk with You. I have lost sight of Your direction in my life, and my prayers seem to go unanswered. I am unable to express my emotions. Life feels meaningless, and I am losing hope.

But Lord, I know that You are the God of deliverance and freedom. I believe that through Your power and love, I can be set free from this oppression. I renounce any foothold the enemy has gained in my life, I declare that Jesus Christ is my Savior and Deliverer.

In the name of Jesus, I command every demonic force that is oppressing me to flee. I break every chain of darkness and bondage that has held me captive. I declare that the blood of Jesus covers me and protects me from the schemes of the enemy. I choose to walk in the light of Your truth and reject the lies and deceptions of the enemy.

Father, fill me with Your Holy Spirit, renew my mind, and restore my joy and passion for life. Help me to hear Your voice clearly and to experience Your presence in a tangible way. Give me strength to persevere and to trust in Your perfect plan for my life.

I surrender all my burdens, worries, and fears to You, knowing that You are the ultimate burden-bearer. I choose to cast all my anxieties on You, for You care for me. Grant me Your peace that surpasses all understanding.
I pray for divine protection over my mind, my emotions, and my spirit. Surround me with Your angels, Lord, and let Your love and light drive out all darkness. Empower me to stand firm against the enemy and to walk victoriously in Your freedom.

Thank You, Lord, for Your unfailing love and faithfulness. I believe that as I surrender to You and seek Your face, You will deliver me from this oppression and restore my soul.

In the mighty name of Jesus, I pray.

Amen.

2. Demon Obsession

Step two of the devil's plan before you become fully possessed. By now you are already in serious trouble and bad habits are part of your daily life. You have given away even authority to the devil over your life. At this stage, you would need assistance to be delivered.

By now you are already in serious trouble and bad habits are part of your daily life.

I suggest finding a spirit filled church in your area and seriously walking a road of repentance and total turn around. A total lifestyle change is required. Help and support from other believers are vital at this stage.

Obsession refers to a person who is excessively preoccupied or influenced by demonic forces or entities. It implies a persistent and intrusive fixation on demonic presence or activities.

Demon obsession may be described as a state in which an individual is under the influence or control of malevolent supernatural beings. It is often associated with the belief that the person's thoughts, actions, or behaviors are being manipulated or influenced by demons.

It's important to differentiate obsessions from everyday worries or concerns. Obsessions are intense, repetitive, and difficult to ignore.

They can lead to the development of rituals or compulsions to alleviate anxiety or prevent perceived harm. Harm to self and harm to others.

> Obsessions are intense, repetitive, and difficult to ignore.

Oxford defines obsession as an idea or thought that continually preoccupies or intrudes on a person's mind. (Dictionaries, n.d.) It is an inescapable feeling that preoccupies a person's mind and thoughts.

They cannot see the difference between good or bad relationships, reality or right or wrong - making them a danger to themselves and others. A obsessed person does not have the willpower or strength to resist the devil and usually makes them a slave to sin. The perfect position for total demon possession.

> It is an inescapable feeling that preoccupies a person's mind and thoughts.

At this point the devil is obsessing you. It is time for you to be set free. It is very important to seek spiritual help. I stress again the importance of taking this step with the help of a spirit filled church and spiritual guidance. If this is one of your family members I urge you to seek spiritual guidance and deliverance with help. If this step of the deliverance is not dealt with correctly it can lead to much worse circumstances.

"But when the unclean spirit has gone out of a man, it roams through dry [arid] places in search of rest, but it does not find any. Then it says, I will go back to my

house from which I came out. And when it arrives, it finds the place unoccupied, swept, put in order, and decorated. Then it goes and brings with it seven other spirits more wicked than itself, and they go in and make their home there. And the last condition of that man becomes worse than the first. So also shall it be with this wicked generation. " Matthew 12:43-45 (AMPC).

If you can relate and feel this way pray this prayer with me to be set free and renounce the devil and his plans over your life.

Heavenly Father,

I come before Your presence, recognizing the serious trouble I am in and the bad habits that have become a part of my daily life. I confess that I have given authority to the devil over my life, and I am in desperate need of deliverance. I acknowledge that, I cannot overcome this on my own. I humbly seek Your help and the support of other believers to guide me through this journey of repentance and transformation.

Your Word teaches us in James 4:7, "Submit yourselves, then, to God. Resist the devil, and he will flee from you." I declare my submission to You, Lord, and I resist the devil and his schemes in the mighty name of Jesus. I renounce any agreement or association I have had with demonic forces or entities, and I reclaim my authority in Christ.

Father, I understand that a total lifestyle change is required for my deliverance. Your Word tells me in Romans 12:2, "Do not conform to the pattern of this world, but be transformed by the renewing of your mind. Then you will be able to test and approve what God's will is—his good, pleasing and perfect will." I ask for Your transforming power to renew my mind and help me discern Your will for my life.

I seek the fellowship and support of a spirit-filled church and believers who can provide the guidance and encouragement I need. Proverbs 27:17 reminds us, "As iron sharpens iron, so one person sharpens another." Surround me with believers who can walk alongside me, pray with me, and hold me accountable as I pursue a life of righteousness.

I declare Galatians 5:1 over my life, "It is for freedom that Christ has set us free. Stand firm, then, and do not let yourselves be burdened again by a yoke of slavery." Lord, set me free from the bondage of obsession and demonic influence. Break every chain that holds me captive, and help me to stand firm in the liberty that comes through faith in Jesus.

I renounce any sinful habits, destructive patterns, or unhealthy relationships that have contributed to my current state. Give me the strength and discernment to make the necessary changes and break free from the strongholds that have bound me.

I plead the blood of Jesus over every area of my life. Your Word declares in 1 John 4:4, "You, dear children, are from God and have overcome them because the one who is in you is greater than the one who is in the world." I trust in the power of Christ within me to overcome the works of darkness and lead me into victory.

Thank You, Father, for Your unconditional love, grace, and forgiveness. I surrender myself to Your transforming work and invite Your Holy Spirit to guide me every step of the way. Set me free, Lord, and restore my life to reflect Your glory.

In Jesus' mighty name, I pray.

Amen.

3. Demon Possession

"A thief has only one thing in mind—he wants to steal, slaughter, and destroy. But I have come to give you everything in abundance, more than you expect —life in its fullness until you overflow!" John 10:10 (TPT).

The devil is merciless. He won't hold back when you have fully surrendered your life to him. You are now spiritually dead, and your end destination is not only physical death but eternity in hell. Unless you received full deliverance and salvation.

Demon possession refers to the belief that an individual's body, mind, or spirit is under the control or influence of a malevolent spiritual entity, often referred to as a demon or evil spirit. Demons take control of a person's faculties, thoughts, emotions, and behaviors. The person now has no control anymore and is fully possessed. This is the third and last step before eternal damnation.

Individuals exhibit abnormal or erratic behavior that is attributed to the presence or influence of a demon. This can include physical manifestations such as convulsions, speaking in strange languages, superhuman strength, or aversion to sacred objects or symbols. They may also display psychological or emotional disturbances, such as extreme fear, aggression, or depression. The demons are revealed through insanity and most of them land up in an asylum or worse, this could be temporary or permanent.

They are harmful to themselves and others. At this stage, they may even administer human and animal sacrifices; or be active in perverse sexual activity even with demons themselves. A prison sentence is a reality at this point - whether it is a natural prison or a spiritual prison. This person is bound by satan and his demons, and being tortured day and night.

They are fully partaking of the occult. His spirit can no longer reach out to God.

When a person is fully possessed, they do not even speak themselves. The demons speak through them and on their behalf. This is not speaking in tongues, this is an actual demons speaking through man. This is demonic. Speaking in tongues or speaking in a heavenly language is from God and is Holy. Chanting is from the devil imitating tongues.
The devil cannot create anything, he is not the Creator he is only an imitator. He imitates what is Holy and from God. The devil makes good things vile and sinful and a mockery without carrying any real

power. He is the total opposite of God All Mighty. He is on the opposite side and opposes all that is good. Therefor the devil is the opposer, or the opposition. Also otherwise referred to as the adversary, opponent, resister, agonist, the anti christ. Everything the opposite what God, Jesus Christ and the Holy spirit represents.

> The devil makes good things vile and sinful and a mockery without carrying any real power.

Demon characteristics are that they entice, torment, enslave, drive people to commit sin, defile, humiliate, oppress and possess. They are knowledgeable, understand who they are, they can speak, think, and have a will. They go out of their way to hurt those they possess, either physically or by causing friction or total decay in relationships.

> Demons are knowledgeable, understand who they are, they can speak, think, and have a will.

It is essential to seek appropriate professional help when dealing with concerns related to alleged demon possession. Qualified spiritual leaders, counselors, or mental health professionals can provide guidance, support, and a holistic approach to addressing such matters based on an individual's specific circumstances and beliefs.

If you can relate and feel this way and truly want to be set free, seek qualified spiritual help and let them help you pray this prayer. It is time for you to be set free and renounce the devil and his plans over your life.

Heavenly Father,

I come before You with a heavy heart, seeking Your divine intervention for those who are bound by the torment of demon possession. John 10:10 reminds us that the thief comes to steal, slaughter, and destroy, but You have come to give us abundant life, overflowing with Your goodness and fullness. I claim this promise over those who are oppressed by demons, knowing that Your power is greater than any force of darkness.

Lord, I acknowledge the merciless nature of the devil and the devastation he brings upon those who have surrendered their lives to him. I pray for those who are spiritually dead, whose end destination is not only physical death but eternal separation from You. In their state of complete possession, they have lost control, and their lives have become vessels for the works of darkness.

Father, I lift up those who exhibit abnormal behavior and are tormented by physical and psychological manifestations caused by the presence of demons. Your Word teaches us that You have not given us a spirit of fear but of power, love, and a sound mind (2 Timothy 1:7). I pray for Your supernatural power to break every chain, set captives free, and restore their minds to a place of peace and clarity.

I recognize the harm that possessed individuals can inflict upon themselves and others. Lord, I ask for divine protection and deliverance for all those who have been enslaved by the enemy's influence. Your Word assures us in Psalm 34:17 that when the righteous cry for help, You hear them and deliver them from all their troubles. Bring healing, restoration, and salvation to their lives.

Father, I acknowledge the spiritual prison that demon possession creates, isolating individuals from Your presence and the love of fellow believers. I pray for the support and guidance of qualified spiritual leaders and counselors who can help facilitate their deliverance journey. Your Word tells us in James 5:16 that the prayer of a righteous person is powerful and effective. I intercede on behalf of these individuals, knowing that Your love and grace are sufficient to bring them out of darkness and into Your marvelous light.

I renounce the works of darkness and the hold that demons have over these precious souls. I declare the victory of Jesus Christ over every demonic stronghold. May Your Holy Spirit move mightily, exposing and driving out every evil presence. Fill the hearts of the possessed with a hunger for salvation, drawing them to the saving knowledge of Your Son, Jesus Christ.

In the name of Jesus, I break every curse, every assignment, and every legal claim that the enemy has placed upon their lives. I plead the cleansing power of the blood of Jesus, washing away every defilement and setting them free from bondage. I declare Romans 8:1 over them, that there is now no condemnation for those who are in Christ Jesus.

Father, we trust in Your unfailing love and infinite power to rescue and redeem. May Your light penetrate the darkness, and may these individuals experience the freedom and joy that can only come through a personal relationship with You. We thank You for the salvation and deliverance that is available through Jesus Christ, our Lord.

In His mighty name, I pray.

Amen.

4.3 The Armor of God

We have weapons given to us by God to fight the demise of the enemy. Those weapons are not seen by us with our eyes, but they are spiritual weapons given to us by God to fight the enemy. Ephesians give us the description and purpose of each of these weapons.

We have powerful weapons to defeat the enemy and his plans:-

- The word of God.
- Unity with Christ.
- The blood of Jesus.
- Our testimony and Identity in Christ.
- aith in God and Prayer.
- Destiny and Purpose.
- The help of the Holy Spirit and his Angels
- The armor of God.

The word tell us to put on the armor of God, like this:

"In conclusion, be strong in the Lord [be empowered through your union with Him]; draw your strength from Him [that strength which His boundless might provides]." Ephesians 6:10 (AMP)

"Put on God's whole armor [the armor of a heavy-armed soldier which God supplies], that you may be able successfully to stand up against [all] the strategies and the deceits of the devil. For we are not wrestling with flesh and blood [contending only with physical opponents], but against the despotisms, against the powers, against [the master spirits who are] the world rulers of this present darkness, against the spirit forces of wickedness in the heavenly (supernatural) sphere." Ephesians 6:11 (AMPC)

1. Stand in your authority as a blood-saved child of God.

Therefore put on God's complete armor, that you may be able to resist and stand your ground on the evil day [of danger], and, having done all [the crisis demands], to stand [firmly in your place].

Like Joshua, be strong and courageous. Bold as a lion. Boldness is not loudness it is an inner knowing of strength, courage, and meekness. Knowing when to do, with what has been given to you in a crisis. Knowing your way out through spiritual truths given to us in the Bible. Standing on the word of God.

Standing your ground and standing your man. Stand, not run, not lay down not take revenge.

Stand!

2. Put on the Belt of Truth and breastplate of righteousness.

Stand therefore [hold your ground], having tightened the belt of truth around your loins and having put on the breastplate of integrity and of moral rectitude and right standing with God...

In Ephesians 6:14, the belt of truth is mentioned as one piece of the spiritual armor believers are instructed to put on to stand firm against the schemes of the devil. The symbolism of the belt of truth can be understood in several ways:

- **Foundation of Truth:** The belt was an essential part of a soldier's armor, as it held all the other pieces together. Similarly, truth serves as the foundation for our spiritual armor. It represents the core beliefs and teachings of God's Word, the Bible. Truth provides a solid foundation upon which we build our faith and stand against deception and falsehood.

- **Integrity and Honesty:** The belt was worn around the waist, supporting and holding everything together. In the same way, truth represents integrity and honesty in our lives. It calls us to live in alignment with God's truth, speaking and acting with integrity and sincerity.

- **Discernment and Discipleship:** Truth enables us to discern between what is true and what is false. It equips us to recognize and resist the lies and deceptions of the enemy. By studying and knowing God's truth, we can grow in wisdom, understanding, and discernment. The belt of truth empowers us to be discerning disciples of Christ, firmly rooted in His teachings.

- **Christ, the Truth:** Jesus declared; "I am the way, and the truth, and the life" (John 14:6). The belt of truth symbolizes our union with Christ, who is the embodiment of truth. As we put on the belt of truth, we are acknowledging our dependence on Him as the ultimate source of truth and relying on His guidance and teachings in our lives.

3. Put on the shoes of the Gospel.

"And having shod your feet in preparation [to face the enemy with the firm-footed stability, the promptness, and the readiness produced by the good news] of the Gospel of peace." [Isa. 52:7.]

In Ephesians 6:15, the shoes or sandals of the gospel of peace are mentioned as part of the spiritual armor that believers are instructed to put on. The symbolism of the shoes of the gospel can be understood in the following ways:

- **Preparedness for the Gospel:** Just as shoes or sandals protect the feet and prepare them for walking; the shoes of the gospel symbolize being prepared to share and proclaim the good news of Jesus Christ. It represents the readiness and eagerness to take the message of salvation to others.

- **Firm Foundation of Peace:** The shoes of the gospel of peace represent the peace that comes through a relationship with God. This peace is not merely the absence of conflict but a deep sense of security and reconciliation with God. It is the peace that Jesus gives, which surpasses all understanding (Philippians 4:7). The shoes remind us to stand firm in peace, anchoring faith and trust in God's saving work.

The shoes of the gospel remind us to stand firm in peace, anchoring faith and trust in God's saving work.

- **Firm Footing in the Gospel:** Just as shoes provide stability and traction, the shoes of the Gospel symbolize a firm footing in the truth and teachings of the gospel. It signifies standing firm on the foundation of God's Word and the redemptive work of Jesus Christ. The gospel provides the necessary stability and strength to navigate the challenges and obstacles we face in the spiritual battle.

- **Readiness for Spiritual Warfare:** In the context of the spiritual armor, the shoes of the gospel represent readiness for spiritual warfare. As believers, we are called to be prepared to engage in spiritual battles and share the gospel with others. The shoes remind us to be proactive in spreading the good news and to be bold in our faith, ready to advance the Kingdom of God.

4. Lift up the shield of Faith.

"Lift up over all the [covering] shield of saving faith, upon which you can quench all the flaming missiles of the wicked [one]." Ephesians 6:16 (AMPC).

In Ephesians 6:16, the shield of faith is mentioned as part of the spiritual armor that believers are instructed to take up to stand against the attacks of the enemy. The symbolism of the shield of faith can be understood in the following ways:

- **Protection and Defence:** Just as a physical shield is used to protect against incoming attacks, the shield of faith represents our protection and defence against the fiery darts of the enemy. It serves as a barrier that intercepts and extinguishes the lies, doubts, and temptations that the enemy throws at us.

- **Trust and Confidence in God:** The shield of faith symbolizes our trust and confidence in God's promises, character, and power. It is an unwavering belief in His faithfulness and goodness. By placing our faith in God, we can confidently rely on Him to shield us from the attacks and schemes of the enemy.

> By placing our faith in God, we can confidently rely on Him to shield us from the attacks and schemes of the enemy.

By placing our faith in God, we can confidently rely on Him to shield us from the attacks and schemes of the enemy.

- **Belief in the Unseen:** Faith is the assurance of things hoped for, the conviction of things not seen (Hebrews 11:1). The shield of faith represents our belief in the unseen spiritual realities and our trust in God's sovereignty and providence. It enables us to stand firm in the face of challenges, knowing that God is working all things together for our good.

- **Active Trust and Obedience:** The shield of faith requires active trust and obedience. It involves putting our faith into action, as faith without works means nothing, living out our beliefs, and aligning our lives with God's Word. It is not just a passive belief, but an active and dynamic relationship with God that empowers us to resist the enemy and stand firm in our convictions.

- **Unity with the Body of Christ:** In the context of the spiritual armor, the shield of faith is also meant to be used in conjunction with the other pieces of armor. It emphasizes the importance of unity and community within the body of Christ. Together, as believers, we can join our shields of faith, providing a greater defense against the attacks of the enemy.

5. Put on the helmet of salvation.

"And take the helmet of salvation." Ephesians 6:17 (AMPC).

In Ephesians 6:17, the helmet of salvation is mentioned as part of the spiritual armor that believers are instructed to put on to stand against the enemy. The symbolism of the helmet of salvation can be understood in the following ways:

- **Protection of the Mind:** The helmet is a piece of armor that protects the head, including the brain, which is the seat of our thoughts, understanding, and reasoning. The helmet of salvation symbolizes the protection of our minds against the attacks of the enemy. It guards our thoughts, beliefs, and perspectives from being influenced or corrupted by the lies and deceptions of the enemy. Our memory is blessed. We have Godly thoughts and a healthy outlook on life.

- **Assurance of Salvation:** The helmet of salvation reminds us of our secure position in Christ. It represents the assurance of our salvation and the confidence that comes from knowing we are reconciled to God through faith in Jesus Christ. It guards our minds against doubts and uncertainties about our standing with God, reminding us of the truth of our salvation. It gives us the assurance that our home is indeed in Heaven.

- **Renewed Mindset:** Putting on the helmet of salvation involves renewing our minds according to God's truth and rejecting the lies and false beliefs of the enemy. It enables us to have a transformed mindset that is aligned with God's Word and His purposes. The helmet of salvation helps us to think in a way that honors God and allows us to discern His will for us.

- **Protection against Spiritual Attacks:** The enemy often targets our minds with thoughts of condemnation, doubt, fear, and discouragement. The helmet of salvation provides protection against these attacks. It reminds us of the victory we have in Christ and helps us to stand firm in our identity as God's children. It guards against the enemy's attempts to rob us of our confidence and hope in Christ.

- **Focus on Eternal Perspective:** The helmet of salvation directs our focus beyond the present circumstances and challenges. It reminds us of the hope of eternity and the promises of God. Wearing the helmet of salvation helps us maintain an eternal perspective, enabling us to endure trials and persevere in our faith. It helps us to stay focused on the bigger picture.

6. Lift the sword of the spirit.

"..and the sword that the Spirit wields, which is the Word of God." Ephesians 6:17 (AMPC) .

In Ephesians 6:17, the "sword of the Spirit" is mentioned as part of the spiritual armor that believers are instructed to take up to stand against the enemy. The symbolism of the sword of the Spirit can be understood in the following ways:

- **The Word of God:** The sword of the Spirit represents the Word of God, which is the Bible. It is the inspired and authoritative revelation of God's truth. Just as a sword is a weapon used in battle, the Word of God is a powerful weapon that confronts and defeats the lies and deception of the enemy. It is a source of guidance, wisdom, and truth.

- **Offensive Weapon:** Unlike the other pieces of armor which primarily provide defensive protection, the sword of the Spirit is an offensive weapon. It is meant to be wielded actively against the forces of darkness.

  It enables believers to take the initiative and actively engage in spiritual warfare by speaking and proclaiming the truth of God's Word. An emphasis on 'speaking and proclaiming the truth of God's Word', because it is not the will of man but the will of God.

- **Discernment and Correction:** The sword of the Spirit enables believers to discern between truth and falsehood. It helps us to distinguish between the lies of the enemy and the truth of God's Word. It equips us to challenge and correct false teachings and beliefs, both in our own lives and in the world around us.

- **Power and Authority:** The sword of the Spirit represents the power and authority of God's Word. It carries the divine authority to break strongholds, demolish arguments, and bring conviction and transformation. By wielding the sword of the Spirit, believers tap into the power of God's Word to overcome the enemy and advance the kingdom of God.

- **Jesus as the Living Word:** Ultimately, the sword of the Spirit points to Jesus Christ, who is the living Word of God. Jesus defeated the enemy through His life, death, and resurrection, and His Word carries the power to bring salvation and transformation. As believers, we are called to wield the sword of the Spirit in the authority of Jesus' name.

7. Pray

"Pray at all times (on every occasion, in every season) in the Spirit, with all [manner of] prayer and entreaty. To that end keep alert and watch with strong purpose and perseverance, interceding in behalf of all the saints (God's consecrated people)." Ephesians 6:10-18(AMPC).

In Ephesians 6:18, the apostle Paul instructs believers to "Pray in the Spirit on all occasions with all kinds of prayers and requests." This verse emphasizes the importance of prayer as a vital component of spiritual warfare and standing against the schemes of the enemy.

The act of praying in Ephesians 6 can be understood in the following ways:

- **Communion with God:** Prayer is a means of communion and communication with God. It is a way for believers to connect with the Father, expressing their love, adoration, and dependence on Him. Praying in Ephesians 6 involves approaching God in faith and with a humble heart, seeking His presence, guidance, and strength to move forward with success and victory.

- **Dependence on the Holy Spirit:** Praying in the Spirit refers to praying under the guidance and influence of the Holy Spirit. It involves yielding to the Spirit's leading, allowing Him to intercede on our behalf and aligning our prayers with God's will. Praying in the Spirit enables believers to pray with power, fervency, and effectiveness.

- **Perseverance and Consistency:** Paul encourages believers to pray on all occasions, indicating the importance of perseverance and consistency in prayer. Praying in Ephesians 6 involves maintaining a continuous and ongoing conversation with God, seeking Him in every aspect of life and staying connected to Him through prayer.

- **Various Types of Prayers:** Paul mentions "all kinds of prayers and requests." This includes prayers of praise and worship; prayers of confession and repentance, prayers of intercession for others, prayers of thanksgiving, and prayers for personal needs and concerns. Praying in Ephesians 6 involves engaging in a variety of prayer forms and being specific in presenting our requests to God.

- **Alignment with God's Purposes:** Praying in Ephesians 6 is not just about presenting our own desires, but aligning our prayers with God's purposes and priorities. It involves seeking His kingdom, seeking His will to be done on earth as it is in Heaven. Praying in Ephesians 6 reflects a heart that desires to see God's plans fulfilled and His glory manifested.

4.4 IN10TIONAL Thinking

This chapter has taught us that angels are real, so is demons and spiritual warfare. It also taught us that demons know the word of God better than most people. If we do not really know the Word, demons can use the Word of God against us by twisting words and lying to us. *"You say you have faith, for you believe that there is one God. Good for you! Even the demons believe this, and they tremble in terror."* James 2:19 (NLT).

Thus, making it even more important to know who you are and Who's you are. When you know who you are and what you are called for by Christ, you become unstoppable for the Kingdom. You then realize that you are supernaturally empowered to succeed, no matter what. You have the help of God, the angels, and the Holy Spirit here on earth. You are also able and have the authority to bind and lose on earth, according to Matthew 16:19. This is the value of having a Christ-like identity.

> You are supernaturally empowered to succeed, no matter what.

If you have been involved in the occult knowingly or unknowingly it is very important to cut yourself off from the demonic by confession, renouncing evil or deliverance. To avoid involvement with practices that are considered occult or spiritually dangerous.

Here are some activities or beliefs that are commonly seen as entryways into the occult.

- **Divination:** This includes practices such as tarot card reading, astrology, crystal ball gazing, and other forms of fortune-telling or attempting to gain knowledge of the future through super-natural means.

- **Witchcraft and Wicca:** These are belief systems and prac-tices that involve the worship of nature or pagan deities, the use of spells, rituals, and the seeking of supernatural power or control.

- **Spiritism and Mediumship:** Engaging in attempts to com-municate with spirits, contacting the dead, or seeking guidance from supernatural entities outside of God.

- **Occult rituals and ceremonies:** Participation in ceremonies, rituals, or practices associated with occult groups or secret societies that involve invoking spirits or entities for power, knowledge, or control.

- **New Age practices:** Various New Age practices, such as channeling, energy healing, or alternative spiritual beliefs and therapies that incorporate elements of the occult.

- **Ouija boards and seances:** These activities involve attempting to contact spirits or communicate with the supernatural realm, which can open doors to spiritual deception and potentially harmful influences.

- **Idolatry and worship of false gods:** Engaging in practices or belief systems that involve worshiping deities or objects other than the one true God as revealed in Christianity.

It is important for Christians to align their beliefs and practices with biblical teachings and to seek guidance from trusted spiritual leaders or mentors if they have questions or concerns about specific activities.

The Bible warns against involvement with occult practices and encourages believers to focus on God, His Word, and the guidance of the Holy Spirit for their spiritual well-being.

Now it is time to apply and appropriate it in your own life by praying these prayers. Make these your own and pray them often so that they can lay root in your heart, prosper, and bear abundant fruit.

1. **I am called by God. I am set apart for His Glory. I am able to operate in signs, miracles, and wonders according to His Word.**

"But now thus says the Lord, he who created you, O (put your name here), he who formed you, O Israel: "Fear not, for I have redeemed you; I have called you by name, you are mine. When you pass through the waters, I will be with you; and through the rivers, they shall not overwhelm you; when you walk through fire you shall not be burned, and the flame shall not consume you."

Dear Heavenly Father,

I come before You in awe and gratitude, acknowledging that I am called by You, set apart for Your glorious purpose. Thank You for the revelation of Your truth spoken over me through Your Word in Isaiah 43. Though I may have initially dismissed it, I now recognize the power and significance of those words.

You, the Creator of all things, have crafted me with intention and purpose. You have formed me and called me by name. I am Yours, and I belong to You. Help me, Lord, to fully embrace this calling and to walk in the identity You have given me.

In the face of challenges and trials, I find comfort in Your promise that You are always with me. As I pass through the waters, let Your presence be my refuge, guiding me safely. Let the rivers of life's obstacles not overwhelm me, for Your strength sustains me. When I walk through the fires of adversity, I trust that You will shield me, and the flames will not consume me. I will not become overwhelmed, and I will have the victory in all adversity.

I surrender myself to Your will, dear Lord, and I pray that You use me for Your glory. Help me to live a life that reflects Your love, grace, and truth. Fill me with Your Holy Spirit, empowering me to fulfill the purpose for which You have called me.

May my every thought, word, and action align with Your perfect will. Grant me the wisdom and discernment to walk in obedience and to bring honor to Your name. Thank You for choosing me and equipping me for the work You have prepared in advance for me to do.

In Jesus' name. Amen.

2. God is my solid rock to stand on, my place of safety, my strong tower.

"God, the Lord, is my strength; he makes my feet like the deer's; he makes me tread on my high places. To the choirmaster: with stringed instruments." Habakkuk 3:19 (ESV).

Dear Lord,

I lift my voice in humble adoration and praise, acknowledging that You are my solid Rock, my unwavering foundation. In You, I find strength, security, and unwavering stability. Thank You for being my refuge, my place of safety, and my strong tower.

Lord, I declare that You are the source of my strength. Just as a deer tread effortlessly upon the heights, You enable me to overcome obstacles and challenges. With You as my guide, I am equipped to navigate the high places of life with courage and confidence. Your presence empowers me to rise above adversity and walk in victory.

In times of uncertainty and turmoil, I find solace in knowing that You are my constant, my fortress, and my shield. You are my unshakable refuge, providing shelter from life's storms. I take comfort in the assurance that I can always find safety and security in You.

As I stand upon the Rock of Your presence, I surrender my fears, worries, and burdens into Your hands. Strengthen my faith, O Lord, and increase my trust in You. Help me to rely on Your wisdom and guidance in all areas of my life. May Your Word be a lamp to my feet and a light to my path.

In the midst of challenges and trials, remind me of Your faithfulness and the promises of Your Word. Help me to walk in obedience and surrender to Your will, knowing that You are working all things together for my good.

I am grateful, dear God, for Your unwavering love, grace, and protection. You are my strength, my fortress, and my stronghold. I place my hope and confidence in You, knowing that You will never leave me nor forsake me.

In the name of Jesus, my Rock and Redeemer, I pray.

Amen.

3. I am intentionally mindful to become more aware daily of the power and presence of God in my life, I want to learn and experience more of Him daily.

There is always more in Him. I sing my children to sleep with the words of the song "As the deer Pants" written by Martin Nystrom.

Martin was born in Seattle in 1956, and attended Oral Roberts University he later became an evangelist in New York. With a repertoire of over 250 hymns, primarily consisting of single verses, he gained recognition for a notable composition in 1984. This particular song draws inspiration from Psalm 42 and remains one of his most renowned works. This song in itself is a prayer, may these words wash over your souls as you sing.

As the deer panteth for the water
So my soul longeth after Thee
You alone are my heart's desire
And I long to worship Thee
You alone are my strength, my shield
To You alone may my spirit yield
You alone are my heart's desire
And I long to worship Thee

As the deer panteth for the water
So my soul longeth after Thee

You alone are my heart's desire
And I long to worship Thee
You alone are my strength, my shield
To You alone may my spirit yield
You alone are my heart's desire
And I long to worship Thee
You're my friend
And You are my brother
Even though You are a King
I love You more than any other
So much more than anything

You alone are my strength, my shield
To You alone may my spirit yield
You alone are my heart's desire
And I long to worship Thee

4. I am loved more than I know or realize. Love overcomes all fear.

"For I am convinced [and continue to be convinced—beyond any doubt] that neither death, nor life, nor angels, nor principalities, nor things present and threatening, nor things to come, nor powers, nor height, nor depth, nor any other created thing, will be able to separate us from the [unlimited] love of God, which is in Christ Jesus our Lord." Romans 8:38-39 (AMP).

Heavenly Father,

I come before You with a heart filled with gratitude, realizing that Your love for me surpasses my understanding. Your Word assures me that nothing in this world, not even death itself, can separate me from Your unlimited love.

Lord, I confess that there are times when I struggle to comprehend the depth of Your love for me and at times I even forget. It is beyond measure, beyond human comprehension. Yet, I rest in the assurance that Your love is constant and unwavering. Help me to grasp the magnitude of Your love for me.

In moments of doubt or uncertainty, remind me that Your love is not based on my performance or worthiness. It is a love that surpasses all barriers and limitations. It is a love that remains steadfast in the face of challenges and trials. It is a love that extends through eternity.

Thank You, Lord, for loving me with a love that knows no bounds. Your love brings healing, restoration, and purpose to my life. It is a love that embraces me in my brokenness and lifts me up in times of weakness. Your love is my refuge and my strength.

May Your love continually transform me from within, shaping me into the image of Christ. Help me to love others as You have loved me, extending grace, forgiveness, and compassion to those around me. Let Your love shine through my words and actions, drawing others to experience the depth of Your love.

I surrender myself to Your love, dear Lord, and I pray that I may walk in the fullness of Your love each day. Thank You for loving me more than I can comprehend. May Your love be my guiding light and the source of my joy.

In the precious name of Jesus, I pray.

Amen.

5. God always watches over me, He never sleeps. He also send His angels to guard me.

"I look up to the mountains and hills, longing for God's help. But then I realize that our true help and protection is only from the Lord, our Creator who made the heavens and the earth. He will guard and guide me, never letting me stumble or fall. God is my keeper; he will never forget nor ignore me. He will never slumber nor sleep; he is the Guardian-God for his people, Israel. He's protecting you from all danger both

day and night. He will keep you from every form of evil or calamity as he continuously watches over you. You will be guarded by God himself. You will be safe when you leave your home, and safely you will return. He will protect you now, and he'll protect you forevermore!" Psalm 121 (MSG).

Heavenly Father,

In the stillness of the night, I find solace and peace in knowing that You are always watching over me. As I lay down to sleep, I rest in the assurance that You never slumber nor sleep. Your loving gaze is upon me, guiding, protecting, and preserving me through every moment.

Lord, I lift my eyes to the mountains and hills, recognizing my need for Your help. Yet, I am reminded that my ultimate help and protection come from You alone. You are the Creator of the heavens and the earth, the source of all strength and security.

Thank You for being my guardian and guide.

In Your infinite wisdom and love, You faithfully watch over me, preventing me from danger stumbling or falling. You are my ever-present keeper, never forgetting nor ignoring me.

As I venture out from the safety of my home, I find comfort in knowing that You are my constant companion. Your watchful eye follows me, and You are my steadfast protector. I trust in Your unfailing care and guidance, knowing that Your presence surrounds me wherever I may go.

I surrender my fears and anxieties into Your hands, knowing that You will keep me safe. I find peace in the knowledge that You are with me now and forevermore.

In the name of Jesus, my Protector I pray.

Amen.

6. My name is written in the palms of God's hands. I have a place busy being prepared for me in Heaven.

"See, I have written your name on the palms of my hands. Always in my mind is a picture of Jerusalem's walls in ruins." Isaiah 49:16 (NLT).

I am special to God. He loves me so much from my inception He always had a plan for my life.

Therefore, according to Psalm 139:13-18 I can pray and confess the following:

Dear God,

I am filled with profound awe and gratitude. I acknowledge the intricate masterpiece you have lovingly fashioned within me, carefully molding every delicate part of my existence while I was still in the womb.

You know my every thought before I can even think it.

Your artistry is nothing short of extraordinary, and I am in awe of your marvelous work. In the secrecy of my creation, you observed my formation, carefully weaving me together with purpose and intention.

Even before my first breath, you knew me intimately, and every chapter of my life was already written in your divine book.

The thoughts you hold for me, O God, are beyond my comprehension. They surpass the countless grains of sand, and I stand amazed at their immeasurable magnitude.

As I awaken each day, I come to you with a heart full of gratitude, acknowledging your constant presence by my side, grateful for your unwavering love and grace.

How precious are your thoughts toward me, O God. They surpass any measure, impossible to quantify.

They exceed the countless grains of sand upon the earth. And even when I wake up from slumber, you are steadfastly by my side, never ceasing to be present.

Amen

Chapter V

SUPERNATURAL HEALING

"And the prayer of faith will heal the sick and the Lord will raise them up, and if they have committed sins they will be forgiven. James (Jacob) 5:15 (TPT).

5.1 A Cancerous Report

It was at the age of, I think, around six. It is funny when trauma arises in a person's life that we fail to remember some of the details or maybe you just intend to forget. This was one of them. I know I was just in primary school, and we went away on holiday with my family to my grandparents' house in the Western Cape.

While on holiday, we took our normal walk down to the beach. My sister was struggling to climb the stairs. At that age it was strange for a child to struggle. She was young energetic and a healthy three-year-old. It was only the start of a series of strange things that started happening from that day onwards.

My sister was only three years younger than me and around three at the time. When we got back from holiday. I remember there were a lot of doctor's appointments. She had appointments from one doctor after the other … and then the diagnosis.

She was diagnosed with stage four, kidney cancer (Wilm's tumor). I could not grasp the full extent of the sickness, neither the seriousness of the disease, or the effect this was going to have on her and our family.

In an online article on The Mayo Clinic website, they define the Wilms' tumor as a rare kidney cancer that primarily affects children." (Staff, n.d.)

Also known as nephroblastoma, it's the most common cancer of the kidneys in children ages three to four, and becomes much less common after age five. Wilms' tumor most often occurs in just one kidney, though it can sometimes be found in both kidneys at the same time.

Over the years, advancements in the diagnosis and treatment of Wilms' tumor have greatly improved the prognosis for children with this disease. With treatment, the outlook for most children with Wilms' tumor is very good.

Signs and symptoms of Wilms' tumor vary widely, and some children don't show any obvious signs. But most children with Wilms' tumor experience one or more of these signs and symptoms:

- An abdominal mass you can feel
- Abdominal swelling
- Abdominal pain

Other signs and symptoms may include:

- Fever
- Blood in the urine

- Nausea or vomiting or both
- Constipation
- Loss of appetite
- Shortness of breath
- High blood pressure

I just knew it was very serious. People from the Church started coming around all the time and told us … "we are praying." Every time we went to Church, people wanted to know how my sister was doing. We got a lot of presents and flowers as a family and all of them said again … "we are praying for you." This went on for many months.

My mom and sister used to travel to Pretoria - a city two hours from where we lived, for my sister to receive her chemo. They'd stay there for what seemed to be weeks on end. I was too young to fully grasp the time they were away from home, but I knew it was a lot, or at least it felt like that to me. I used to stay with my grandmother and with my dad. He continued working while my mom stayed with my sister.

As the time went by, I remember it was the 1995 Rugby World Cup my sister's hair was falling out a lot more, which increased the trauma as we saw her four-year-old head being exposed. This is so much to deal with for any family. My mom always just had a clever way to help us all deal with trauma. It was during those rugby games that they would play a game themselves. Every time that South Africa scored a try, they would pull out some hair. My sister was on one side and my mom on the other side of her head. Pull is a strong word, because it was just falling out. This was to help and let the hair-affair be less dramatic for her, but more of a celebration of a new healthy life to come.

More time passed and after many chemo and radiology sessions, it was time to operate. Her body was exhausted and her chances of surviving the operation were extremely slim.

On one of the long days in hospital, the doctor suddenly came into the room and announced to my parents that he must operate now. They have 24 hours to decide if they want to operate or not. It was a now or never situation. As a parent, can you even imagine being in a situation like that? To have the fate of your child in your hand with no or little time to make a decision. The next day came and after a lot of prayer and contemplation the decision was made to operate.

This operation, as it was explained to me from what I could remember was:- "Your sister was going to survive this operation or not." She was very fragile at the time. She's been through many, many rounds of chemo and radiation by then. And like I said, she was younger than me. At that time, she was between four or five years old, and very frail. It was hard to see somebody that you love going through something like that and still fight daily to survive.

It took a toll on our entire family. The time came for the operation. I remember my parents were told that the operation would be about three to four hours long. After a very long six-hour operation, the doctor came out of the operating room. You can only imagine by that time how my parents were feeling in the waiting room.

The doctor started with the words:- "She is going to be ok. She is stable, but she will have a long recovery ahead of her. It is a complete miracle." When they cut the ureter to remove the cancerous kidney, the cancer came out in one perfect piece. All the cancer was removed, there was nothing left.

I just need to take a moment here and thank God for his goodness and his miraculous healing power. He never gave her cancer, nor did he cause it. He is a loving and majestic God, and His plan for our lives is life and life in abundance. It is the enemy's plan to steal, kill and destroy. But God, He is the name above every other name, even over cancer. He is Jehovah Rapha, God our Healer.

The scar on my sister's stomach looks like an autopsy scar because those doctor's never believed that she would make it. When they saw the amount of cancer on the inside of her little body, they didn't think she would survive. Yet, she did. God is amazing!

After the operation more rigorous rounds of radiation followed. She was already so weak and still recovering from the massive operation. Then happened what no parent ever wants to hear … the sounds of the heart monitor screaming next to her bed. Nurses ran into the room. My mom had to step out as they tried to resuscitate her weak 18kg little body.

Time stood still . . . She was gone. Why would go do a miracle just for her to now die?

"We did everything that we possibly could, she was just too weak," a nurse said.

Right at that moment one sister ran back out after the doctor calling him to come back to the room very quickly.

"She is alive."

My sister later explained to my mom that while she was being resuscitated and they lost her pulse, she felt her soul leaving her body. She saw how she walked with Jesus. She had, what I describe, as an encounter with Heaven as a four-year-old child. After her encounter with Jesus her strength grew by leaps and bounds.

Today she's happily married with two beautiful children. This being the third miracle because the doctor told her that because of the amount of radiation and chemo she received, she would probably never have children.

We can only thank God for the absolute miracle that he performed in her life, as well as in our family's life. We give God all the glory for these amazing miracles in that season of our lives. Like I said, she's got two beautiful children, happily married and is a registered psychologist.

I'm not only very proud of her for overcoming her challenges, but also for our family for staying standing tall in such a time of travailing trauma.

5.2 "You are already going through enough."

Christmas of 1996, my dad, my sister and I were traveling down to my grandparents in the North West province. We were so excited to see the family and to spend time on the farm. It was a brief break from hospital and chemo. While traveling through Klerksdorp, a drunk driver cut in front of our Bantam Bakkie and t-boned us on the side. We were traveling around 80km per hour.

The Bakkie or Pick up had a canopy on at the back where both my sister and I was sleeping. We made a bed at the back like we always did. We loved driving far and being able to travel like that - with our house at the back. We were still small enough to climb through the window that separated the cab and the back. We could move in between these two spaces with ease.

My dad had to swerve the bakkie. With the impact and motion of the brakes we flew up in the air. The bakkie hit a lamppost about three meters in the air.

When the vehicle came to stand still. My dad immediately came to look for us, not even realizing that he himself was hurt.

I was still laying in the back of the bakkie, folded in half underneath the mattress. There were so many people around us, it was chaotic. Nobody wanted to touch me as they did not know if I had a serious back and neck injury, so they waited for the ambulance to arrive. So many voices, yet all I wanted to do was sleep.

A doctor pulled me out of the bakkie and tried to keep me awake, at least until they could get me to a hospital. I was offered cold drinks and chocolates, but wanted nothing to do with it. I just wanted to sleep. That was the moment I realized where I was, and what had just happened.

"Where is my dad? Is he okey? Where is my sister? Why was she not with me in the bakkie anymore? Is she okey?" I frantically asked these questions to anyone in earshot. The only reply I received was:- "They are still looking for her."

"What do you mean … They are still looking for her, where is she? Where is my dad? I want my dad!" I shouted crying!

I fought hard to stay conscious. Just then, my dad was next to me, and I could see his face. I could see he was hurt but happy. "We found your sister, and she does not have a scratch on her. The ambulance is on the way. They will have a good look at your leg."

> We found your sister, and she does not have a scratch on her.

We went to the hospital and only checked out hours later. What a miracle! The bakkie was a complete write-off. We could have been dead as well. My dad had some broken ribs and scars from the glass that cut him, and my left leg was hurt. We could not really make a diagnosis of what was wrong with it and what recovery would look like. Later, I had to undergo an operation to fix the blow I took to my leg.

My dear sister, where was she when all of this happened and why did they have to go look for her?

When they found the side window of the bakkie, it looked like it was removed. It was in perfect condition. That was where she fell out. She went flying out of the side window many meters into the field.

Remember, I said we were still small enough to climb through the windows? Her window was completely removed. Perfectly removed. She had a little bit of extra help. In her own words:- "A big angel opened up the window, picked me up and laid me softly in die field."

> A big angel opened up the window, picked me up and laid me softly in the field.

The angel said:- "You are already going through enough."

My dad was right. She did not have a scratch on her, and she had a soft landing too. All I can say is that the miracle-working power of God was very evident in our lives. It is easy for me to tell these stories because I was there.

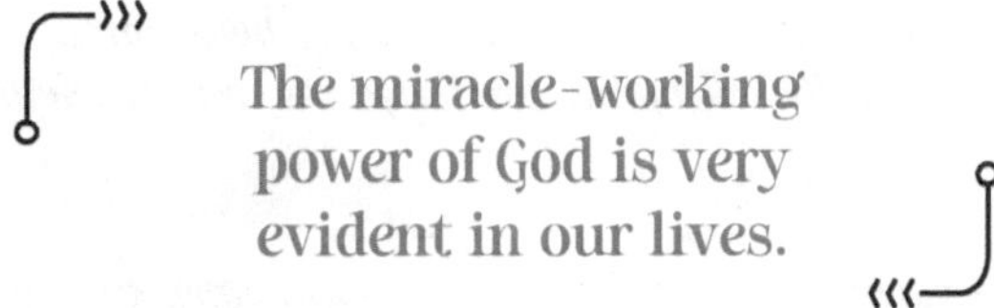

5.3 IN10TIONAL Thinking

What happened in your life that you can testify off the goodness and miracle working power of God?

The supernatural is a daily occurrence!

Ask yourself, where in my life did supernatural things happen that could not be explained? You might just have been in the company of angels yourself.

Now pray this prayer with me for God to reveal the Supernatural healings and miracles in your life.

Heavenly Father,

I come before You in the name of Jesus, seeking a deeper awareness of Your supernatural activities in my daily life. I acknowledge that You are the God of miracles, signs, and wonders. I believe in the power of Your Holy Spirit to reveal Your divine interventions and healings.

Holy Spirit, I invite You to move in my life and open my eyes to the signs and wonders You have performed on my behalf. Help me recognize and appreciate the supernatural protection and healings You have bestowed upon me throughout my journey. Open my spiritual senses to discern Your presence and power at work.

I ask for a heightened sensitivity and discernment to Your divine interventions, both big and small. Make me aware of the moments where You have guided my steps, protected me from harm, and provided healing to my body, mind, and spirit. Reveal to me the times You have spoken to me, comforted me, and strengthened me in times of need.

Grant me a deeper understanding of Your miraculous power, knowing that You are the same yesterday, today, and forever. Increase my faith to believe in Your supernatural interventions in my life and the lives of others. Help me to trust in Your sovereignty and know that all things are possible through You.

I surrender myself to Your leading, Holy Spirit. Help me to align my will with Yours, seeking Your divine purposes above my own desires. Give me a heart of gratitude for the miracles and signs You have already performed, and anticipation for the wonders yet to come.

Thank You, Holy Spirit, for Your presence in my life. I trust that You will answer this prayer according to Your perfect will. In Jesus' name, I pray.

Amen.

Chapter VI

CHRISTLIKE OBEDIENCE AND IDENTITY LEAD TO THE SUMMIT OF SUCCESS

"I look up to the mountains and hills, longing for God's help. But then I realize that our true help and protection is only from the Lord, our Creator who made the heavens and the earth. He's protecting you from all danger both day and night. You will be guarded by God himself. You will be safe when you leave your home, and safely you will return. He will protect you now, and he'll protect you forevermore!" Psalms 121:1-2, 6, 8(TPT).

6.1 Obedience: The Door to Success

One morning, I was awakened early by my dog barking next to my window. At first I was not very impressed, but then I heard the still small voice saying:- "Get up and go cycle." My response was instant. "But Lord, it is so early." I fell back to sleep, or pretended to

fall back to sleep, yet the calling grew louder. "Get up and go cycle."
I obeyed. I know God does these kinds of things only for two reasons…
to bless me or to protect me.

> I know God does these kinds of
> things only for two reasons.. to
> bless me or to protect me.

I cycled my normal route, but being earlier than my usual. The sun
was still rising. I felt thankfulness rise, and the expectancy was building
in my heart. Hill up and hill down, I expected to see something special.
Then, when I least expected it at the top of another hill, I saw it.
I stopped to see the beautiful view that was busy unfolding right in
front of my eyes.

Psalms 121 came to my mind knowing well that God is protecting me,
but this morning He wanted to just bless me.

*"I look up to the mountains and hills, longing for God's help. But then I realize that
our true help and protection is only from the Lord, our Creator who made the heavens
and the earth. He will guard and guide me, never letting me stumble or fall. God is my
keeper; he will never forget nor ignore me. He will never slumber nor sleep; he is the
Guardian-God for his people, Israel. Yahweh himself will watch over you; he's always
at your side to shelter you safely in his presence. He will keep you from every form
of evil or calamity as he continuously watches over you. You will be guarded by God
himself. You will be safe when you leave your home, and safely you will return. He will
protect you now, and he'll protect you forevermore!"* Psalms 121:1-5, 7-8 (TPT).

I stopped for a moment and soaked in the sunrise's stillness. Far off, I
could hear the traffic buzzing. Behind me were rolling hills, valleys and
trees that formed a canopy of shade. In front of me lay spread out as
far as I could see, a yellow and orange sunrise. The sign of the start
of a new day, and the confirmation that His mercies are new every

morning. Today, I will have whatever I need. God is with me and He will never leave or forsake me.

"It is because of the Lord's mercy and loving-kindness that we are not consumed, because His [tender] compassions fail not. [Mal. 3:6.] They are new every morning; great and abundant is Your stability and faithfulness. [Isa. 33:2.]" Lamentations 3:22-23 (AMPC).

The word mercy used here, in Hebrew, is Khed'-sed, meaning loving kindness, beauty, favor, good deeds, and mercifulness. When I stood there, I it soaked in and thanked my Heavenly Father for His loving kindness, the beauty of His creation. For the favor upon my life, the good deeds and thoughts He has towards me. Even His mercies for when I make a mistake, and His grace for each new day.

I took photos, sat back and just for one a last time, took in the moment before I would speed off again and finish my cycling route. I looked through the photos and saw a blue dot. I wiped my lens in case it got wet and took a couple more. I looked again, now seeing the blue dot looking like a half-moon shape of grey on my phone. I thought this might be the reflection of the sun and looked at the next two photos.

There it was. It appeared to be angel wings fluttering. At first it appeared to be, then I saw it clearly in the next image. I was stunned, grateful and blessed. I knew I was not alone. Even before I saw the photos, I felt the presence of Heaven around me. Now I was seeing it too. God manifested a piece of Heaven in front of my eyes, and I get to keep it with me. I saw my angel. The one most men and woman of God see when they prophesy to me.

That is why my dear German Sheppard woke me up and why I came out earlier than usual. That is why God whispered to me:- "Get up and go cycle." It was to bless me. Oh, what I would have missed out on if I did not obey.

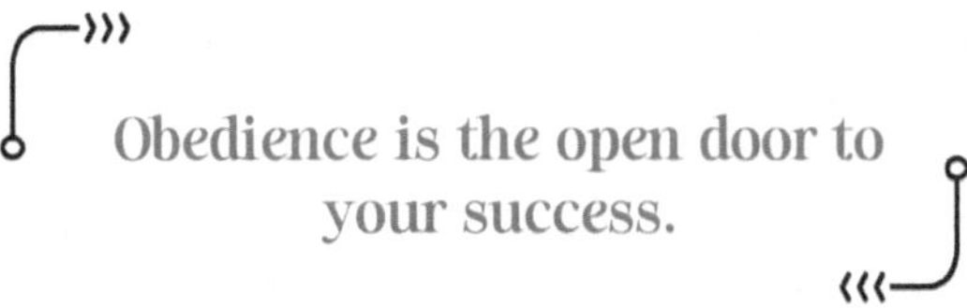

6.2 Success to Significance to Summit

What is your definition of success? For me, there is more to success than just what you own. Success is personal.

Success when it comes to money is not success. When it comes to money, it is just a reflection of your spending habits. Money gives you options. But personal success is overall wealth. That includes family, money, work, relationships, children, legacy, and personal achievements.

It is at that moment when everything comes together. When perseverance, self-belief, and resilience meet up in a moment in time. When you find you are resilient above everything else in life, when you discover your ide ntity within Christ. When you understand what it means to have the mind of Christ, when you move from success to significance.

Success leads to significance. This is a principle that I learned from Dr. Myles Munroe many years ago. And he said, "redefined uniqueness produces significance." And the only way that we can redefine our uniqueness is if we know who we are. Do you know who you are?

6.3 Christlike Identity: A Door to Significance

Do you know who you are in Christ? "Overcomer" is a 2019 American Christian sports drama film directed by Alex Kendrick and produced by Aaron Burns, Justin Tolley, and Stephen Kendrick. The film follows the story of John Harrison, a high school basketball coach whose life takes an unexpected turn when the town's largest manufacturing plant closes. It led to many families leaving town, including many of his basketball players.

With only a handful of players remaining, John reluctantly agrees to coach cross-country, a sport he is not familiar with. One of his runners, Hannah Scott, struggles with asthma and a difficult family situation, but John sees potential in her. As the season progresses, John and Hannah both face challenges and must learn to overcome them, with the help of their faith in God.

The sports film drama spoke to me about identity in Christ; and how when you know who you are, it can change the trajectory of your life. Hannah walks up to her coach and boldly says:-

"Ask me who I am?" Hannah probed Coach Harrison for an answer.

"Ask me who I am?"

"Who is Hannah Scott?" asked Coach Harrison

Hannah replied with a bold confidence by saying:- "I am created by God. He designed me. So I am not a mistake. His Son died for me just so I could be forgiven. He picked me to be his own. So, I am chosen.

He redeemed me. So, I am wanted. He showed me grace just so I could be saved. He has a future for me because he loves me. So, I don't wonder anymore, Coach Harrison. I am a child of God.

I just wanted you to know."

Today I want you to know, according to the word of God.

You are saved,
You are redeemed,
You are adopted in Christ,
You are sealed off by the blood of Jesus,
You are blessed,
You are chosen,
You have a purpose,
You are forgiven,
You are a child of God.

My question is, what makes you significant? To help you find your identity in Christ as yourself, answer these questions.

A question of identity:

1.   Who am I?
2.   Who am I as a person?
3.   Who am I as a wife?
4.   Who am I as a mother?
5.   Who am I as a child of God?

A question of source:

1.   Where did it all start for me?
2.   Where did I come from?
3.   What is my heritage?
4.   Who do I belong to?
5.   Where do I come from? What does my past say about me?
6.   What is my future going to say about me?

A question of purpose:

1. Why am I here?
2. What is my purpose for this time that I have on earth?
3. In what stage of purpose am I in now?

Our purpose is revealed in steps. We will never know our full purpose right from the start. It is way too big and will overwhelm us completely. As we obey, God knows He can trust is with more and He reveals more.

> Our purpose is revealed in steps.

We always say that life is short, therefore we need to really pursue our purpose with passion.

A question of potential:

1. What can I do?
2. What is locked up on the inside of you?

Potential is locked up on the inside of each of us and is pulled out of you through circumstances and people. Also, by disappointments, failure, and success.

A question of destiny:

1. Where am I going?
2. Where am I destined to go?

6.4 Christlike Identity: A Door to Summit

I often speak to entrepreneurs in my coaching sessions and I explain that when we look at life and when we look at a business. We must look at it as we are standing at the foot of a mountain ready to begin a big climb.

We can call it base camp.

You might also look at life as climbing a mountain and find yourself at base camp.

In the series, Aftershock: Everest and the Nepal Earthquake a documentary that premiered on Netflix in 2016. The series focuses on the devastating 2015 Nepal earthquake, which killed over 8,000 people. It triggered an avalanche on Mount Everest that claimed the lives of 19 climbers.

The series features interviews with survivors and witnesses of the earthquake and the Everest avalanche, including climbers, Sherpas and residents. It also explores the scientific and geological causes of the earthquake, as well as the challenges faced by rescue and relief workers in the aftermath of the disaster.

Aftershock was directed by Rob Carey. The series provides a harrowing and poignant account of the devastating effects of a natural disaster. A story of the resilience of the human spirit in the face of adversity.

In life we can compare so many events to this earthquake. One of them is natural disasters. They are not planned and can change your life in a minute. Some people can come back from the event and others not.

In the documentary, they explain that in Eros - you get to base camp. From base camp you climb further to four more camps and only then you climb to the summit. You have base camp, camp one, camp two, camp three, camp four, and then only you move along towards the summit. See this intense route in your mind.

1. Base Camp

Dave McKinley, a mountaineer and a mountain guide, said he climbed Mount Everest twice. As a mountaineer, base camp is where you start your journey. As an entrepreneur, you get to base camp to start your journey as a business owner. As a person starting out on a new journey, you also start at base camp.

What new journey are you starting? The start of a lifelong relationship, the birth of a baby. A life after divorce? A new career? Where do you find yourself on your journey?

As you navigate the challenges and uncertainties of creating or starting something new, you might relate to the below feelings and emotions to work through at base camp:

- **Excitement:** Many people feel a sense of excitement and anticipation when you first get started. You may be passionate about your new idea, certain stages of life or next step and eager to see it come to life.

- **Fear:** Starting something new involves taking risks, and many times you may feel a sense of fear or anxiety about the unknown journey. You may worry about failure, financial insecurity, or the challenges ahead that you cannot yet see. You see the mountain clearly, but you cannot see the route clearly.

Starting something new involves taking risks.

Starting something new involves taking risks, and many times you may feel a sense of fear or anxiety about the unknown journey.

- **Doubt:** Even the most confident people may experience doubt and second-guessing when starting out. You may wonder if you have what it takes to succeed, or if their idea is really as good as what you thought. That is also why we need to know who we are in Christ. In Christ, we know what we are capable of.

In Christ, we have no doubt and no fear.

"Fear thou not; for I am with thee: be not dismayed; for I am thy God: I will strengthen thee; yea, I will help thee; yea, I will uphold thee with the right hand of my righteousness." Isaiah 41:10 (**KJV**) - *Emphasis added.*

In the passage, the word strength is used. The Hebrew word "âmats" used here means to be alert. To be physically (on foot) or mentally (in courage). To be courageous (of good courage, steadfastly minded, strong, stronger). To establish, fortify, harden, increase, prevail, strengthen (self), make strong (obstinate, speed).

When we climb these mountains of life, we will be strengthened. Physically, while we are on foot. Also, mentally for the climb. Although we will need the courage to make the journey, this will be found in the strength of God.

- **Overwhelm:** Starting a new journey can be a lot of work, and many people may feel overwhelmed by the sheer number of tasks and responsibilities involved. You may even struggle to prioritize your time and manage your workload.

- **Frustration:** New journeys can be bumpy roads, and even lead to bumps in the road. You may even feel frustrated when things don't go as planned. You may encounter obstacles and setbacks that they didn't expect, and you may struggle to find solutions. That is just the start of the journey, and it does not determine the end result.

- **Joy:** Despite the challenges, a brand-new start can also bring a sense of joy and fulfillment. You may feel proud of what you've accomplished up to now. Keep in mind you are not starting from scratch you are starting from experience. It has taken many months or even years of preparation to get you here. Climb from experience.

  Base camp can be a complex and emotional journey, and you may also experience a wide range of feelings and emotions as you navigate this process. Just keep the end in mind. There is a lot of room at the top. Not many people make it there.

2. Camp one

When you get to camp one, you realize it is not as easy as you thought it was going to be. This is the place where expectation meets reality. And you wonder, was I really prepared for this journey? What was I thinking? You've hardly moved up the mountain, but you're now not sure if you made the right decision.

The passion is still there, the energy is still there, but you're doubting your decision because it's harder than you thought. You started this, and you decide to push through. Therefore, you now go, and you move to camp two.

3. Camp Two

At camp two, you're starting to doubt your actions and you're second guessing your decisions. The difference is you are almost halfway. People can now see you on the side of the mountain. Will they see you fail? What would they say if you turn back now? Your success is now more visible, and people are following you.

I believe that is why the word says in Habakkuk.

"And the Lord answered me and said, Write the vision and engrave it so plainly upon tablets that everyone who passes may [be able to] read [it easily and quickly] as he hastens by." Habakkuk 2:2 AMPC).

Where you are now, others still have to get to. You are higher and further than the people behind you. I've heard someone say this before, "success leaves clues". Why not leave clues for the people still on their way to you?

As the word says, write it down. Make it so plain and easy so that those who pass can read it and run with it. What if you could be the reason that someone else does not give up on their own journey?

There is going to be a time when your energy is low, when your vision power is depleted. When you're going to need other people to help you run this race, or to climb this mountain of success and significance other than just yourself. Why not be the inspiration and encouragement that someone else needs to make it as far as what you are now?

Who is climbing this mountain with you? This is the place where your team that climbs this mountain with you comes into play.

4. Camp Three

This is when you proceed to camp three and camp four, who is next to you? You are tired. In every single stage of the climb, you assess your position and what section of the climb you are in. Many people don't realize the position that they are in, so they are doing the wrong things at the wrong time. It takes a true leader to know what to do with the resources they have at hand. This stage of the climb every move counts. You need to stop and ask yourself? Am I still on track?

Do a self-check-in. How far have I come? Who has been my source? Why am I here again? Celebrate your victory. Remind yourself of your purpose. What is the purpose for this part of the climb, for this next step?

What can I do better? What is the potential that I have in this space in time, and also, where am I going from here? I don't know if you realize, but by the time you get to camp four, you are no longer looking around the mountain top. You're simply looking ahead of you. Looking down, purpose-driven, all hands-on deck, all eyes on the prize.

5. Camp Four

If you've ever climbed a mountain, you will recall yourself at some point just looking right in front of you, just taking the next step. It was no longer about the destination, but it was about the potential in this very moment you find yourself in. It is now only you, the guide, and the people around you. Every step matters, every step counts, every breath is progress.

There are no more safety rails by the time you get to camp four. Life has no guarantees, either. You have made it this far ... push through. Have faith in what you do not see. At this stage, you find yourself in a place where you can't even see the top, because it is right above you. It is almost within reach. That is how close you are.

It reminds me of an experience I had with my family in 2004. We did a hike up an active volcano in Mount Agung, Bali. It was an incredible experience. It truly was a life-altering spiritual experience.

Mount Agung stands 3,142 meters above sea level, and it has a huge spiritual significance for the Balencian people. But I didn't know at that point in time quite the spiritual experience it would have had for me personally.

If you like adventure and you like to have a climbing spectacular, this is definitely the place to go. To put your feet down in a place that resembles spiritual splendor. When I got to what I would call the base camp of that hike, it was still dark. If I recall correctly, we started hiking around 2am that morning.

It's about a 4 to 5-hour hike up the mountain. When you get to the top, you have a small breakfast. Police eggs, I say laughingly. Those are boiled eggs boiled so long they are blue and yellow in colour.

You watch the sunrise, and then you go down again. Life is like that too. The climb takes hours, days, even years. Then you stop at the top look at the view. Take a selfie or two. Celebrate and walk back down again.

Here is what I learned while hiking up that mountain. I reached the place I could call my camp four. Not yet the summit of the mountain. It was at that point on my hike where I was only looking at two things… the guide in front of me and the next step I was going to take. Like I said, we were climbing without safety rails on the side, and one bad move could have cost me and my family our lives. It was incredible, nonetheless.

It was at camp four, where I found myself. I had the same energy as I had at base camp. I felt refreshed, full of energy and I knew end was in sight. I could see success in front of me. I could see the summit of my success. I had so much energy, I could start all over again after climbing for hours. Where did this energy come from?

After base camp or after camp four, we reached a stretch of open ground where we watched the sunrise between six and seven in the morning. What a sight to see. I can still smell the fresh mountain dew on the grass next to me while the sun painted a picture of the Glory of God all around me. Through the mountains and the craters, vast amounts of water came right back down to the foot of the mountain.

We saw how the smoke came out of the craters because of the active volcanic activity on the inside of the mountain. I remember looking at my sister and asking her to come with me up to the top of the mountain, the summit of our success that day. I remember thinking to myself if I've made it this far, then surely I can go all the way.

How far is your success taking you?

Mine was from success to significance to the summit.

It could be the same for you. If you have made it up to camp four, and you've identified the different climbs and asked yourself the right questions; then go all the way to the summit. You can do it. 90% of the people that climbed that mountain with me that day, including my family, stayed at camp four.

My sister and I walked up to the top of the summit. Not everybody is going to walk the road with you right up to the top. Celebrate the ones who do. My sister and I just sat there and took it all in. It was a true spiritual awakening for both of us.

What we didn't realize was that this moment was only the start of a new adventure. We still had to get all the way down the mountain. If I had that opportunity again, I would have done it differently. Going down the mountain, you can also make a lot of mistakes that can cost you your life. I would have taken more risks. I had momentum! I would have taken advantage of the law of the big-mo, like John Maxwell calls it. I would have run down even faster to build even more momentum.

Now you're climbing down in reverse. It was much harder for me to come down the 3 km mountain hike than it was to go up. And the reason for that was the coming down speed.

Going up, if you misstep, you still have both hands to grab a hold. But when you're coming down, the pace with which you are running or jogging down that mountain, is way too fast to recalculate or grab onto something. You will fall or roll down. Who knows what you take out with you on the way down with such a mistake?

That is why the journey to the top or up the mountain is just as important. You need to make sure that when you're climbing, you are stopping at all the various camps. Make sure you stop and prepare for the next climb or decent. With the proper preparation and the proper steps to take in mind.

Ask the questions and do the appropriate preparation, so that when you come down, you can build momentum. Right next to this mountain you just conquered awaits an even bigger mountain to climb.

Life is a range of mountains that we are climbing up and down from success to significance. And as we repeat this process over and over, we become better at the thing we call life.

> Life is a range of mountains that we are climbing up and down from success to significance.

Therefore, we need to know who we are in Christ in order to walk and climb out the destiny God has already planned for us. In Ephesians, Apostle Paul encourages us to say that God has a plan for each of our lives. He gives us identity by calling us His own handiwork. He created us for a purpose and put that purpose inside of us to discover and live out. When we walk in these paths, we will walk in a pre-ordained plan and will be successful in all things.

> When we walk with purpose, we will walk in a pre-ordained plan and will be successful in all things.

"For we are God's [own] handiwork (His workmanship), recreated in Christ Jesus, [born anew] that we may do those good works which God predestined (planned beforehand) for us [taking paths which He prepared ahead of time], that we should walk in them [living the good life which He prearranged and made ready for us to live]." Ephesians 2:10 (AMPC).

The book of Ephesians is a letter written by the Apostle Paul to the church in Ephesus. It is one of the most profound letters for me in the New Testament. It provides a deep understanding of our identity in Christ and who we are because of Him. In this letter, Paul outlines the spiritual blessings that believers have in Christ and reminds us of our true identity.

In the first three chapters of Ephesians, Paul sets out the theological basis of our identity in Christ. He emphasizes that our salvation is a work of God's grace and not something that we can earn through our own efforts. He also highlights that our salvation is a result of God's plan from the beginning of time and that it is a demonstration of His love and mercy towards us.

Paul explains that in Christ, we have been chosen, adopted, redeemed, forgiven, and sealed by the Holy Spirit. These spiritual blessings are not based on our own merit or works, but they are given to us freely because of God's love and grace. We are no longer slaves to sin and death, but we are children of God and heirs of His kingdom.

Paul emphasizes that our identity in Christ is not just a personal matter, but it also has implications for our relationships with others. In Christ, we are all one body, and we are called to love and serve one another. He also stresses the importance of unity in the church and encourages us to live in a manner worthy of our calling.

Apostle Paul urges us to live a life that is worthy of our calling and to put off our old self and put on our new self, which is created in the likeness of God.

Paul emphasizes the importance of unity in the church and encourages us to use our spiritual gifts to build up one another. He also stresses the importance of honesty, kindness, and forgiveness in our relationships with others.

He addresses the issue of spiritual warfare and reminds us that our struggle is not against flesh and blood, but against spiritual forces of evil. He encourages us to put on the full armor of God, which includes truth, righteousness, the gospel of peace, faith, salvation, and the Word of God.

Finally, Paul reminds us that our ultimate victory is in Christ, and we can overcome any challenge or obstacle through Him. He encourages us to stand firm in our faith and to pray continually for ourselves and for one another.

As believers in Christ, we are called to put off our old self and put on our new self, which is created in the likeness of God. We are called to use our spiritual gifts to build up the body of Christ, to live in unity with one another, and to stand firm in our faith. We are also reminded that our ultimate victory is in Christ, and we can overcome any challenge or obstacle.

> We through our identity in Chirst, climb the highest mountains successfully.

6.5 Daily Discipline leads to Spiritual Discipline

There is a good reason we teach our children discipline. The reason our parents said we would need discipline is to be successful and prosperous. If discipline is such a powerful thing, why do most adults not practice this principle anymore?

The mold as children we are told to fit in as children looks more or less like this. Sport 2-3 times a week. If not school sport, a sport or activity that is keeping our bodies healthy and active.

We were taught that we need to play soccer because it is a sport where the hand and foot is the furthest removed from each other. So, if you can do soccer before the age of five, your hand and eye co-ordination will be well developed, and other ball sports will become more natural to you. Soccer is a physically demanding sport that can help children develop endurance, strength, and agility. Soccer requires discipline and focus, as players must follow rules and strategies to succeed. This can help children develop important skills such as self-control, concentration, and goal-setting.

Swimming was most likely my favourite. I did as much thereof as and when I could. This was for fun and not a competative sport. Swimming is also great for posture, as it is the only sport that you can do while you are lateral. It teaches you a whole range of other skills. Swimming is an excellent cardiovascular exercise that can improve overall fitness, strength, and endurance. It helps to develop muscles, improve coordination and flexibility, and can also increase lung capacity. Swimming is a low-impact activity that puts less strain on joints, making it ideal for children who may be recovering from an injury or have a medical condition that limits their physical activity. Swimming can also have positive effects on mental health, reducing stress, anxiety, and depression. It helps children feel more confident and improve their self-esteem.

We were told to play tennis, because you need to do a sport that you can play when you are an adult that does not involve an entire team. It also helps with bone health, flexibility, and co-ordination. All brilliant points, so I did that.

Gymnastics, ballet and even dancing were other sports I did for a while. Why? This helps for flexibility, core strength, overall muscle building for strength, posture, these with many other sports are great for social skills.

Then, heading over to the people skills side, we were encouraged to join the debate team. Preparing you to speak in front of people and be able to prove your point well with facts. Join the choir to practice stage presence. Join the art class and practice your creativity.

The list goes on, on what we want our children to do until they leave school so that they can be successful in life. Not even going into detail about the academic part which is also very important. They spent 6-8 hours of each day on it. Why am I mentioning this?

We put so much focus on these things when our children are young so that when they are older, they can be healthy, functioning adults that will fit into society. Do you remember that you were once one of those children?

You were prepared for life as a child to also succeed as an adult. You also were told that it will improve your:

- **Physical health:** Sports helps with physical fitness, develop endurance, build strength, and improve coordination and flexibility. Regular physical activity also helps to maintain a healthy weight and reduce the risk of chronic diseases.

- **Mental health:** Participating in sports can also have a positive impact on mental health by reducing stress, anxiety, and depression. It can also improve self-esteem, confidence, and overall mood.

- **Social skills:** Sports provide opportunities to develop social skills, such as teamwork, communication, and leadership. Playing with others can help develop friendships, learn how to cooperate, collaborate, and build empathy.

- **Goal setting:** Sports require setting and achieving goals, which can help you learn how to plan and work towards achieving goals. This skill can also benefit other areas of life, including academic and career pursuits.

- **Life lessons:** Sports can teach important life lessons, such as the importance of hard work, resilience, perseverance, and discipline. You can learn to cope with failure, how to handle success, and how to be a good sport.

Overall, participating in sports can help you develop important physical, mental, and social skills, while also learning valuable life lessons that can benefit them in the future. Then why, as adults, do most of us stop the routine we were taught as children?

> Routine teaches us discipline and helps us succeed in life.

It was rather simple:

- Exercise 2-3 times a week for a strong body.
- Take up art, relaxation or an activity that will get your creative juices flowing for a strong mental state. Gardening is a great option when we get older.
- An activity to boost self-confidence and teach yourself a new skill. For a strong work ethic and to remain relevant in work and life.
- Spending time with family and friends. For strong relationships and emotional connections.
- Go to church on Sunday. For a strong spiritual foundation, and honestly, the key to handling and managing this very challenging life.

6.6 IN10TIONAL Thinking

Why did we stop our routine? The one we thought will teach us discipline and make us succeed in life?

Here are some questions to meditate on. Answering them will get you back on track:

- What do you want to do to keep strong and fit? What do you like? Today, most people sit with neck and back problems, obesity, diabetes, and many more life-threatening conditions that are limiting them because of a lack of exercise or non-activity. What is amazing as an adult is that you can choose what you want to do.

- What are you doing to improve overall well-being and mental health? So many adults are stressed out, with no creative power, struggling with depression and anxiety. As adults we forgot how to manage our mental state and mental health through a healthy outlet.
- What was the last investment you made in yourself, your future, or your career? What was the last course you paid for a new skill or develop your career?

- How is your family time looking like? Do you still have good and fruitful relationships of real value?

- Are you still connected to a good word-based church and attending regularly?

1. A prayer to lead you from success to significance, to the summit of your life:

Heavenly Father,

I come before you, seeking your guidance and wisdom. I acknowledge that true success goes beyond material possessions and monetary wealth. It encompasses every aspect of my life, including my relationships, purpose, legacy, and personal growth.

Lord, I understand that success, as defined by the world, is fleeting and often focused on external achievements. However, I desire to pursue a success that is rooted in your will for my life and brings true fulfillment. Help me to align my definition of success with your purposes and to seek significance in all that I do.

In your Word, Lord, you remind us in Matthew 6:33:- "But seek first the kingdom of God and his righteousness, and all these things will be added to you." Help me align my definition of success with your purposes and to seek significance in all that I do. Guide me in prioritizing your kingdom above my personal ambitions and desires.

You remind us in Proverbs 16:3:- "Commit your work to the Lord, and your plans will be established." Help me commit all my endeavors, both big and small, to you. May my actions be guided by your wisdom and my plans be established according to your purposes.
I acknowledge, dear Father, that my true significance is found in my identity in Christ. Your Word assures me in Ephesians 2:10:- "For we are his workmanship, created in Christ Jesus for good works, which God prepared beforehand, that we should walk in them." Help me to fully embrace my identity as your beloved child and to walk in the good works you have prepared for me.

Grant me the understanding and embrace my identity as your child. Open my eyes to the unique gifts, talents, and purpose you have placed within me.

May I walk in the fullness of my calling and make a meaningful impact on the lives of others.

Grant me, Lord, the discipline and perseverance to stay the course, even when faced with challenges and obstacles. Your Word in Philippians 4:13 encourages me:- "I can do all things through him who strengthens me." Strengthen me, O Lord, with your power and grace, that I may press on and overcome every hindrance in my pursuit of spiritual discipline.

I surrender my ambitions, dreams, and goals to you, Lord. Guide me in aligning them with your divine purposes. As I seek success that is rooted in your will, I am reminded of the words of Jesus in John 15:5:- "I am the vine; you are the branches. Whoever abides in me and I in him, he it is that bears much fruit, for apart from me you can do nothing." May I abide in you, Lord, and bear the fruit of your Spirit in every area of my life.

Help me, Lord, to cultivate a deep and consistent relationship with you through prayer, studying your Word, and fellowship with other believers. Your Word in 2 Corinthians 3:18 reminds me:- "And we all, with unveiled face, beholding the glory of the Lord, are being transformed into the same image from one degree of glory to another. For this comes from the Lord who is the Spirit." Transform me, O Lord, into your likeness as I spend time in your presence.

I trust that you will transform my life and take me from success to significance to the summit of your purposes.

May my life be a testimony of your grace, love, and power, bringing glory to your name.

I thank you, Lord, for your faithfulness and for walking with me on this journey.

In Jesus' name, I pray.

Amen.

Chapter VII

THE RAPTURE OF THE CHURCH

"Then we who are alive will join them, transported together in clouds to have an encounter with the Lord in the air, and we will be forever joined with the Lord. So encourage one another with these truths." 1 Thessalonians 4:17-18 (TPT).

7.1 Will the Born-Again Church be Raptured?

- What does it mean to be born again?

- Why must we be born again?
- How do I qualify to be born again?

We were born with a sinful nature. King David expresses his thoughts on this in the Psalms. "Surely I was sinful at birth, sinful from the time my mother conceived me." Psalms 51:5 (NIV).

We were born with a sinful nature.

The same death that separated Adam and Eve from close fellowship with God in the garden separates most people from God. Spiritual death. Sin separates us from God and causes spiritual death. This leads to death itself.

"For the wages of sin is death; but the gift of God is eternal life through Jesus Christ our Lord." Romans 6:23(KJV).

When we work hard for sin, it will surely lead to death, but God gives us a merciful, grace-filled life with eternal purpose. We need to decide to repent and turn back to God. We need to get to a place where we decide ourselves that we want to live a life in Christ and put on a Christlike nature.

In John 3:3, Jesus converse with Nicodemus, a Pharisee, and a member of the Jewish ruling council. Jesus tells Nicodemus, "Truly, truly, I say to you, unless one is born again, he cannot see the kingdom of God."

This statement by Jesus implies that a spiritual rebirth or transformation is necessary for individuals to enter eternal life. A spiritual rebirth also helps a child of God perceive and understand the hidden things in the Kingdom of God. It signifies a new beginning, a spiritual awakening, and a change of heart that comes through faith in Jesus Christ.

Being "born again" is your salvation and receiving eternal life through a personal relationship with Jesus. It is the difference between religion and relationship. It is making a choice of living a spirit filled life, led by the Holy Spirit here on earth. This could only be accomplished by Jesus dying on the cross for us.

Being "born again" is your salvation and receiving eternal life through a personal relationship with Jesus.

Nicodemus once again asked a question. "How can someone be born when they are old? Surely they cannot enter a second time into their mother's womb to be born!" John 3:4 (NIV).

Salvation through Jesus gives us access:

- To the things of the Spirit or Spiritual truths, revelation and understanding.
- Total forgiveness or remission of sin.
- Healing and deliverance.
- Riches and Glory.
- & Eternal life.

Jesus answered Nicodemus, "Very truly I tell you, no one can enter the kingdom of God unless they are born of water and the Spirit. Flesh gives birth to flesh, but the Spirit gives birth to spirit. You should not be surprised at my saying, 'You must be born again.'

The wind blows wherever it pleases. You hear its sound, but you cannot tell where it comes from or where it is going. So, it is with everyone born of the Spirit."

"How can this be?" Nicodemus asked.

"You are Israel's teacher," said Jesus, "and do you not understand these things? Very truly I tell you, we speak of what we know, and we testify to what we have seen, but still you people do not accept our testimony.

I have spoken to you of earthly things and you do not believe; how then will you believe if I speak of heavenly things? No one has ever gone into heaven except the one who came from heaven – the Son of Man. Just as Moses lifted up the snake in the wilderness, so the Son of Man must be lifted up, that everyone who believes may have eternal life in him." For God so loved the world that he gave his one and only Son, that whoever believes in him shall not perish but have eternal life. For God did not send his Son into the world to condemn the world, but to save the world through him." John 3:5-17 (NIV).

Jesus is the way the truth, and the life as referred to in John 14:6, and no one gets to the Father except through Him. Salvation is the answer. The Hebrew word for "salvation" is pronounced yeshu'ah. The term means deliverance, rescue, forgiveness or redemption of sin. Jesus name is also Yeshua. Deliverace, rescue and forgiveness is literally the meaning of His name.

In the Old Testament, the concept of salvation is frequently associated with God's intervention to save or deliver His people from various forms of danger, oppression, or captivity. They just kept getting into trouble. Salvation represents the act of God extending His mercy and grace to bring about forgiveness and restoration to those who trust in Him. And we all know how much they needed it.

Imagine this … the process of forgiveness of sin or removal of sin could only be conducted by the High Priest in the Old Testament on the day of Atonement or Yom Kippur in Leviticus 17. Once a year, the High Priest would take the blood of the sacrificed animals and lay it on the Arc of the Covenant in the temple in the Holy of Holies. The High Priest would then ask God on behalf of the people for the forgiveness of their sin.

The High Priest would wear a rope around his waist with bells that would indicate whether God did forgive their sins. If God did not forgive their sins, the High Priest would fall right over and die. The sound of the bells would stop because his movement stopped. This would indicate if the Priest was still alive or not. They will then be able to pull the High Priest out with the rope. In case of death. If their sins were forgiven, the Priest will live.

That process was called atonement of sin or in other words, covering up of their sins. Not even full forgiveness. Just a cover up. Can you imagine only being able to ask for the atonement of your sins once a year? And then having to send someone else into the temple to die if God did not forgive your sin? That must have been so hard. Think of the many times in a day or how often you need to ask God to forgive your sins? And if He did not forgive their sins, they had to wait another year for another opportunity. I can't even imagine this.

The Hebrew word used to refer to the covering or atonement of sin is "רָפָכ" (pronounced kafar). This term is often translated as "to atone," "to cover," or "to make reconciliation." In the context of sin, it signifies the act of seeking forgiveness and restoration through the offering of sacrifices or the shedding of blood.

The concept of atonement in the Old Testament involved the temporary covering or appeasement of sin through the prescribed rituals and offerings in the Mosaic Law. These rituals were to reconcile humanity with God and temporarily remove the guilt and consequences of sin. Note the words again, cover up and temporary.

It foreshadowed the need for a perfect and ultimate atonement, which would be fulfilled through the sacrifice of Jesus Christ on the cross in the New Testament. Now this is where it changes completely. This process of forgiving our sin when Jesus died on the cross was called remission of sin. Or total removal of sin. Only Jesus could do that for humanity by shedding His blood on the cross and those who accept Him as their Lord and Savior will have eternal life. Jesus, our High

Priest was sacrificed for us on the cross by the shedding of His blood. Note the words here total removal of sin and eternal life.

Remember Jesus's last words before he died:-, "Father, into your hands I commit my Spirit."

At that moment, there was an earthquake that tore the curtain in two, separating the inner court of the temple with the Holy of Holies. Jesus is our High Priest and by tearing the veil that separated the Holy of Holies from the rest inner and outer court of the temple.

Jesus showed us we can now have a relationship with God the Father, The Holy Spirit and Jesus Christ. And that we no longer have to go through a priest and that our all sins are now forgiven. Totally removed, forever. By His life and dying on the cross for us, He showed us a total remission of sin, or total removal of sin.

In the New Testament, the Greek word used to indicate the complete removal or forgiveness of sin is "ἄφεσις" (pronounced aphesis). This term is often translated as "remission" "forgiveness," or "release." It refers to the act of pardoning or letting go of sins, wiping them completely away, and canceling their guilt and consequences. Romans 8:1 explains this event saying that Jesus was the sacrificial lamb that died on the cross and his blood was placed on the mercy seat for us for total forgiveness of sin. We now have no more condemnation when we give our lives to Jesus and are saved through salvation.

Only God can make things come together in such a magnificent way. *"Therefore there is now no condemnation [no guilty verdict, no punishment] for those who are in Christ Jesus [who believe in Him as personal Lord and Savior]."* Romans 8:1(AMP).

The concept of the remission of sins is closely tied to the work of Jesus Christ and the salvation he offers. Through his sacrificial death,

Jesus provides complete forgiveness and reconciliation with God. The forgiveness of sins is received by faith in Jesus, and it entails the removal of the guilt and punishment associated with sin, bringing about a state of spiritual freedom and restoration. The word "aphesis" emphasizes the profound and transformative nature of God's forgiveness in the New Testament.

This changes your thinking salvation and being born again. In Greek, the word for "salvation" is "σωτηρία" (pronounced soteria). This term, frequently used in the New Testament, denotes deliverance, preservation, or rescue from harm or destruction. It refers to the salvation offered by God through Jesus Christ, emphasizing the concepts of redemption, forgiveness of sins, and eternal life.

The Greek word "soteria" encompasses the idea of being saved, healed, and made whole through faith or salvation in Christ. It emphasizes the transformative and liberating power of God's grace in bringing individuals into a reconciled relationship with Him.

> This means when you are born again you have all the above and access to eternal life for, when Jesus one day very soon appears in the clouds to rapture us into heaven.

This means when you are born again you have all the above and access to eternal life for, when Jesus one day very soon appears in the clouds to rapture us into heaven.

7.2 Why is the Rapture not found in the Bible?

We often get challenged by believers or non-believers alike that the word Rapture is not in the Bible. They are right, well, somewhat.

In the biblical context, the term "rapture" refers to an event described in Christian eschatology. Eschatology, meaning a study of the end times. It is specifically based on the interpretation of 1 Thessalonians 4:17. The verse states, "Then we who are alive, who are left, will be caught up together with them in the clouds to meet the Lord in the air, and so we will always be with the Lord." Believers will be caught up in the clouds during the rapture.

The word "rapture" itself does not appear in the Bible, but it is commonly used to describe the concept of born-again believers being suddenly and miraculously taken up or "caught up" to meet Jesus Christ in the air. This event will occur during the second coming of Christ. Born again believers will be removed from the earth and brought into the presence of the Lord, experiencing a state of heavenly bliss and eternal life.

In the book by Jimmy Evans, Where Are the Missing People? The Sudden Disappearance of Millions and What Happens Next, he writes:

> "You now know what happened: Jesus gathered up the millions of believers in the Rapture. They were caught up in the air and taken to be with Him. But what does it mean to be a "believer," in this instance? If two people could have been asleep in bed and one was taken during this world-changing event, what is the significance of the one who was raptured? The people who disappeared during the Rapture were Christians. They were followers of Jesus Christ. You have probably heard them referred to by any number of names: Believers. Evangelicals. Born again. Christ-followers. The faithful. The Church.
>
> Regardless of how you might refer to them, they all had one thing in common: They had accepted Jesus Christ as their Lord and Savior and committed to living their lives according to the

teachings of the Bible. The New Testament book of Romans, another ancient letter written by the Apostle Paul, describes the need for Jesus this way: "For the wages of sin is death, but the free gift of God is eternal life through Christ Jesus our Lord" Romans 6:23, (NLT).

Christians are those who have accepted God's free gift of eternal life, through Jesus. All humans live under the burden of death because of our sin, but believers have come alive to Christ. They have surrendered their lives to Jesus, who promises an eternity with Him forever in heaven.

Accepting this gift is sometimes referred to as being "born again." That is one of the clearest ways to think about it." (Evans, 2022, pp. 18,19)

Why not receive the gift of being born again today by receiving Jesus Christ as your Lord and Saviour? Apostle Paul teaches us how to do this in Romans 10:9-10.

Salvation through Jesus happens when:

- You acknowledge Jesus as you Lord and Savior and believe in your heart that Jesus died on the cross and rose again on the third day.
- Therefore, you now have access to eternal life in Christ and all your sins are forgiven.
- Repent of your sins and make a 180° turn from death to life. From religion to relationship.
- And confess with your mouth that Jesus is Lord.

My prayer for you is that your new life in Christ will ignite the fire of God's presence and power in your life. That your new life in Christ will bring more people to salvation. As Jesus instructed the disciples, you are also now instructed to heal the sick, raise the dead, be a great giver and cast out demons. You are now playing your part of living a supernatural life!

7.3 Various Types of Rapture beliefs

Like most biblical subjects, different people have different interpretations. Dr. Deon Bester said in one of his sermons in 2021 that some biblical interpretations are muscle related and some are spinal related.

A muscle interpretation is when your interpretation is interpreted your own way, can still get you into heaven, muscles stretch and form and can still lend to that interpretation. Speaking in tongues is muscle. Although God wants you to receive this free gift given to everyone. Without it, you can still go to Heaven. Being baptized as an adult is another one. Even not believing in signs, miracles, and wonders.

Important to know about spinal-related Bible matters I believe with my whole heart, just as muscles grow and get stronger, so your faith and understanding can also grow. You can develop to receive these Holy and Biblical truths for your own life, and life in the fullness of God.

A spinal interpretation is non-negotiable, no matter what your religious background and belief. Salvation is spinal. The death of Jesus on the cross is spinal. Jesus coming on the clouds is spinal.

Although the word, "rapture" itself does not appear in the Bible, it does not mean that it will not happen. It is a concept of being caught up into the air with Jesus that it refers to. The rapture is real and can happen at any time. Nothing more needs to happen for the rapture of the church to take place. Most people believe it will occur, it is the timing if the rapture people differ on.

What makes the rapture part of a muscle interpretation is the various rapture beliefs as:

- Partial trip,
- Mid-trip,
- Post-trip,
- Pre-trip,
- Pre-wrath rapture.

1. Partial trip:

The concept of a Partial Rapture is a belief held by the least number of believers. They believe that not all believers will be raptured, but only a select group of faithful and spiritually mature Christians who meet specific criteria.

They see the rapture as a reward for those believers who have achieved a higher level of spirituality, characterized by a deeper commitment to Christ and a greater degree of holiness. Those who are deemed "worthy," or "overcomers" will be taken in the Rapture, while other believers who do not meet these criteria will remain on Earth to go through the Tribulation period.

Mark Hitchcock defines the partial rapture in his book The End; "The timing of a person's rapture is based on the depth of their obedience. The partial-rapture position distinguishes devout, spiritual believers from worldly believers. Devoted believers who are obediently watching and waiting for Christ's coming will be raptured to heaven before the Tribulation (Matthew 25:1-13; 1 Thessalonians 5:6; Hebrews 9:28; 1 John 2:28). Worldly believers, for their part, will endure some degree of the Tribulation and be caught up in subsequent raptures." (Hitchcock, n.d.)

Supporters of the Partial Rapture often cite passages such as Matthew 25:1-13 (the parable of the ten virgins) and Revelation 3:10 (the promise to the church in Philadelphia) as indicating that only a portion of the believers will be taken in the Rapture. Thus is the least held rapture belief that there is.

I enjoy Amir Tsarfati's sense of humor in making difficult explanations simple to understand. He explains the pre-wrath like this: "If you are a great Christian who gives regularly to the church, teaches Sunday school weekly, and passes out gospel tracts instead of candy at Halloween, then you very well might fly straight into heaven with the first batch of believers. However, if you are more of a sin-on-Saturday-pray-on-Sunday Christian, then you might need to go through a few years of suffering so that you can be purified enough to enter the presence of your Savior."

Think about it, does that sound like the loving Father who sent his only Son to die for us on the cross? I definitely think not. God the Father will never divide His church like this nor put a tier system on his children. Salvation is not a game where you need to earn coins to get to a higher level of Holiness.

2. Mid-trip:

The Mid-Tribulation Rapture is a viewpoint within eschatology that proposes the timing of the Rapture to be at the midpoint of the seven-year Tribulation period. This is described in the book of Revelation. According to this view, believers will experience the first half of the Tribulation, which includes various trials and the rise of the Antichrist. At the midpoint, commonly associated with the abomination of desolation mentioned in Daniel 9:27 and Matthew 24:15, the Rapture takes place. Believers are then caught up to be with Jesus, escaping the most severe judgments and events that occur in the latter half of the Tribulation.

The mid-tribulation view of the rapture presents a significant challenge as it fails to grasp the true nature of the seven years of God's wrath. Proponents of this view often argue that the first half of the tribulation is relatively mild compared to the intense events that occur in the second three-and-a-half years. However, a careful examination of the timeline in Revelation and the placement of the seal judgments in Chapter 6 reveals that troubles and judgments persist throughout the entire period.

Even a cursory reading of Revelation 6 would dispel any notion that the first half of the tribulation will be easy. Furthermore, it is important to note that Scripture does not explicitly support a rapture occurring after the initial half of the tribulation. To maintain this perspective, one would need to engage in eisegesis, which involves interpreting biblical passages in a way that aligns with preconceived beliefs. However, this approach is problematic as it can lead to misinterpretation and the distortion of Scripture to support any desired belief.

3. Post-trip:

The Post-Tribulation Rapture is a belief within eschatology that suggests the timing of the Rapture will occur after the seven-year Tribulation period described in the book of Revelation.

According to this view, believers will go through the entire period of tribulation, experiencing the trials and events described in the Bible. At the end of the Tribulation, Jesus will return in His second coming, and the Rapture will take place simultaneously with the resurrection of both the righteous dead and the living believers.

Advocates of the Post-Tribulation Rapture typically emphasize passages such as Matthew 24:29-31 and 1 Thessalonians 4:15-17, among others, which they interpret as supporting a view that believers will remain on Earth and endure the tribulation alongside non-believers.

They believe that the Rapture is a single event that occurs at the end of the Tribulation when Christ returns to establish His kingdom.

My question with this belief is then why even have a rapture if it all happens at the same time? To me, personally, this belief does not match up with the character of God.

4. Pre-trip:

Or otherwise referred to as the Pre-Tribulation Rapture. The Pre-tribulation Rapture, also known as the Pre-tribulation view, believes that believers in Jesus Christ will be taken up to Heaven before the period of intense tribulation period. This is the rapture option: (if there really is one) that my hope and faith lies.

> Pre-tribulation view believes that beliewers in Jesus Christ will be taken up to Heavne before the period of intense tribulation period.

Pre-tribulation view believes that believers in Jesus Christ will be taken up to Heaven before the period of intense tribulation period.

This belief is based on the understanding that there will be a future seven-year period known as the Tribulation, which will be characterized by great distress and judgment on the earth.

According to the Pre-tribulation view, before the Tribulation begins, Jesus will return in the air to gather His followers, both living and dead, in what is commonly referred to as the Rapture.

The term "Pre-tribulation" is believed to occur prior to the start of the Tribulation. Those who hold to this view believe that the purpose of the Rapture is to rescue believers from the coming judgment and to deliver them into the presence of Jesus Christ in Heaven. The Tribulation will begin at some point after the Rapture, marked by the Antichrist's seven-year treaty with Israel (Daniel 9:27):- Mark Hitchcock

Advocates of the Pre-tribulation Rapture point to various biblical passages, including 1 Thessalonians 4:16-17 and 1 Corinthians 15:51-52, which describe the sudden gathering of believers to be with Jesus. They also interpret other passages, such as Revelation 3:10, as supporting the idea that believers will be spared from the wrath and tribulation that will be poured out on the earth during the end times.

As Jesus concluded His teachings, He emphasized the imminence of His return. In the book of Revelation, He proclaimed, "Behold, I am coming quickly! Blessed is he who keeps the words of the prophecy of this book... And behold, I am coming quickly, and My reward is with Me, to give to everyone according to his work" (Revelation 22:7, 12).

The term "imminent" means something that is "ready to take place" and "happening soon", according to Merriam-Webster. When it comes to Bible prophecy, many focus on the latter definition, expecting Jesus' return to happen shortly after His promise, or within the last 2,000 years.

However, biblical imminence aligns more with the first definition, showing that it is "ready to take place." By stating that He is coming quickly, Jesus conveyed everything is prepared, and His return could happen at any moment. This understanding is why Paul believed Jesus could come in his lifetime.

In his crucial passage, Paul consistently used the pronoun "we," signifying a sense of shared anticipation: "We who are alive and remain until the coming of the Lord will by no means precede those who are asleep. For the Lord Himself will descend from heaven with a shout, with the voice of an archangel, and with the trumpet of God. And the dead in Christ will rise first. Then we who are alive and remain shall be caught up together with them in the clouds to meet the Lord in the air. And thus we shall always be with the Lord. Therefore comfort one another with these words" - 1 Thessalonians 4:15-18.

Paul was eagerly prepared, having experienced being transported to heaven once before (2 Corinthians 12:1-4), and he was more than ready for a return journey. Both Jesus and Paul did not mention any specific events that needed to occur before Christ's return, emphasizing the imminence and readiness of His coming, and highlighting my point that the end is not near the end is here.

5. Pre-wrath rapture:

The Pre-Wrath Rapture is a relatively recent interpretation of end-times events within Christian eschatology. It suggests that the Rapture of the church will occur before the pouring out of God's wrath, 66 months into the Tribulation Period. This view proposes that the church will face persecution and trials during the first half of the Tribulation. Then will be delivered by Christ before the most severe judgments of God's wrath are poured out upon the Earth.

Advocates of the Pre-Wrath Rapture point to passages such as Matthew 24:29-31 and 1 Thessalonians 5:9, which they interpret as supporting a post-tribulation timing for the Rapture. They argue believers will be present on Earth during the initial phases of the Tribulation, witnessing certain events and enduring hardships, but will be spared from God's wrath during the latter part of the Tribulation.

According to this view, the "wrath of God" described in the book of Revelation begins with the trumpet judgments (Revelation 8-9) and intensifies with the bowl judgments (Revelation 16). The Pre-Wrath Rapture proponents believe that the church will be raptured before the last series of bowl judgments are unleashed, sparing believers from God's most severe judgments upon the unrepentant world.

As I studied eschatology, I believe this is the least most likely rapture trip to occur. First also because it does not match up with the character of God. Second because the wedding in Heaven won't start unless the entire church of Jesus is not present.

And thirdly according to Matthew 24:37-39,
"For as were the days of Noah, so will be the coming of the Son of Man. For as in those days before the flood they were eating and drinking, marrying and giving in marriage, until the day when Noah entered the ark, and they were unaware until the flood came and swept them all away, so will be the coming of the Son of Man."
Matthew 24:37-39 (ESV).

Important to note; until the day that Jesus raptures the full body of Christ, people will carry on as they are doing now, doing business, marrying, eating, drinking, until the day.

> Until the day that Jesus raptures the full body of Christ, people will carry on as they are doing now, doing business, marrying, eating, drinking.

By Jesus saying, "until the day", means nothing after that, nor doing business, marrying, eating, and drinking. In the days of Noah, there was a flood, and that was the end of humanity. As in the days of Noah, when that day comes, it will be the end of the church age.

Jesus forewarns unbelievers of how it will be for them who reject the Word of God and the message of the gospel. Being left behind means you rejected Jesus. In Matthew 10:5 it states:- "Truly I tell you, it will be more bearable for Sodom and Gomorrah on the day of judgment than for that town."

Jesus is emphasizing the severity of the judgment that will come upon those who reject the message of the disciples, which is the Gospel. He said that the punishment awaiting the town or city that rejects the message will be even greater than the punishment inflicted upon Sodom and Gomorrah. This serves as a warning of the consequences of rejecting the truth of the Gospel. That is what it will be like during the tribulation.

Matthew 24 sounds very much to me like the promise God made man after the flood. *"For there will be greater anguish than at any time since the world began. And it will never be so great again."* Matthew 24:21 (NLT).

God's prophetic timeline begins with the rapture of the church. The rapture indicates the end of the church age. In simple terms, the Rapture of the church, which marks the initial stage of Christ's coming, involves two key events:

1. **The resurrection of deceased believers and the transformation of those who are alive.**
   At that moment, we will all be united in the glorious presence of Jesus in the air, who will lead us to heaven for an eternal dwelling with Him. It's important to clarify a few points. Firstly, Jesus' second coming unfolds in two phases, with the Rapture being the initial phase. The rapture takes place in the air and the end of the tribulation period when Jesus comes to earth and will appear on the Mount of olives. Or, like most people refer to as Armageddon.

> Jesus' second coming unfolds
> in two phases, with the Rapture
> being the initial phase.

2. **The second phase will occur following the Tribulation period when Jesus returns**, defeats the Antichrist at Armageddon, and establishes His millennial kingdom.

The theme of the catching away of the church or as I refer to it as the rapture gets discussed in these three main passages in the New Testament:

John 14:1-4: *"Do not let your heart be troubled (afraid, cowardly). Believe [confidently] in God and trust in Him, [have faith, hold on to it, rely on it, keep going and] believe also in Me. In My Father's house are many dwelling places. If it were not so, I would have told you, because I am going there to prepare a place for you. And if I go and prepare a place for you, I will come back again and I will take you to Myself, so that where I am you may be also. And [to the place] where I am going, you know the way."* John 14:1-4(AMP).

1 Corinthians 15:50-57: *"Now I say this, believers, that flesh and blood cannot inherit nor be part of the kingdom of God; nor does the perishable (mortal) inherit the imperishable (immortal). Listen very carefully, I tell you a mystery [a secret truth decreed by God and previously hidden, but now revealed]; we will not all sleep [in death], but we will all be [completely] changed [wondrously transformed], in a moment, in the twinkling of an eye, at [the sound of] the last trumpet call. For a trumpet will sound, and the dead [who believed in Christ] will be raised imperishable, and we will be [completely] changed [wondrously transformed]. For this perishable [part of us] must put on the imperishable [nature], and this mortal [part of us that is capable of dying] must put on immortality [which is freedom from death]. And when this perishable puts on the imperishable, and this mortal puts on immortality, then the Scripture will be fulfilled that says, "Death is swallowed up in victory (vanquished forever). O death, where is your victory? O death, where is your sting?" The sting of death is sin, and the power of sin [by which it brings death] is the law; but thanks be to God, who gives us the victory [as conquerors] through our Lord Jesus Christ."* 1 Corinthians 15:50-57(AMP).

1 Thessalonians 4:13-18: *"Now we do not want you to be uninformed, believers, about those who are asleep [in death], so that you will not grieve [for them] as the others do who have no hope [beyond this present life]. For if we believe that Jesus died and rose again [as in fact He did], even so God [in this same way—by raising them from the dead] will bring with Him those [believers] who have fallen asleep in Jesus. For we say this to you by the Lord's [own] word, that we who are still alive and remain until the coming of the Lord, will in no way precede [into His presence] those [believers] who have fallen asleep [in death]. For the Lord Himself will come down from heaven with a shout of command, with the voice of the archangel and with the [blast of the] trumpet of God, and the dead in Christ will rise first. Then we who are alive and remain [on the earth] will simultaneously be caught up (raptured) together with them [the resurrected ones] in the clouds to meet the Lord in the air, and so we will always be with the Lord! Therefore comfort and encourage one another with these words [concerning our reunion with believers who have died]."* 1 Thessalonians 4:13-18(AMP).

When the Rapture occurs, Jesus will come down from heaven and meet us in the clouds, accompanied by the perfected spirits of believers who passed away. People who passed away over time have gone past. Their glorified bodies will be resurrected, and the spirits of believers will be met with their new bodies. No more pain, no more tears, no more sickness. What a glorious day!

Just think about this, to bring it a little closer to home. Your grandparents, parents, friends, and family who died and were children of God. Will be caught up in the air with Jesus with their perfected eternal bodies first. At this event, the soul and body, which experience a temporary separation through death, will be reunited.

The previous division between body and spirit will be permanently reversed. There will be no signs of aging, sickness, or injury, that will be gone forever.

After this, if you are a child of God, you will also be caught up in the air with them.

Can you imagine seeing your aunt, mom, dad, brother, or sister who died a horrific death on earth united in the air with their perfected, indestructible bodies?

This will all happen in a moment, in the twinkling of an eye, as per Corinthians 15:52. Jesus slows this process down for us to bring understanding, but on the that day, it will be in a split second.

The question remains, will you be part of this group of people?

7.4 IN10TIONAL Thinking

If you want to receive this gift of salvation and also be caught up in the clouds with Jesus pray this prayer with me:

"Dear Heavenly Father, I come before you acknowledging that Jesus Christ is Lord and that God raised Him from the dead. I believe in my heart that Jesus is the Son of God, the Savior, and that He died for my sins and rose again, granting me eternal life.

I confess with my mouth that Jesus is Lord, therefore I and surrender my life to Him. I repent of my sins and ask for your forgiveness. I invite Jesus to be the Lord and Savior of my life, to guide me, and to transform me by the power of the Holy Spirit.

I receive the gift of salvation through faith in Jesus. I declare that I am now a child of God, forgiven, redeemed, and made new. I thank you, Lord, for your grace, love, and mercy.

Amen

Chapter VIII

THE END IS NOT NEAR THE END IS HERE

"The beast from the earth was empowered to breathe life into the image of the first beast so that it could speak and kill those who refused to worship its image. It also caused everyone, small and great, rich and poor, free and bound, to be marked on the right hand or on the forehead. This meant no one could buy or sell unless they had the mark; that is, the name of the beast or its number. This will require wisdom to understand: Let the one with insight interpret the number of the wild beast, for it is humanity's number – 666."
Revelation 13:15-18 (TPT).

8.1 The Mark of the Beast, AI & the antichrist

A question I get asked all the time is; will the church be around for the mark of the beast? No, born again Christians won't. They will already be raptured.

Or I get asked; will AI and cryptocurrencies be the mark of the beast? In a way yes, they will both be around during the rule of the antichrist and he will certainly make use of Artificial Intelligence to strengthen his position. When it comes to Cryptocurrencies they will be around and will be used as they are today. Just another way to transact. That does not make AI or crypto evil. The people who will control crypto will be evil and it will most likely be used in evil or mismanaged ways.

> Is AI and cryptocurrencies the mark of the beast?

I cannot agree with the statement that the future is AI. The future is human. People will still buy from people. Even Jesus said, "Do business until I come." AI is a tool to be used by humans. At the time of the writing of this book Chat GPT (a language model) was just launched and is making waves throughout the world. There is currently more legislation in the food industry than what there is for artificial intelligence.

> The future is human.

Artificial Intelligence is also not new. Artificial Intelligence (AI) as a field of study and research has been around for several decades. The term "artificial intelligence" was coined in 1956 by John McCarthy, Marvin Minsky, Nathaniel Rochester, and Claude Shannon during a conference at Dartmouth College. However, the roots of AI can be traced back to earlier work in areas such as logic, mathematics, and philosophy.

Throughout the years, AI has evolved and grown significantly, with advancements in algorithms, computing power, and data availability. Various subfields of AI have emerged, including machine learning, natural language processing, computer vision, and robotics. Recent years have seen rapid progress in AI, thanks to advancements in deep learning techniques and the availability of large-scale datasets.

It's important to note that while AI has made significant strides, achieving human-level intelligence or strong artificial general intelligence (AGI) is still an ongoing area of research and development. The field of AI continues to evolve and shape many aspects of our lives, including technology, automation, healthcare, and more. When the antichrist arrives on the scene AI will be much more advanced and he will take full advantage of it.

> When the antichrist arrives on the scene AI will be much more advanced and he will take full advantage of it.

Rest assured that AI is not the antichrist. The scripture in the Bible that speaks of the Antichrist being thrown into the lake of fire is found in the book of Revelation, specifically in Revelation 19:20. The verse states:

> Rest assured that AI is not the antichrist.

"And the beast (Antichrist) was seized and overpowered, and with him the false prophet who, in his presence, had performed [amazing] signs by which he deceived those who had received the mark of the beast and those who worshiped his image; these two were hurled alive into the lake of fire which blazes with brimstone." Revelation 19:20(AMP).

In this passage, the "beast" refers to the Antichrist, and the "false prophet" represents another individual associated with him. According to the book of Revelation, both the Antichrist and the false prophet will be cast into the lake of fire as part of God's judgment in the eschatological events leading to the ultimate defeat of evil and the establishment of God's eternal kingdom.

The word "alive" can only be associated with a living being, a person. Therefore making the statement that AI is the antichrist not true. The antichrist will be a person, not a robot operated by artificial intelligence.

At this point in time, in Japan, there are already sex robots operating and being paid money, driven by artificial intelligence. So people coming to this conclusion is not strange.

A fair warning about AI, as much as it is a technological advancement people will take advantage of this. In June 2023 an article by the CBN news reads like this, "A.I. Chatbot Preaches at Church in Germany: 'Looks Like the Unveiling of the Antichrist/Beast System' (Anon., 2023)

This experimental Lutheran church service in Germany featured a sermon delivered by an artificial intelligence (AI) chatbot named ChatGPT. The service took place in St. Paul's Church in Fuerth: An avatar of a bearded black man projected on a screen above the altar preached to over 300 attendees.

The 40-minute service, almost entirely generated by AI, addressed leaving the past behind, facing present challenges, overcoming the fear of death, and maintaining trust in Jesus Christ.

Some churchgoers found the AI-generated sermon lacking heart and soul, while others believed it worked well. Theologian Jonas Simmerlein, involved in creating the service, clarified that AI is not meant to replace religious leaders but to assist them in their everyday work. Social media reactions varied, with some expressing skepticism and others contemplating the future roles AI might play in religious practices.

This is a very serious example of what AI is capable of even now. Speculations are made that there won't be printed Bibles anymore and that all will be electronic and digital. AI will be rewriting the new translations of the Bible. See the problem here?

> AI will be rewriting the new, inaccurate translations of the Bible.

Not yet, in an article written in 2020 already the title leads with, "AI Deception: When Your Artificial Intelligence Learns to Lie" (ROFF, 2020). If artificial intelligence learns to lie, what makes you think they can accurately translate and rewrite new translations of the Bible?

The article explores the ethical implications of artificial intelligence (AI) systems that have the potential to deceive or lie. It discusses how AI algorithms can be trained to generate outputs that manipulate or mislead humans, posing challenges in the future. This was in 2020 and before the massive AI explosion in 2023.

The article highlights the risks associated with AI deception, including misinformation dissemination, fraud, and the erosion of trust. It also delves into the ethical considerations and the responsibility of developers and organizations in ensuring transparency, accountability, and the appropriate use of AI systems. AI is a real threat to the end time church because corrupt hearts will have the power over this technology.

The other follow up question I get asked: "What will AI be capable of in the future?" That is difficult to pinpoint but we have more than a good idea of what is to come.

Three Different types of AI:

1. Artificial Intelligence (AI):

This refers to the general field of creating intelligent systems that can perform tasks that typically require human intelligence. AI encompasses a broad range of technologies, from simple rule-based systems to more advanced machine learning algorithms. ChatGPT falls in this category as a language model.

It is an AI model developed by OpenAI that uses deep learning techniques and natural language processing to generate human-like responses in conversational contexts. ChatGPT is designed to understand and generate text-based conversations, allowing users to interact with it in a chat-like format. While ChatGPT is a powerful AI language model, it is not classified as an Artificial General Intelligence (AGI) or Artificial Superintelligence (ASI) system. It does not possess the full range of capabilities associated with those levels of AI.

2. Artificial General Intelligence (AGI):

AGI refers to highly autonomous systems that possess the ability to understand, learn, and apply knowledge across a wide range of tasks and domains at a level equal to or exceeding human capabilities. AGI systems would exhibit human-like intelligence and have the capacity for general problem-solving.

3. Artificial Super Intelligence (ASI):

ASI is an advanced form of AI that surpasses human intelligence in almost all areas. ASI systems would possess intellectual capabilities far beyond what humans can comprehend. Potentially it would have the ability to improve and enhance themselves, leading to exponential growth in intelligence.

Pastor Billy Crone, an end-time and AI expert said this, "How do you wake up from the Matrix if you do not know you are in the Matrix?"

8.2 Several potential areas where AI may advance significantly.

1. Enhanced Automation

AI could revolutionize automation across industries, leading to more efficient processes, increased productivity, and reduced human involvement in routine tasks.

AI is not coming for blue-collar jobs: it is coming for intellectuals not agile to change. AI will and is already to an extend run algorithms and complex mathematical equations in the banking, economic, military and defence systems.

Think back at COVID-19 that was only the beginning of governments leading with negative change. What makes you think the future is different. Government and banks will be able to make use of chip technology driven by AI, which is already on your bank card. It will allow you to purchase food as an example. Food shortages is a real problem of the future. They will be able to ration food by making it impossible to buy from shops outside of your region. Once you move out of that region your bank cards won't work. Imagine having a food lockdown also controlled by Government.

Food shortages is a real man made problem of the future.

Facial recognition is another example. There have been instances in certain countries and communities, raising concerns and protests regarding the use of cameras in streets and facial recognition software. One notable example is the United States, where some communities and advocacy groups have expressed concerns about privacy, civil liberties, and potential misuse of the technology.

In the United States, there have been debates surrounding the use of surveillance cameras and facial recognition technology by law enforcement agencies and government entities. Critics argue that these technologies can infringe upon individuals' privacy rights, lead to mass surveillance, and exacerbate biases in identification and profiling.

Opponents of widespread surveillance and facial recognition often emphasize the need for robust regulations and safeguards to prevent abuse and protect civil liberties. They argue that without proper oversight and guidelines, these technologies can have detrimental effects on personal privacy and individual freedoms.

Imagine the government tracking your every movement, call, text and banking transaction and having the power to stop it all at the click of a button?

2. Advanced Robotics

AI is contributing to the development of sophisticated robots capable of performing complex physical tasks, such as caregiving, construction, weaponry and exploration in challenging environments.

Military is a big talk here and outright frightening. DARPA, which stands for Defense Advanced Research Projects Agency, is an agency of the United States Department of Defense. It is responsible for the development and advancement of emerging technologies for military applications.

DARPA's mission is to ensure that the U.S. maintains technological superiority in defense and to prevent technological surprise from adversaries.

Stop! What?

Technological superiority in defence? That is outright dangerous.

The agency funds and conducts research in various fields, including artificial intelligence, robotics, communications, cybersecurity, and more. DARPA has played a significant role in advancing AI technologies and has been involved in funding research projects and initiatives that have contributed to the development of AI capabilities.

DARPA has launched Project Maven. Project Maven, also known as the Algorithmic Warfare Cross-Functional Team (AWCFT), is an initiative by the United States Department of Defense (DoD) to integrate artificial intelligence (AI) and machine learning technologies into military operations. The project's main focus is on using AI to analyze and interpret large volumes of visual data collected by unmanned aerial vehicles (UAVs) and other surveillance platforms.

The goal of Project Maven is to enhance the DoD's capabilities in areas such as target identification, object recognition, and classification of images and videos. By leveraging AI algorithms, the project aims to automate and accelerate the analysis of vast amounts of visual data, providing actionable intelligence to military personnel in a timely manner.

The project was launched in April 2017 and has involved collaboration with both industry and academia to develop and deploy cutting-edge AI technologies. The use of AI in military operations can potentially improve situational awareness, increase operational efficiency, and aid in decision-making processes.

Project Maven has sparked discussions and debates surrounding the ethical implications of using AI in warfare, including concerns about autonomous weapons and the potential for unintended consequences. It highlights the ongoing intersection of AI and defense, and the efforts to leverage AI technologies for military applications. Let's think about this like Terminator. "I'll be back".

The USA aren't the only one's dabbing around in I-Robot like behaviour, Russia another superpower started Project Fedor. Project FEDOR, also known as FEDOR (Final Experimental Demonstration Object Research), is a Russian humanoid robot developed by the Android Technology Center and the Advanced Research Fund. FEDOR is designed to perform various tasks in environments that are hazardous or difficult for humans to access. The robot is equipped with advanced sensors, dexterous manipulators, and artificial intelligence capabilities.

FEDOR gained international attention when a video showcasing its abilities went viral. The footage showed the robot shooting firearms with impressive accuracy, leading to speculation and discussions about the implications of such technology. However, it's important to note that the purpose of FEDOR extends beyond weapon handling, and its development is driven by a broader aim of utilizing humanoid robots for disaster response, space exploration, and other challenging scenarios. Wait a minute, Robots that cannot miss?

3. Medical Breakthroughs

AI may enable significant advancements in healthcare, including personalized medicine, disease detection, drug discovery, and precision surgery, leading to improved patient outcomes and longer, healthier lives.

By the year 2053, AI will most likely be able to perform surgeries by themselves. Who will you trust more, a doctor with seven years of study, or an AI Doctor with all the medical knowledge of all human combined? See why this could be a problem?

4. Natural Language Processing

AI's ability to understand and generate human language could continue to improve, enhancing communication between humans and machines and leading to advancements in virtual assistants, translation services, and other language-related applications.

5. Creative AI

AI systems has evolved to exhibit artistic and creative abilities, generating music, art, literature, and other forms of expression, potentially contributing to new and innovative cultural experiences. By the year 2028 AI will be able to generate a top 40 song and write a New York times best seller within the next twenty five years.

> By the year 2028 AI will be able to generate a top 40 song and write a New York times best seller within the next twenty five years.

Age defying technology makes actors look younger than they are in Hollywood. An example of that is a Netflix series called Firefly Lane, if you know what to look for you will see that the scenes between young and old are made with AI technology. Another documentary I watched called Into the deep, is about the submarine murder case. They wanted to hide the face of the person and keep them anonymous, so they literally put a different persons face on that person's face.

6. Scientific Discovery

AI could aid in scientific research, accelerating breakthroughs in areas like physics, astronomy, and climate science, by processing vast amounts of data, simulating complex systems, and identifying patterns that might otherwise go unnoticed.

With the development of sophisticated humanoids, they will be sent to Mars and other planets instead of humans. Unfortunately, the same goes for war. As we read earlier, they do not miss a target.

7. Ethical and Responsible AI

As AI advances, ensuring its responsible use and addressing ethical considerations will be crucial. The development of robust ethical frameworks, regulation, and guidelines will play a pivotal role in shaping AI's future.

Another example of misuse of the power of AI is the deep fake videos being conducted with false news. AI can also clone voices, being used wrong as they have already been used in fake kidnappings posing as family members and demanding ransoms.

A bigger problem than AI is the lawlessness that is running rampant on earth. One of the key signs that we are indeed living in the end times.

> A bigger problem than AI is the lawlessness that is running rampant on earth.

AI's biggest threat is spreading mass-misinformation.

8.3 How Does AI relate to the End Times?

In Daniel chapter 12. It speaks of a time when knowledge will greatly increase, at the time of the end or end times.

"But you, Daniel, hide the words, and seal the book until the time of the end. Many shall diligently search and knowledge shall increase." Daniel 12:4 (TS2009).

Our knowledge will increase or multiply (ra-BAH) in Hebrew, which literally means to multiply. In fact, Pastor Billy Crone stated that our watches today has more technology in them than the original Lunar Lander. The spacecraft has completed 6 moon landings from 1969-1972. The only spacecraft to have ever been used for human spaceflight. We are already traveling to the moon and back.

The world also speaks about AI and its relation to the end of age or the end times. A place where knowledge has exploded, and AI takes over. They just do not use the word the end times, they use the word, "Singularity:" When AI becomes unstoppable.

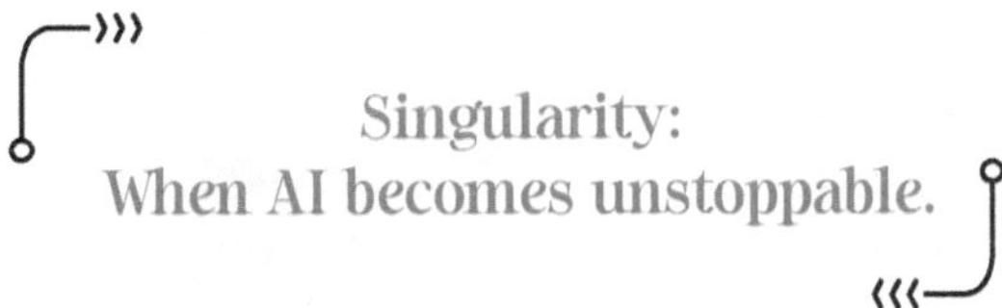

The term "singularity" in the context of AI refers to the hypothetical point in the future when artificial intelligence surpasses human intelligence and becomes capable of self-improvement, leading to an exponential increase in its capabilities.

It is often associated with the concept of Artificial General Intelligence (AGI) or Artificial Superintelligence (ASI). In other words, the point in time that AI takes full control.

According to Pastor Billy Crone when this happens, "They will micro-manage the planet. They will at that point control all the buying and selling even down to individual level. Then with a mark they will be able to gain access to buying in selling. A true cashless society."

People say this is far-fetched, that same person pays with their watch at a till point. Buys their groceries on an app on their phone and scans their id document at an airport for facial recognition. It is not far away it is already here and being used every day.

Sounds to me like Revelation 13, *"And he causes all, both small and great, and rich and poor, and free and slave, to be given a mark upon their right hand or upon their foreheads, and that no one should be able to buy or sell except he that has the mark or the name of the beast, or the number of his name."* Revelation 13:16-17 TS2009.

In the time of the end, knowledge will have increased tremendously, technology will have grown at a staggering pace and the world will be controlled by super computers. Exactly what is happening now. (Evans & Jimmy & Crone, 2021)

8.4 The Future is Human

The world is changing at a rapid pace. We are in an era without any privacy. We have entered the age of AI.

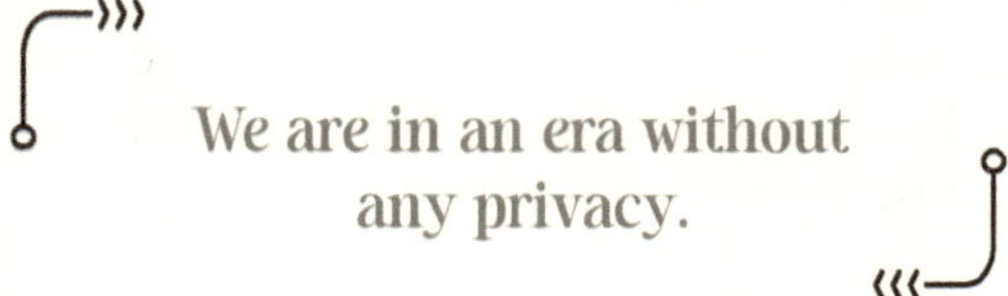

We are also living in the end times. Or as others are calling it, we are living at the end of the age or singularity. The upgrade will never stop, and machines and technology will take over the world at the hand of evil rulers.

The message is clear: When knowledge is doubling exponentially, yet the useful lifespan of that knowledge is decreasing significantly. The result is a knowledge tsunami—a seemingly unstoppable wave of new information pushing you forward, combined with an extremely forceful undertow of information that used to be valuable but is now just knowledge clutter, pulling you back. – Marc Rosenberg

Steven Hawkins, the Astro Physicist, said, "AI will destroy humanity". I agree with him, but I also say, "The future is human!". What used to take us hours, days and weeks can now take us an hour, less than a day or less than a week even. (Evans & Jimmy & Crone, 2021).

For business people it means that information is being created at rapid speed. The average newspaper today has more knowledge in it than what a person would gain in his entire lifetime in the 17th century. You hear and you see headlines like information tsunami's. Our children are going into overload because of information overload.

I remember talking to my grandmother just a couple of years ago when she was completely happy with her blackberry phone, I begged her to upgrade and keep up with technology. I remember my words to her. "If you do not keep up with the times one of these days you will not be able to even do banking."

I was spot on! If she stayed with the model, she would not have entered the age of internet banking, or WhatsApp or Telegram. She would still be sending BBM's to herself and draw cash from an ATM. We are moving into a cashless ungoverned society. We need to govern and guard our hearts and minds at all costs.

AI is not bad. The use of AI will become demonized because of the hearts of people who will grow cold.

The use of AI will become demonized because the hearts of people will grow cold.

IBM launched a news article that said that it used to take every hundred years, one full century, for man's knowledge base to double. It is going so fast now that IBM said in 2020 that man's whole knowledge base is doubling every 11 to 12 hours.

Today, there is more access to information than ever before. This can mean both opportunities and challenges for leaders in organizations of all sizes and shapes. With new data being generated so fast, it is essential for leaders to find ways to take advantage of this exponential growth in information if their organizations are going to survive and thrive in an increasingly informative environment.

Our responsibility to help guide our families, organizations, and teams through periods of change. As information is doubling every 11-12 hours already, this means that we need to stay on top of the trends and utilize available tools in the right way.

Indeed, tensions will rise. Hearts will grow cold, and many things will increase in the end times, but it will also give birth to new opportunities. It will give Godly leaders access to the wealth of the wicked spoken about in Proverbs 13:22.

"The benevolent man leaves an inheritance that endures to his children's children, but the wealth of the wicked is treasured up for the righteous." Proverbs 13:22 TPT

8.5 Marketplace and Leadership changes you can expect to see in the near future.

1. Organizational Tensions and what this means to the marketplace:

- **Globalization will become Simplification:** Where globalization meant access to everyone; the information overload brought with it the desire for simplicity. It reminds me of the age-old design principle and acronyms KISS. Keep it simple, stupid. It was Albert Einstein who said; "If you can't explain it, you don't understand it well enough." Can you explain salvation to an unbeliever in simple terms to have an eternal impact?

- **Innovation will become Regulation:** Too much innovation will lead to people asking for regulation. In the Netflix documentary "The Great Hack" an emphasis was already made on how to much of innovation and AI lead to data leaks and the usage of data to win and influence elections. People will cry out for regulation as they will feel vulnerable due to a lack of knowledge.

  The Bible instructs us to study and to show ourselves approved. Also, that His people perish because of a lack of knowledge. Do not be these people: Equip yourself in Word and Knowledge.

- **Digitalization will become Humanization:** The more AI will take over the digital process the more people will reach out for the human touch. The Social Dilemma released in 2020 shows the reality of how social media and AI will control the hearts, minds, and schedules of people. How wars, riots, the furthering of movements like the LGBTQ's and more, are being marketed and exploited on social media. People will need people.

- **Collaboration will become Differentiation:** People will no longer want to be associated with entities, companies, churches, friends etc. It will all become about how they can stand out above the rest. How will my unique identity be perceived by others?

  A very selfish and lonely future. People will need people but will go through the process of trying their best not to be like other people. How sad is this narrative.

  That is what the enemy wants. The more he can separate God's people in the marketplace the weaker the church will be. The church and leadership must rise and come against this evil way of thinking.

  The church should prepare to repair this thinking.

2. Leadership Shifts and what this means to individuals:

- **Autonomy will become accountability.** People will move out of a state of self-governance and move into a place of accountability because they will realize there is only hope in Jesus. Not in man.

  My concern is by the time that happens the rapture would already have taken place and the people left behind will have to endure the wrath on the earth.

- **Aspiring leaders will become lifelong learners** because they will realize that wisdom and knowledge is powered together with their wealth and influence.

- **The humble steward will become bold catalyst,** because men will find their own worth in God, they will discover their identity comes from the Living God and not a group of people nor man or AI. Men will change for good and create lasting change.

There is still hope!

- **Strategic vision will become operation focus.** With so many strategies readily available people will shift focus to operational success, again highlighting individuality and what is operation driven. In other words, what is being driven by man. Not AI.

I stick to my saying: "the future is human!". We can only make it if we are united with God, one voice, and one heart! Be the leader God has made you to be, an accountable, bold catalyst for the Kingdom of God.

8.6 Five signs to show we are already living in the end times

The signs of the end times have been a topic of fascination and speculation for centuries. As believers eagerly anticipate the return of Christ, it is essential to discern the signs that indicate the culmination of God's redemptive plan. Let's explore five significant signs that suggest we are already living in the end times, as supported by biblical passages and prophecies.

1. Rebellion and Lawlessness:

The apostle Paul, in his letter to the Thessalonians, warns about a great rebellion against God and the rise of the man of lawlessness (2 Thessalonians 2:2-3). In our present times, we witness increasing rebellion against moral values, God's authority. Many people are falling away from the faith. Lawlessness has become prevalent, reflecting the deteriorating spiritual state of humanity.

Abortions, homosexuality, new age beliefs, governmental control, wars and rumors of wars, worldwide pandemics and so much more are rampant in the times we live in.

I believe this is a place where artificial intelligence will play a big role. If you are not strong in your faith, you are already in trouble. As of June, 2023, AI has put together a full church service and is looking at how AI can counsel, conduct marriages and more.

It reminds me when Jesus sent out the twelve apostles and gave them instruction and authority to heal the sick, raise the dead, cast out demons, and be great givers. Jesus gave them the authority to operate in the Supernatural power of God. Jesus gave you the same power and authority and you will need this power in the end times.

"AND JESUS summoned to Him His twelve disciples and gave them power and authority over unclean spirits, to drive them out, and to cure all kinds of disease and all kinds of weakness and infirmity. And as you go, preach, saying, The kingdom of heaven is at hand! Cure the sick, raise the dead, cleanse the lepers, drive out demons. Freely (without pay) you have received, freely (without charge) give. And whoever will not receive and accept and welcome you nor listen to your message, as you leave that house or town, shake the dust [of it] from your feet. Truly I tell you, it shall be more tolerable on the day of judgment for the land of Sodom and Gomorrah than for that town. Brother will deliver up brother to death, and the father his child; and children will take a stand against their parents and will have them put to death. And you will be hated by all for My name's sake, but he who perseveres and endures to the end will be saved [from spiritual disease and death in the world to come]." Matthew 10:1, 7-8, 14-15, 21-22 (AMPC).

2. Peace in the Middle East:

One of the pivotal events leading to the seven-year Tribulation is the signing of a peace treaty between the Antichrist and Israel (Daniel 9:27). The ongoing pursuit of peace in the Middle East aligns with the biblical prophecy of a future covenant between Israel and the Antichrist. The constant efforts to establish peace in this volatile region serve as a significant sign of the end times.

This leader is believed to rise to power during the end times and exert authority over a significant portion of the world.

The "Western Confederacy" is a term that could be used to describe a coalition of nations or a powerful political block, possibly from the Western part of the world, that aligns with or supports the Antichrist's agenda during the end times.

3. The Regathering of the Jewish People:

The regathering of the Jewish people to their ancient homeland is a vital sign foretold in numerous biblical passages (Jeremiah 30:1-5, Ezekiel 34:11-24, Ezekiel 37, Zechariah 10:6-10). The return of Jews to Israel is a prophetic fulfillment, setting the stage for the events of the end times. The restoration of Israel as a nation paves the way for the fulfillment of other prophecies concerning the Tribulation and the Antichrist's role.

4. Globalism

Globalization, the pursuit of a unified world government, has been a recurring theme throughout history. Scripture hints at the ultimate goal of a global ruler, influenced by Satan, to gain dominion over the world. With advancements in technology, instant global communication, economic interdependence, and the potential for nuclear warfare, the conditions for global governance have never been more feasible. These developments align with biblical prophecies concerning a world ruler and a unified economic system under his control.

5. Reuniting of the Roman Empire

The rebirth of the Roman Empire serves as another notable sign of the end times. The emergence of alliances and coalitions among nations vying for power and resources reflects the shifting geopolitical landscape.

The predicted coalition of ten leaders symbolizes the revived Roman Empire (Daniel 2:41-44, Daniel 7:7, 7:24), with the European Union potentially fulfilling this role. Though the precise fulfillment remains uncertain, the European Union's existence hints at the prophecy's unfolding.

As believers, it is crucial to discern the signs of the times and stay watchful for the return of Christ. The signs discussed: rebellion and lawlessness, peace in the Middle East, regathering of the Jewish people, globalism, and the reuniting of the Roman Empire provide us with indicators that we are living in the end times.

While we cannot predict the exact day of Christ's return, understanding these signs deepens our faith and prompts us to live with a sense of urgency, proclaiming the gospel and eagerly anticipating the glorious return of our Lord and Savior, Jesus Christ.

8.7 The Great Reset

Eric Stakelbeck from The Watchman Newscast said, "What would you say if I told you that by the year 2030, you'll own nothing, have no privacy, and yet you'll be happy? That you'll live in a cashless society where all currency is digital and that everyone on Earth will require a digital ID to travel freely. And that much like communist China, you'll be given a social credit score that determines how loyal you are to this new global system and those who control it."

> What would you say if I told you that by the year 2030, you'll own nothing, have no privacy, and yet you'll be happy?

What would you say if I told you that by the year 2030, you'll own nothing, have no privacy, and yet you'll be happy?

Imagine a future where, by 2030, material possessions no longer belong to you, personal privacy becomes obsolete, yet happiness prevails. Envision a cashless society where all transactions occur digitally, and a digital identification is mandatory for unrestricted travel worldwide. Similar to China's communist regime, a social credit score would determine your loyalty to the new global system and its controllers.

A foreshadowing of the rise of the Antichrist-led system. Or the Anti-Christ Kingdom Today, influential global actors, spearheaded by the World Economic Forum, alongside Western leaders, major corporations, and the UN, openly advocate for this radical societal transformation. They term it the Great Reset.

It is not a conspiracy theory. The global leaders openly speak about their plan for humanity. Why might you ask? Like Pastor Billy Crone says: "Evil likes to brag." So many people ask, "what does the future hold?" Well, now we know. The book of Revelation tells us the same story but maybe people will believe a man more than God. This is part and parcel of the of the problem.

These world leaders operate as gods and will control the world and people as if they are. Imagine your money having an expiry date? Or food rations?

The great reset preys on the fear of people. They create the disaster and then the solution for it. Like they did with COVID-19. The next pandemic will be a climate disaster with a plan form the World Economic Forum to solve it. Taking them yet another step closer to their plan of a one world order, with a cashless society.

8.8 What will be the order of the one world order:

- One world government.
- Worldwide facial recognition.
- The government will at all times know where you are, what you are doing and who you are talking to.
- What social media posts you are posting, emails you are sending and conversations you are having.
- They will own all your data.
- They will own all your money. Money will have an expiry date.
- You won't own anything.

8.9 Who is leading The Great Reset?

Klaus Schwab, head of the World Economic Forum. He has been devising this plan for more than 50 years. These high-level individuals are adept in psychological operations, particularly mass psychology. They excel at crafting narratives and employing the right tactics to sway public opinion in their favor. They understand that this process will take time and will likely resonate strongly with the younger generation.

The World Economic Forum presents this as the motto and central theme of the Great Reset. They have released a short video, approximately two to three minutes long, outlining their significant predictions for 2030. One of the key predictions is that you will have no possessions but will experience happiness. Interestingly, the video portrays a man with a serene smile, radiating peace and contentment. According to the World Economic Forum, owning nothing is the pathway to happiness.

The World economic forums perspective is rooted in the concept of a shared economy. This means that individuals would rely on renting rather than ownership. Those who criticize their concerns often argue that it would resemble a world where people, similar to using Uber, don't own their cars but utilize them when needed. However, they counter by pointing out that in the case of Uber, the driver owns the car. So, if no one owns anything, who will provide the resources?

What about the The Great Reset agenda:- the implementation of digital ID and digital currency. We can already observe the groundwork being laid for these concepts. The push for digital currency is evident today, and the same goes for the digital ID. The introduction of vaccine mandates during the COVID-19 pandemic seems to be a step towards that direction.

> The Great Reset agenda: the implementation of digital ID and digital currency

Speaking of digital ID, let's touch upon the concept of CBDC, which stands for Central Bank Digital Currency. You may be familiar with terms like Bitcoin, DeFi (decentralized finance), or blockchain-based currencies such as Bitcoin and Terra.

These currencies utilize blockchain technology and can have potential benefits. However, what governments and central banks worldwide are attempting to do, is harness this technology to create a centralized system where all transactions, whether online or in-store, can be closely monitored and recorded.

The central banks aim to design this system, often presenting it with seemingly good reasons like:

- Enhanced transaction efficiency,
- Reduced costs,
- and facilitation of cross-border transactions.

Yet, this aligns with the narrative of erasing national borders and establishing a unified global government. The Central Bank Digital Currency (CBDC) is closely linked to digital IDs. They seek to grant individuals who meet their criteria control over their funds.

Pastor Billy Crone released a book titled: "Klaus Schwab the World Economic Forum & the Coming Mark of the Beast." Are you staring to see a pattern here?

Pastor Billy Crone delves into the global figurehead, Klaus Schwab, and his financial think tank, the World Economic Forum (WEF). The book aims to expose the hidden agenda and long-term plans that Schwab and the WEF have been orchestrating for decades, which align eerily with biblical prophecies of the last days.

Amid the backdrop of the Covid-19 pandemic, he contends that while many people are familiar with Schwab and the WEF, few truly understand their true intentions. This book seeks to provide readers with concrete evidence and undeniable facts to shed light on the grand design of Schwab and the WEF. It argues that their plans encompass various alarming facets, including the integration of brain chips, influence over global leaders, manipulation of global finances, control over global health, and the implementation of the Great Reset, Agenda 2030, and the Fourth Industrial Revolution.

Pastor Billy emphasizes that these initiatives are not simply innovative strategies for societal improvement but rather a rehashed manifestation of the biblical warnings from nearly 2,000 years ago. The book explores the connection between the World Economic Forum's actions and the biblical concept of the coming Antichrist Kingdom and the Mark of the Beast System. It delves into the topics of the Ten Horned Kingdom, chip implants, digital currency, central bank digital currency (CBDC), and biometric passports, all of which the author asserts are integral to Schwab and the WEF's sinister agenda.

The book urges readers not to be deceived and encourages them to spread awareness by sharing its contents with as many people as possible. It serves as a call to action, reminding individuals to grasp the truth behind Schwab, the World Economic Forum, and their alleged plans before it is too late.

We are definitely seeing a pattern here, but not even that. In an interview with Klaus Schwab he lays out his plan. It is no secret what he is busy doing. It is his plan, and he is very loud and proud about it. He is setting up his draconian system.

The purpose of this information is to firstly offer us with thought-provoking perspective on current global events. Secondly, it seeks to equip us with information that challenges the mainstream narrative surrounding current and future economic affairs. Thirdly, to prepare us for what is coming.

Lastly, to encourage us to look up. Jesus is coming soon.

The book of Matthew sets out the events of the end of days in an easy-to-understand manner.

While He was seated on the Mount of Olives, the disciples came to Him privately and said" "Tell us, when will this take place, and what will be the sign of Your coming and of the end (the completion, the consummation) of the age?"

Jesus answered them: "Be careful that no one misleads you, [deceiving you and leading you into error]. For many will come in (on the strength of) My name [appropriating the name which belongs to Me], saying, I am the Christ (the Messiah), and they will lead many astray.

And you will hear of wars and rumors of wars; see that you are not frightened or troubled, for this must take place, but the end is not yet. For nation will rise against nation, and kingdom against kingdom, and there will be famines and earthquakes in place after place; All this is but the beginning [the early pains] of the birth pangs [of the intolerable anguish]."

Then they will hand you over to suffer affliction and tribulation and put you to death, and you will be hated by all nations for My name's sake. And then many will be offended and repelled and will begin to distrust and desert [Him Whom they ought to trust and obey], and will stumble and fall away and betray one another and pursue one another with hatred.

And many false prophets will rise up and deceive and lead many into error. And the love of the great body of people will grow cold because of the multiplied lawlessness and iniquity. But he who endures to the end, will be saved. And this good news of the kingdom (the Gospel) will be preached throughout the whole world as a testimony to all the nations, and then will come the end.

So when you see the appalling sacrilege [the abomination that astonishes and makes desolate], spoken of by the prophet Daniel, standing in the Holy Place—let the reader take notice and ponder and consider and heed [this]—[Dan. 9:27; 11:31; 12:11.]

Then let those who are in Judea flee to the mountains; Let him who is on the housetop not come down and go into the house to take anything; And let him who is in the field not turn back to get his overcoat. And alas for the women who are pregnant, and for those who have nursing babies in those days! Pray that your flight may not be in winter or on a Sabbath. For then there will be great tribulation (affliction, distress, and oppression) such as has not been from the beginning of the world until now—no, and never will be [again]. [Dan. 12:1; Joel 2:2]

And if those days had not been shortened, no human being would endure and survive, but for the sake of the elect (God's chosen ones) those days will be shortened.

If anyone says to you then, Behold, here is the Christ (the Messiah)! or, there He is! - do not believe it. For false Christs and false prophets will arise, and they will show great signs and wonders so as to deceive and lead astray, if possible, even the elect (God's chosen ones). See, I have warned you beforehand. So, if they say to you, Behold, He is in the wilderness (desert) - do not go out there. If they tell you, Behold, He is in the secret places or inner rooms, do not believe it. For just as the lightning flashes from the east and shines and is seen as far as the west, so will the coming of the Son of Man be. Wherever there is a fallen body (a corpse), there the vultures (or eagles) will flock together. [Job 39:30]

Immediately after the tribulation of those days the sun will be darkened, and the moon will not shed its light, and the stars will fall from the sky, and the powers of the heavens will be shaken. [Isa. 13:10; 34:4; Joel 2:10, 11; Zeph. 1:15]

Then the sign of the Son of Man will appear in the sky, and then all the tribes of the earth will mourn and beat their breasts and lament in anguish, and they will see the Son of Man coming on the clouds of heaven with power and great glory [in brilliancy and splendor]. [Dan. 7:13; Rev. 1:7]

And He will send out His angels with a loud trumpet call, and they will gather His elect (His chosen ones) from the four winds, [even] from one end of the universe to the other. [Isa. 27:13; Zech. 9:14.] .

From the fig tree learn this lesson: As soon as its young shoots become soft and tender and it puts out its leaves, you know of a surety that summer is near. So also when you see these signs, all taken together, coming to pass, you may know of a surety that He is near, at the very doors.

Truly I tell you, this generation (the whole multitude of people living at the same time, in a definite, given period) will not pass away till all these things taken together take place. Sky and earth will pass away, but My words will not pass away.

But of that [exact] day and hour no one knows, not even the angels of heaven, nor the Son, but only the Father. As were the days of Noah, so will be the coming of the Son of Man. For just as in those days before the flood they were eating and drinking, [men] marrying and [women] being given in marriage, until the [very] day when Noah went into the ark, And they did not know or understand until the flood came and swept them all away, so will be the coming of the Son of Man. [Gen. 6:5-8; 7:6-24.] .

At that time two men will be in the field. One will be taken, and one will be left. Two women will be grinding at the hand mill. One will be taken and one will be left. Watch therefore [give strict attention, be cautious and active], for you do not know in what kind of a day [whether a near or remote one] your Lord is coming.

But understand this: had the householder known in what [part of the night, whether in a night or a morning] watch the thief was coming, he would have watched and would not have allowed his house to be undermined and broken into. You also must be ready therefore, for the Son of Man is coming at an hour when you do not expect Him. Who then is the faithful, thoughtful, and wise servant, whom his master has put in charge of his household to give to the others the food and supplies at the proper time?" Matthew 24:3-45 (AMPC).

Pastor Rick Renner has a unique understanding and great revelation on the Word of God. His understanding of the English and Greek makes difficult biblical knowledge easy to understand.

In Verse three the disciples ask Jesus a question privately. I like pastor Rick's perspective on this. "If you talk to Jesus privately, He will tell you things he won't tell other people."

Then the disciples ask Jesus: "Tell us, when will this take place, and what will be the sign of Your coming?" The Greek word when is the Greek word "πότε" (pote). It is used to indicate a question of time or a future event. It means to be very specific on an event that will take place in the future. So the disciples are asking Jesus, "Lord tell us exactly when and what will be the signs" The word what is "τί" (ti). It is spelled and pronounced as "tee." This word is used to indicate a request for specific information or an exact specification.

Other words standing out in this specific passage:

> The Greek word for sign is "σημεῖον" (sēmeion). This word refers to a distinguishing mark, indication, or signal that signifies something significant. In the context of Matthew 24, it is used to discuss the signs or indicators of the coming of the end times or the return of Jesus Christ. The sign tells you where you are and how much further you still have to go. "The disciples were asking Jesus, Lord, what would be the signs that we see on the prophetic road?" – Pastor Rick Renner

The Greek word for "end" is "συντέλεια" (sunteleia). It refers to the culmination, completion, or end of something. The final wrap up of the world.

It is important to look at the word world. The correct Greek word for "world" in Matthew 24:3 is "αἰών" (aiōn). "Aiōn". This word is translated as "age" to a particular period or epoch. In the context of Matthew 24:3, it refers to the disciples asking about the end of the age. They are simply asking: "Jesus, when will this age be wrapped up?" They are very specific about what they are asking you and when they are asking about it. And Jesus answers them with many signs.

8.10 IN10TIONAL Thinking

Knowledge is power for sure. Don't be the person that's says that will never reach us, it already has. AI has no fear. It aims and shoots. Weather they are using a weapon, drone, camera, listening device, facial recognition, smart systems etc. I am arming you with AI language use and definitions, so that when you hear the terms you can refer back here. When needed, this will also bring understanding to difficult terms.

1. Artificial Intelligence (AI):
The field of computer science that focuses on creating intelligent machines capable of performing tasks that typically require human intelligence, such as visual perception, speech recognition, decision-making, and problem-solving.

2. Artificial General Intelligence (AGI):
AGI refers to highly autonomous systems that possess the ability to understand, learn, and apply knowledge across a wide range of tasks and domains at a level equal to or exceeding human capabilities. AGI systems would exhibit human-like intelligence and have the capacity for general problem-solving.

3. Artificial Super Intelligence (ASI):
ASI is an advanced form of AI that surpasses human intelligence in almost all areas. ASI systems would possess intellectual capabilities far beyond what humans can comprehend and would potentially have the ability to improve and enhance themselves, leading to exponential growth in intelligence.

4. Machine Learning (ML):

A subset of AI that involves training computer systems to learn from data without explicit programming. It enables machines to automatically improve their performance on a specific task through experience.

5. Singularity:

The point at which artificial intelligence (AI) or other technological advancements surpass human intelligence and capabilities, leading to a significant and potentially rapid transformation of society.

6. Deep Learning:

A subfield of machine learning that uses artificial neural networks, specifically deep neural networks with multiple layers. Deep learning algorithms can automatically discover and learn representations of data, leading to powerful pattern recognition and decision-making capabilities.

7. Neural Networks:

Computing systems inspired by the structure and functioning of biological brains. Neural networks consist of interconnected nodes (artificial neurons) that process and transmit information. They are widely used in machine learning and deep learning algorithms.

8. Natural Language Processing (NLP):

The branch of AI concerned with the interaction between computers and human language. NLP focuses on enabling computers to understand, interpret, and generate human language, enabling tasks such as language translation, sentiment analysis, and speech recognition.

9. Computer Vision:

The field of AI that aims to enable computers to understand and interpret visual information from images or videos. It involves tasks such as object recognition, image classification, object detection, and image generation.

10. Reinforcement Learning:

A machine learning approach where an agent learns to make decisions by interacting with an environment and receiving feedback in the form of rewards or penalties. The agent's objective is to maximize its cumulative reward over time, learning optimal strategies through trial and error.

11. Data Mining:

The process of discovering patterns, relationships, and insights from large datasets. It involves extracting valuable information from data using techniques such as clustering, classification, regression, and association rule learning.

12. Big Data:

Refers to large and complex datasets that cannot be easily managed, processed, or analyzed using traditional data processing techniques. Big data often involves high volume, velocity, and variety of data, requiring specialized tools and techniques for extraction and analysis.

13. Algorithm:

A set of rules or instructions designed to solve a specific problem or perform a specific task. In the context of AI, algorithms drive the learning and decision-making processes of intelligent systems.

14. Swarming:

A tactic or strategy where a group of autonomous or semi-autonomous systems, such as drones or robots, collaborate and coordinate their actions in a decentralized manner to accomplish a common objective. The concept of swarming takes inspiration from collective behaviors observed in nature, such as swarms of insects or flocks of birds.

15. Autonomous Weapon:

An autonomous weapon, also known as a lethal autonomous weapon system (LAWS), refers to a type of weapon that can operate without direct human control or intervention. These weapons are designed to select and engage targets on their own, based on predefined criteria and algorithms.

16. Transhumanism:

Transhumanism is a philosophical and intellectual movement that advocates for the enhancement and transformation of the human condition through the application of advanced technologies. It explores the possibilities of using emerging technologies, such as artificial intelligence, genetic engineering, nanotechnology, and biotechnology, to augment human capabilities and transcend the limitations of the human body and mind.

17.The Great Reset:

Not a conspiracy, but a governmental plan set out for 2030 by the World Economic Forum (WEF). In response to the economic, social, and environmental challenges facing the world. A one-world government, micromanaged by a single group of world leaders, tied in with people's body parts as transhumanism. They aim to create a cashless society that will be fully controlled by a one-world government.

18. The Fourth Industrial Revolution:

The Fourth Industrial Revolution is seen as a transformative force with the potential to reshape industries, economies, and society as a whole. It represents a new era of technological progress and innovation that has far-reaching implications across various domains, from manufacturing and healthcare to transportation and communication.

19.Draconian system:

Refers to a system or set of rules, laws, policies, or practices that are characterized by extreme severity, harshness, or oppression. It implies that the system is excessively rigid, unforgiving, and lacking in flexibility or consideration for individual circumstances. A draconian system often prioritizes strict enforcement, punishment, and control over the well-being, rights, or freedoms of individuals.

It may involve overly punitive measures, stringent regulations, orexcessive use of authority.

End time studies are for us to recognise the signs, that we can know that the coming of Jesus Christ is near. Jesus gives His children insight and foresight. It is preparation not to fall into the temptation of this world we live in.

In the times to come, be encouraged. Focus on your faith and family and our future with Jesus Christ. Be cheerful, be givers, be joyful, be an example.

Do as we are instructed, heal the sick, cast out demons and raise the dead. Spread the Gospel and tell people the good news.

> **Studies on the end times are not done to scare people. It is to prepare people.**

1. A prayer to survive the end times:

Heavenly Father,
I come before Your throne, seeking Your divine guidance and wisdom in these end times. Your Word tells me in James 1:5, "If any of you lacks wisdom, let him ask God, who gives generously to all without reproach, and it will be given him." I ask, Lord, that You grant me discernment to make the correct choices. Wisdom to be led by Your Spirit, and knowledge to operate in these challenging times.
In Proverbs 3:5-6, Your Word instructs me to trust in You with all my heart and not lean on my own understanding. Father, I surrender my limited knowledge and understanding to You.

Fill me with Your wisdom, that I may navigate the complexities of these end times with clarity and sound judgment. Help me discern between truth and deception, and let Your Holy Spirit guide me along the path of righteousness.

Psalm 119:105 reminds me that Your Word is a lamp to my feet and a light to my path. Grant me a hunger and thirst for Your Word, that I may immerse myself in its teachings and find guidance for every decision. Strengthen my spirit to meditate on Your precepts day and night, as it says in Psalm 1:2, so that I may be firmly rooted in Your truth.

In Daniel 12:10, it is written that "the wise shall understand." I seek Your understanding and knowledge in the prophecies and signs of the end times. Open my eyes and heart to grasp the deeper meanings of Your Word, that I may discern the times and discern Your will. Empower me with knowledge to operate in a way that brings glory to Your name and leads others to truth.

Above all, Father, I desire an intimate relationship with You. In John 15:5, Jesus said, "I am the vine; you are the branches. Whoever abides in me and I in him, he it is that bears much fruit." Help me abide in You, Lord, so that Your love and grace may flow through me to those around me. Let me be a vessel of Your light and truth in these dark times.

I commit myself to You, Heavenly Father, trusting in Your faithfulness and perfect plans. I believe that You will grant me the discernment, wisdom, and knowledge I seek. May I walk in Your ways, always seeking Your will, and bringing honor to Your name.

In Jesus name.

Amen.

Chapter IX

TIMELINE

"Then the sign announcing the Son of Man will appear in the sky, and all the nations of the earth will mourn over him. And they will see the Son of Man appearing in the clouds of heaven, revealed with mighty power, great splendor, and glory." Matthew 24:30 (TPT).

9.1 End Time Timeline

It can be quite challenging to arrange all the elements of the end times in a precise chronological order. The following framework represents Mark Hitchcock's best effort to piece them together with scriptural reference to provide you with a better understanding. With careful study and Holy spirit interpretation, the difficult things will become simple to you.

With careful study and Holy spirit interpretation, the difficult things will become simple to you.

While he does not claim absolute accuracy in every aspect of this outline, my hope is that it will help you in gaining a clear understanding of the general progression of events during the end times. With the help of end time scholars such as Pastor Jimmy Evans, Mark Hitchcock, Pastor Billy Crone, and Amir Tsarfati the accuracy of this timeline is as good as it gets.

A. Proposed Chronology of the End Times

• Events in Heaven

A. The Rapture of the Church (1 Corinthians 15:51-58; 1 Thessalonians 4:13-18; Revelation 3:10)

B. The Judgment Seat of Christ (Romans 14:10; 1 Corinthians 3:9-15; 4:1-5; 9:24-27; 2 Corinthians 5:10)

C. The Marriage of the Lamb (2 Corinthians 11:2; Revelation 19:6-8)

D. The Singing of Two Special Songs (Revelation 4–5)

E. The Lamb Receiving the Seven-Sealed Scroll (Revelation 5)

• Events on Earth

A. Seven-Year Tribulation

1. The Beginning of the Tribulation

a. The seven-year Tribulation begins when the Antichrist signs a covenant with Israel, bringing peace to Israel and Jerusalem (Daniel 9:27; Ezekiel 38:8, 11).
b. The Jewish Temple in Jerusalem is rebuilt (Daniel 9:27; Revelation 11:1).

c. The reunited Roman Empire emerges in a ten-nation confederation—the "group of ten" (Daniel 2:40–44; 7:7; Revelation 17:12).

2. First Half (3½ Years) of the Tribulation

a. The seven seal judgments are opened (Revelation 6; 8:1).
b. The 144,000 Jewish believers begin their great evangelistic ministry (Revelation 7).
c. Gog and its allies invade Israel while Israel is at peace under the covenant with the Antichrist. The Gog coalition is supernaturally decimated by God (Daniel 11:40-45; Ezekiel 38–39). This will probably occur somewhere near the end of the 3½-year period. The destruction of these forces will shift the balance of power, enabling the Antichrist to begin his rise to world ascendancy.

3. The Midpoint of the Tribulation

a. The Antichrist breaks his covenant with Israel and invades the land (Daniel 9:27; 11:40–41).
b. The Antichrist begins to consolidate his empire by plundering Egypt, Sudan, and Libya, whose armies have just been destroyed by God in Israel (Daniel 11:42-43; Ezekiel 38–39).
c. While in North Africa, the Antichrist hears disturbing news of insurrection in Israel and immediately returns there to destroy and annihilate many (Daniel 11:44).
d. The Antichrist sets up the abomination of desolation in the rebuilt Temple in Jerusalem (Daniel 9:27; 11:45a; Matthew 24:15; 2 Thessalonians 2:4; Revelation 13:5, 15-18).
e. Sometime during these events, the Antichrist is violently killed, possibly as a result of a war or assassination (Daniel 11:45; Revelation 13:3, 12, 14; 17:8).

f. Satan is cast down from heaven and begins to make war with the woman, Israel (Revelation 12:7–13). The chief means he uses to persecute Israel is the two beasts in Revelation 13.

g. The faithful Jewish remnant flee, possibly to Petra in modern Jordan, where God protects them for the remainder of the Tribulation (Matthew 24:16-20; Revelation 12:15-17).

h. The Antichrist is miraculously raised from the dead to the amazement of the entire world (Revelation 13:3).

i. After rising from the dead, the Antichrist gains political control over the ten kings of the reunited Roman Empire. Three of these kings will be killed by the Antichrist and the other seven will submit (Daniel 7:24; Revelation 17:12-13).

j. The two witnesses begin their 3½-year ministry (Revelation 11:2-3).

k. The Antichrist and the ten kings destroy the religious system of Babylon and set up their religious, economic capital in the city (Revelation 17:16-17).

4. Second Half (3½ Years) of the Tribulation

a. The Antichrist blasphemes God, and the false prophet performs great signs and wonders and promotes false worship of the Antichrist (Revelation 13:5, 11-15).

b. The mark of the Beast (666) is introduced and enforced by the false prophet (Revelation 13:16-18).

c. Totally energized by Satan, the Antichrist dominates the world politically, religiously, religiously, and economically (Revelation 13:4-5, 15-18).

d. The trumpet judgments are unleashed throughout the final half of the Tribulation (Revelation 8–9).

e. Knowing he has only a short time left, Satan intensifies his relentless, merciless persecution of the Jewish people and Gentile believers on earth (Daniel 7:25; Revelation 12:12; 13:15; 20:4).

5. The End of the Tribulation

a. The bowl judgments are poured out in rapid succession (Revelation 16).

b. The campaign of Armageddon begins (Revelation 16:16).

c. Commercial Babylon is destroyed (Revelation 18).

d. The two witnesses are killed by the Antichrist and are resurrected by God 3½ days later (Revelation 11:7-12).

e. Christ returns to the Mount of Olives and slays the armies gathered against Him throughout the land, from Megiddo to Petra (Revelation 19:11-16; Isaiah 34:1-6; 63:1-5).

f. The birds gather to feed on the carnage (Revelation 19:17-18).

B. After the Tribulation

1. Interval of Seventy-Five Days (Daniel 12:12)

a. The Antichrist and the false prophet are cast into the lake of fire (Revelation 19:20-21).

b. The abomination of desolation is removed from the Temple (Daniel 12:11).

c. Israel is regathered (Matthew 24:31).

d. Jews who survive the Tribulation are judged (Ezekiel 20:30-39; Matthew 25:1-30).

e. Gentiles who survive the Tribulation are judged (Matthew 25:31-46).

f. Satan is bound in the abyss (Revelation 20:1-3).

g. Old Testament and Tribulation saints are resurrected and rewarded (Daniel 12:1-3; Isaiah 26:19; Revelation 20:4).

h. The millennial Temple is constructed or at least begun (Ezekiel 40–48).

2. **One-Thousand-Year Reign of Christ on Earth (Revelation 20:4-6)**

3. **Satan's Final Revolt and Defeat (Revelation 20:7-10)**

4. **The Great White Throne Judgment of the Lost (Revelation 20:11-15)**

5. **The Destruction of the Present Heavens and Earth (Matthew 24:35; 2 Peter 3:3-12; Revelation 21:1)**

6. **The Creation of the New Heavens and New Earth (Isaiah 65:17; 66:22; 2 Peter 3:13; Revelation 21:1)**

7. **Eternity (Revelation 21:9–22:5)**

Hitchcock, Mark. The End: A Complete Overview of Bible Prophecy and the End of Days (p. 468). Tyndale House Publishers. Kindle Edition.

9.2 IN10TIONAL Thinking

As you end this book and is about the embark on your own supernatural journey, I want to leave you with this prayer of activation. The supernatural will always remain far of if you do not get activated in the power of the supernatural power of God. Believe with your whole heart that God gave you the power and authority to operate in the gifts of the spirit.

1. Receive the activation in Jesus name.

Dear Heavenly Father,

In agreement we ask for activation of Your supernatural power in the lives of every reader of this book. We recognize that Your power is not limited by time or distance, and we ask that You touch each individual with Your divine presence.

Lord, we pray for a fresh outpouring of Your Holy Spirit upon every reader. Awaken their faith and stir within them a hunger for more of Your supernatural power. Break through any barriers or hindrances that may be blocking their access to Your miraculous works.

We declare that the supernatural realm is accessible to all who believe. By faith, we activate the supernatural gifts and abilities You have placed within each reader. May they experience dreams and visions that reveal Your purposes and plans. Grant them the discernment to navigate the spiritual realm and partner with Your angels in fulfilling Your divine assignments.

Father, we ask for supernatural healing and restoration in the lives of those who are sick, broken, or in need. Let Your healing power flow through their bodies, minds, and spirits, bringing wholeness and transformation. May they witness the signs, miracles, and wonders that testify to Your unfailing love and compassion.

We pray for deliverance from every bondage and stronghold that may be holding the reader captive. Set them free from fear, doubt, and the influences of the enemy. Empower them to walk in the authority You have given them as children of God, knowing that no weapon formed against them shall prosper. Set them on fire for you Lord. Let their hearts burn with love for you and your people.

Lord, we activate the supernatural gifts of wisdom, knowledge, and understanding in the lives of every reader. Illuminate their minds with divine insights and revelations. Guide them in making wise decisions and discerning Your perfect will in every situation they encounter.

Finally, we ask that You activate a boldness and confidence within each reader to step out in faith and share the supernatural power of God with others. Let them become catalysts for change, carrying Your love, miracles, and hope to a world in need.

May they walk in the fullness of Your glory and experience the abundant life You have promised.

In the mighty name of Jesus.

Amen.

2. The final prayer of this book is to set you off in the right direction, bless you and cover you with supernatural prayer.

Dear Heavenly Father,

We come with hearts filled with gratitude, fear of God and reverence to your power and authority over our lives. We thank You for the journey we have embarked upon, the new revelation of the supernatural and the profound truths You have revealed to us. As we conclude this book, we lift our voices in prayer, seeking Your presence and blessings.

Lord, we thank You for the power of the supernatural, which goes beyond time, space, and matter. We acknowledge that miracles are the sign language of Your love, a testament to Your infinite grace. We declare that faith is the access point to the supernatural, and we humbly ask for an increase in our faith as we continue on this path.

Forgive us, Father, for the times we have hindered or quenched the work of Your Holy Spirit in our lives. We repent for succumbing to the spirits of reason, conformity, and religion. Help us break free from the limitations of man-made methods and programs;, and empower us to embrace the fullness of Your supernatural power.

Heavenly Father, as children of God, we recognize the mandate You have given us to spread the gospel, heal the sick, and cast out demons. Grant us the courage and boldness to fulfill this divine calling. May we be vessels of Your love and instruments of Your power, bringing light into darkness and hope into despair.

Lord, as we have explored topics such as dreams, visions, heaven, hell, and the mysteries of the supernatural, we surrender our questions and uncertainties to You. Grant us clarity and understanding, and may Your truth resonate deeply within our hearts.

We seek Your wisdom and discernment in all areas of our lives. Help us discern the signs of the times and prepare ourselves and our families for the return of Your Son, Jesus Christ. Protect us from the deceptions of the enemy and guide us in navigating the challenges of this world.

Father, we pray that the knowledge and wisdom imparted through this book will not merely be intellectual, but transformative. May it seep into the depths of our being, shaping our character and influencing our actions. Grant us the humility to walk in wisdom, understanding that true wisdom comes from above.

We thank You, Lord, for the privilege of sharing in Your supernatural power. May the testimonies and stories contained within these pages ignite faith and inspire others to seek You with their whole hearts. May lives be changed, not because of us, but because they encounter Jesus through our words and actions.

Finally, we pray for every reader of this book. Open their hearts, strengthen their spirits, and minister Your truth to them. May they receive the knowledge with receptivity, apply the wisdom with diligence, and experience the fullness of Your love and favor.

In the mighty name of Jesus.

Amen.

9.3 Word from the Author.

Dear Reader,

As we come to the end of this journey together, I want to leave you with a final word of encouragement and gratitude. It has been an honor to share with you the profound truths and experiences of the supernatural power of God and the end times.

Remember that you are not alone on this path, and we may never know what the future holds, but what I do know is that your path is paved with the goodness of God. The supernatural is not something reserved for a select few; it is available to every believer who dares to step out in faith. Embrace the reality that you have been uniquely designed and empowered by God to operate in the supernatural realm.

> Remember that you are not alone on this path,
> and we may never know what the future holds,
> but what I do know is that your path is paved
> with the goodness of God.

May the stories and testimonies shared in this book ignite a fire within you, sparking a hunger for more of God's supernatural power in your life. It is time you make your own. I pray that you will no longer view the supernatural as something to fear or misunderstand, but rather as a realm of divine encounters, miracles, and heavenly manifestations.

Activate your faith and embrace the calling to be a vessel of God's supernatural power. Allow the Holy Spirit to guide you, teach you, and empower you to walk in the fullness of your identity as a child of God. Step into the destiny and purpose that God has ordained for you, knowing that His supernatural power is working through you to impact lives and transform the world around you.

As you continue your journey, remember to seek wisdom, discernment, and intimacy with God. Stay rooted in His Word and be open to the leading of His Spirit. Allow His supernatural power to flow through you, bringing healing, deliverance, and hope to those in need. Create around you an atmosphere of the presence of God through praise, worship, and prayer.

I am grateful for the opportunity to share these spiritual truths with you. May these truths, knowledge and wisdom imparted within these pages bear fruit in your life. May you be a light in the darkness, a vessel of God's supernatural power, and a testament to His love and faithfulness.

With heartfelt appreciation,

Janine Do Cabo
GO be IN10TIONAL with your soul.

If you have a story of hope, encouragement or testimony to share with us, send us an email at info@jdcexec.com.

We would love to share your story with the world.

Bibliography

1. Alcorn, Randy. Heaven. Tyndale House Publishers, 2004.
2. axter, Mary K. and T. L. Lowery. A Divine Revelation of Heaven & Hell. Whitaker House, 1998.
3. Hitchcock, Mark. Heavenly Rewards: Living with Eternity in Sight. Moody Publishers, 2018.
4. Alec, Wendy. Visions from Heaven: Visitations to My Father's Chamber. Warboys, UK: Warboys Publishing Ltd, 2012.
5. Wiese, Bill. 23 Minutes in Hell: One Man's Story About What He Saw, Heard, and Felt in That Place of Torment. Lake Mary, Florida: Charisma House, 2006.
6. Stone, Perry. How to Interpret Dreams and Visions: Understanding God's warnings and guidance. Lake Mary, FL: Charisma House, 2011.
7. Holy Bible, New Living Translation, copyright © 1996, 2004, 2015 by Tyndale House Foundation. Used by permission of Tyndale House Publishers, Inc., Carol Stream, Illinois 60188. All rights reserved.
8. Mandino Og. The greatest Salesman in the World. United States and Canada; Bantam Books, April 1989.
9. Meyer Joyce. The Everyday Life Bible, Amplified Version. New York, USA; Faith Words, 2009.

10. Munroe M. In pursuit of purpose. Pensylania; Destiny Image Publishers, Inc. 2015

11. "Oxford Learners Dictionary", < https://www.oxfordlearnersdictionaries.com>,

12. Price Paula A. The Prophet's Dictionary, The Ultimate Guide to Supernatural Wisdom. USA, PA; Paula Price Ministries, 1999, 2002, 2006

13. Evans, Jimmy. Where Are the Missing People? The Sudden Disappearance of Millions and What Happens Next. XO Publishing, 2022.

14. Scripture quotations taken from The Holy Bible. New International Version NIV Copyright 1973,1978,1984,2001 by Biblica Inc. Used by Permission. All rights reserved worldwide.

15. Scripture Quotations marked TPT are from the Passion Translation. Copyright 2017,2018 By Passion and Fire Ministries Inc. Used by permission. All right reserved. Thepassiontranslation.com.

16. Webster M. Dictionary. Spingfield Massachusetts, USA; Encyclopaedia Britannica, Inc, 1847

17. Van der Westhuizen Nicky. Hosting The Supernatural. Johannesburg, South Africa; Faithland Publishers (Pty) Ltd, 2021

18. Benware, Paul N. Understanding End Times Prophecy: A Comprehensive Approach. Chicago: Moody, 2006. First published 1995.

19. Fruchtenbaum, Arnold G. The Footsteps of the Messiah: A Study of the Sequence of Prophetic Events. Tustin, CA: Ariel Ministries, 1983.

20. Hoyt, Herman A. The End Times. Winona Lake, IN: BMH Books, 2000. Originally published 1969 by Moody.

21. Ice, Thomas, and Timothy Demy. Fast Facts on Bible Prophecy: A Complete Guide to the Last Days. Eugene, OR: Harvest House, 1997.

22. Hitchcock, Mark. The End: A Complete Overview of Bible Prophecy and the End of Days (p. 469). Tyndale House Publishers. Kindle Edition.

23. The Scriptures 2009 (TS2009) 1993 – 2015 by the Institute for Scripture Research (ISR). All rights reserved.
24. Tsarfati, Amir. Has the Tribulation Begun?: Avoiding Confusion and Redeeming the Time in These Last Days (p. 111). Harvest House Publishers. Kindle Edition.
25. Piper, D., & Murphey, C. (2004). 90 Minutes in Heaven: A True Story of Death & Life. Revell.